# Hard Looks

## Masculinities, Spectatorship and Contemporary Consumption

Sean Nixon
*University of Essex*

St. Martin's Press
New York

St. Martin's Press, Scholarly and Reference Division, 175 Fifth Avenue, New York, N.Y. 10010

First published in 1996 by UCL Press
The name of University College London (UCL) is a registered trade mark used by UCL Press with the consent of the owner.

First published in the United States of America in 1996

Printed in Great Britain

ISBNs: 0-312-16332-0 (cloth)
0-312-16333-9 (pbk)

Library of Congress Cataloging-in-Publication Data

Nixon, Sean (Sean James), 1966–
Hard looks : masculinities, spectatorship and contemporary consumption / Sean Nixon.
p. cm.
Includes bibliographical references and index.
ISBN 0-312-16332-0 (cloth). – ISBN 0-312-16333-9 (pbk.)
1. Men consumers–Great Britain–Attitudes. 2. Middle aged men–Great Britain–Attitudes. 3. Men's clothing industry–Great Britain. 4. Advertising–Clothing and dress–Great Britain.
I. Title.
HF5415.33.G7N59    1996
658.8'348–dc20
96-21862
CIP

# Contents

v

# Acknowledgements

Many intellectual and personal debts have been accrued in the course of completing this book. I am firstly grateful to the Economic and Social Research Council for a postgraduate training award which funded the first three years of the doctoral research on which the book is based. The practitioners who populate my account were also extremely generous with their time. For putting time aside to talk to me I am grateful to: Bill Webb, Fitch-RS, London; Mark Landini, Fitch-Rs, London; Liz Watts, Bartle Bogle Hegarty, London; Neil Saunders, Grey Advertising, London; Paul Keers, Condé Nast (*GQ*), London; Sue Oriel, FCO, London; Adam Lury, Howell Henry Chaldecott Lury, London; Rasheid Din, Din Associates, London; Gill Daniels, Yellowhammer, London; Dylan Jones, Wagodon (*Arena*), London; Rod Sopp, Wagadon (*The Face/Arena*), London; Elizabeth Nelson Taylor-Nelson, Epsom and Dan O'Donahugue, Publicis, London. I am particularly grateful to Gill Daniels for supplying me with some useful material. My parents, Carole and John Nixon, were generous throughout this project with their support. I also owe more than I can say to Claire Manning for her support and love.

The ideas developed in the book have been shaped by conversations with both colleagues and students at The Open University, Portsmouth Polytechnic, South Bank Polytechnic, Liverpool Polytechnic, the University of North London and the University of East London over the past seven and a half years. I am grateful in particular to Paul Du Gay, Adrian Mellor, Andrew Winder, Elizabeth Wilson, Sheila Henderson, Bill Schwarz, Roberta Garrett and Robert Kincaid.

David Oswell has been a consistent source of both stimulating and perceptive comment and friendship. Frank Mort provided good practical advice from early on concerning the business of research and thesis writing. Together with Peter Jackson, he was also a supportive series editor in the final stages of the book's production. Bob Bocock and Angela McRobbie were stimulating examiners when the material was presented as a thesis. Angela McRobbie has continued to offer a critical sounding board for the ideas developed in the book and I am grateful to her for her support. Thanks are also due to Sheila Knight and Aisling Ryan at UCL Press for the excellent job they have done in shaping the production of the book. A final special acknowledgement is due to Stuart Hall. The generosity and rigour of his comments throughout this project have been – in the full sense – exemplary. Without his guidance and support, the research might have come to nothing.

Earlier and substantially different versions of some of the material presented in the book have already been published. These can be found in: "Have you got the look? Masculinities and shopping spectacle", in *Lifestyle shopping, the subject of consumption,* R. Shields (ed.), 149–69 (London: Routledge, 1992); "Distinguishing looks: masculinities, the visual and men's magazines", in *Pleasure principles, politics, sexuality, ethics,* V. Harwood, D. Oswell, K. Parkinson, A. Ward (eds), 54–70 (London: Lawrence & Wishart, 1993); "Looking for the Holy Grail: publishing and advertising strategies and contemporary men's magazines", *Cultural Studies* 7(3), 466–92, 1993.

# Introduction

Imagine the following scene:

The door of an urban launderette opens. Marvin Gaye's song "I heard it through the grapevine" starts up on the soundtrack, its taut, soulful groove laying across the unfolding scene. A row of arcane looking washing machines fill the space the camera has entered. The launderette is busy, and steam rises from the machines. Two young women sit together on chairs reading magazines. One wears crazy, white framed "3-D" glasses. Both are in long, flared skirts and wear their hair in high pony-tails. The camera introduces other users of the launderette: a pair of brothers in red reversed baseball caps who are restless and inquisitive in this functional adult domain; their mother, wearily attentive to her sons' movements and to the washing to be overseen and tended. A grumpy-looking fat man in a hat sits just down from the two young women; a bespectacled lady reads next to him.

By now the visual scenario is established. The camera has opened up a scene that is not recognizably of the present. We have entered a space whose key signifiers (the washing machines, the women's hairstyles, clothes, the music) allude to a glamorized 1950s/early 1960s cultural landscape.

The anonymous hand that has opened the door and led us into this urban launderette is revealed to us: it belongs to a striking looking young man. He pauses inside the doorway. His appearance confirms the historical periodization already established by the music, the set and costume: his hair is greased in a soft quiff, and he is wearing a plain T-shirt and denim jeans.

He nonchalantly removes the sunglasses he is also wearing and glances around the launderette, taking in the situation. The camera moves onto him in close-up: his skin is seamless, olive-brown and glistening; his eyes are dark. None of the other users of the launderette appears to know or recognize him. A danger and tension is marked around him as he moves towards a machine. Eyes begin to turn to him. The mother pulls her boys away from gawping at the young interloper, as he pours nuggets of soap powder into a machine.

The slightly troubling self-containment – and self-consciousness – of the young man becomes clearer as the narrative unfolds. Where are his bags of washing? Where is the unglamorous weight of domestic laundry? With one more controlled glance across the launderette, the young man pulls off his T-shirt to reveal a firm, smooth torso. He then undoes and slides off the belt to his jeans, unbuttons them and pulls them down and off over his boxer shorts and thighs. Both items are thrown into the washing machine. Confident in this performance, he casually takes up a seat amidst the gaping mouths, giggles and frowns of the other users of the launderette.

A final shot of our young "hero" sitting in his white boxer shorts and white socks is framed by a line of copy and the trademark label of the object of his daring washing ritual: the red tab 501 shrink-to-fit indigo-blue jeans.

Why start with this invocation of a 50-second television and cinema advertisement that ran in the UK from Boxing Day 1985 through until the Autumn of 1986? The advert is important to the story this book sets out to tell for a number of reasons. First, it brings together a particular and distinctive set of codings of masculinity that occupy a central place in the book as a whole. The foregrounding of the surface of the body is central to "Launderette's" representation of masculinity. Through the choice of camera shots, an intensity is produced in the framing of the masculine body in the advert. As Nick Kamen, the model, undresses a series of looks are formally established that bring the viewer's eye close up to his face, chest, arms, thighs and bottom. A fragmentation of his body is produced in these shots that undercuts the more established codes of aggression and power associated with masculine display. The revealed torso and Kamen's features combine to allow the display of both developed (but not too hard) muscularity and a marked softness and sensuality connoted through his soft lips, eyes and skin-tone.

Individualism is also key to the representation of masculinity in "Launderette". The narrative of the advert and its *mise en scène* signify the young hero as stylistically self-conscious and, through this, as separate from the dreary adults who sit and watch him in this functional domain. After all, the ritual that we witness is guided by his desire to achieve the perfect fit to his jeans through the shrinkage produced by washing. The shrink-to-fit jeans, the button-fly, the connotations of the model's "look" and the setting of the launderette, together signal a pre-permissive moment that is also important to "Launderette's" distinctiveness. It is precisely this ensemble of codings of masculinity in the field of vision, the modes of spectatorship associated with them and the pleasures forged in relation to them that this book is concerned with interrogating.

In setting about this task, the account developed in the book has been shaped in relation to a range of other interpretations of these same visual codings. These other readings bring us to the second reason for choosing to begin with "Launderette". Immediately upon its broadcast, the advert (together with its companion advert "Bath") prompted a plethora of commentary and analysis. Crossing over from the narrow confines of the advertising and marketing trade press, this commentary featured in the popular and quality press, in consumer magazines and academic articles. What these often diverse commentaries shared was the sense that "Launderette" was in important ways exemplary of some wider decisive shifts occurring in popular representations of masculinity. These were shifts that by late 1986 could be confidently condensed in the figure of the "new man".[1]

One account offered a particularly lucid reading of "Launderette" and the shifts in masculine scripts connected to style and individual consumption associated with the "new man". In an important article, Frank Mort argued that what marked out the new imagery was the way it offered a more sexualized representation of the male body in ways which drew on the codings traditionally associated with representations of femininity in consumer culture and, in addition, resisted the assertion of a fixed or true sense of maleness in its styling of appearance. The significance of this for Mort was that such codings pointed the way to a radically different version of masculinity; one characterized by a more self-conscious sense of maleness. He developed his argument about the significance of the "new man" imagery through a particular conceptualization of the problem of masculinity; a conceptualization rooted within the injunctions of contemporary sexual politics to problematize dominant and exclusive forms of masculinity and heterosexuality. Drawing upon an argument put forward by Rosalind Coward and Maria Black, Mort argued that at the heart of the contemporary problem of masculinity was a set of discursive practices that positioned the masculine as the social norm; that is, as embodying the human or universal experience. For Mort, these unmarked positions (which Coward & Black specify in relation to discourses of citizenship, the law, anthropology and sexuality) (Coward & Black 1981: 83), made it possible for men not to recognize the problem of their masculinity for women or to take responsibility for it. His central contention about the "new man" imagery was that it precisely spoke to men "through their gender – as a community of men" (Mort 1988: 212). In other words, he saw the new codings as making it possible for men to live out their masculinity in more provisional, gendered terms. This lay at the root of the ruptural potential of the profusion of the "new man" imagery for him.

My account takes its cue from Mort's reading and is driven by a similar politically engaged concern to push at the significance of the "new man" imagery in relation to contemporary formations of masculinity and masculine culture. The central narrative thrust of the book is focused around a concern to open out in some detail the moment of the break in popular representations of masculinity most clearly identified by Mort and others around the Levi's adverts. I explore at some length the novelty of these representations and reflect on how deep rooted the shifts were. Embedded in this analysis is an assertion about the need to grasp the proliferation of this imagery as a regime of representation. To this end, I reflect on four key sites of cultural circulation across which the "new man" imagery signified: television advertising, press advertising, menswear shops and popular magazines for men. One of these sites – that of popular magazines for men – occupies a particular significance in my account. I argue that the magazines were not only the cultural form responsible for carrying the greatest volume of these new representations, but that it was within the fashion photography of these magazines that the new codings of masculinity were most extensively elaborated. Accordingly, it is in relation to this representational form that I primarily pursue the visual distinctiveness of the "new man" and advance an argument about its cultural significance. In Part IV, I detail the importance, in particular, of the "style press" between 1984–6 in establishing the precepts of this new regime of representation. I chart the formative moment of this regime of representation and its development and consolidation up until 1990 in a reading of the magazines' fashion photography.

The periodization of the formation and consolidation of the "new man" imagery that I advance is central to the story the book sets out to tell. What the books recounts, in fact, is best read as a cultural history of a very specific moment – a moment with an identifiable beginning and identifiable end. Developments since the end of 1990 in the men's markets related to style and individual consumption that I centre-stage, have given a sharper edge and sense of specificity to the period detailed in Parts II, III and IV. Looming large in this have been developments associated with the men's magazine market. The launch of four major new titles since the beginning of 1991 – National Magazines' *Esquire*, Northern Shell Plc's *Attitude*, IPC's *Loaded* and Wagadon's *Arena Homme Plus* – together with some significant rethinks in the editorial focus of the magazines launched at the end of the 1980s, have thrown up some new versions of masculinity to those I detail in Part IV. Significantly, these shifts have impacted on the visual codings of masculinity produced within the magazines fashion photography. In the conclusion to the book I reflect on the nature of this second break as it casts illuminating retrospective light over the period that the book details. However, in insisting on the specificity of the moment of representation between 1984–90, it would be wrong to read me as inferring that more recent developments in the visual coding of masculinity associated with style and individual consumption mark a complete reversal of the shifts associated with the "new man". Far from it. The display of men's bodies and the continuing centrality of certain physical attributes (notably, developed chest, arm and upper-body muscles and highly groomed hair and skin) across a wide range of popular representations underline the importance of this earlier break. In this sense, the visual codings that I begin this introduction with in my comments on the Levi's advert and which I elaborate upon in the course of the chapters that follow, continue to exert a considerable influence over a range of contemporary representations of masculinity. It is both the legacy of and the discontinuities between these moments of the mid to late 1980s and the 1990s, then, that frames my cultural history of the "new man".

An evaluation of the cultural significance of the "new man" imagery in relation to formations of masculinity and masculine culture is not the only concern that shapes this book. The book is also concerned to set out an argument about the factors that drove the formation of the new representations of masculinity. In this sense, the book is a response to the question, "Why did these images emerge in the mid to late 1980s?" In answering this question, I have focused upon a specific set of factors: the role of a set of consumer institutions. It is in this third sense that the Levi's advert has been an instructive place to start this book. In representing masculinity through the advertising of jeans, "Launderette" points us towards these institutional practices of cultural production and circulation. Three sets of institutional practices, in fact, dominate the book. In Part II, I look at the way developments in the design and selling of menswear set important terms for the formation of the "new man" imagery. In Part III, it is developments in advertising and market research that are my focus, while in Part IV, I chart the developments within magazine publishing that bore upon the forging of the "new man" imagery. In putting together accounts of these consumer institutions, I argue that it was the specific practices internal to each institutional nexus and the ways in which they interconnected that set the terms for the production of the regime of "new man" representations.

In privileging these practices I have deliberately bent the stick of the analysis towards an account of the production and circulation of the "new man" imagery and have put to one side important questions about its consumption. However, given the emphasis in recent years on the moment of consumption in accounts of commercial cultural forms – and specifically the questionable emphasis on "consumption as resistance" within some of this work – there is much to be gained from such a shift of emphasis onto the more neglected moments of production and circulation within these circuits of culture. Bringing to the fore these institutional practices within advertising, magazine publishing and the menswear business further underlines the weight I give in the book to the period between 1984–90. One of the underlying themes of the book concerns the significance of the developments within consumer institutions that took place during the mid to late 1980s. Economic and business historians have yet to produce a fully grounded picture of the transformations in commercial organizations across the main consumer sectors of the economy in this period. It is one of the contentions of the book that this period will repay repeated attention from these quarters over the comings years.

In setting out my account of the "new man" imagery, the question of space has also emerged as an important theme. Space, as Doreen Massey has noted, is very much on the agenda these days in the human and social sciences (Massey 1994: 289). The way in which this new attention to spatiality informs my account stems from the argument – put by radical geographers like Massey in the 1970s – that space is not a blank inert backdrop against which the dynamic processes of culture are played out. Rather it shapes the very organization and experience of these processes. This sense of the spatial dimension of culture registers in three ways in the book. The first concerns the representations of masculinity I discuss. One of the characteristic features of these images concerns the way they place or locate masculinity within a specifically metropolitan context. This rendering of the "new man" as a metropolitan masculinity was underscored, for example, by the editorial focus of the magazines I discuss in Part IV. A common theme across them was the interweaving of representations of the "new man" with distinct languages of metropolitanism – that is, particular ways of imaginatively apprehending the city in the form of places, sights, events and people.

The second way in which the spatial informs my account has been in relation to menswear retailing. In Part II, I advance an argument about the way cultural practices associated with the retailing of menswear helped to fix the meaning of particular garment designs. Central to this argument is an attention to retail design and its coding of shop frontages and interiors. In attending to the role of retail design, I draw out the way it worked not simply to establish certain cultural values around the garments being sold, but did this through the coding of shop space. Opening up the spatial dynamics of shops is important to my argument about the forms of looking that were staged within these retail outlets. I argue that a specific spatialization of spectatorship was produced within and around menswear shops.

The third way in which the question of space surfaces in the book relates to a larger spatial scale. Specifically, it relates to the spatial or geographical dimensions of economic restructuring in the consumer sectors focused on by the book. This is clearest in relation to developments within the clothing industry, though it also figures in my account of institutional developments in advertising and marketing services. What is at stake is the way these sectors of the economy fitted into a reconfiguring global economy and the consequences this had for the spatial relations within these industries and in intersectoral relations. As I suggest in Part III, for example, the increasing globalization of production and the formation of new global markets threw up organizational challenges for British advertising agencies; challenges that related to the stretching out of commercial relations between agencies, clients and consumers over larger geographical distances.

Being sensitive to the spatial dimension of culture forms part of my ambition to piece together a mode of cultural analysis that moves beyond the familiar terms of reference of cultural criticism. As such, it compliments the concern I have already stated of holding together in the same analytic frame an attention to the cultural significance of the "new man" codings and an account of the institutional practices that underpinned them. Bringing together these lines of enquiry is central to the book's reading of the "new man". In particular, the central ambition not to reproduce the conventional bifurcation (prevalent within media and cultural studies) between "texts" and "institutions" has given shape to the story the book tells. One consequence of this analytic move has been that I have drawn on a range of literatures and theoretical arguments. In Part I, I open out in more detail two sets of these conceptual frameworks that have had a major impact in shaping this project: concepts drawn from theories of representation and subjectivity; and arguments about the restructuring of consumer markets on the back of new production technology in the literature on flexible specialization. It is to these conceptual arguments that I now turn.

# PART I

# Masculinities, commercial culture and cultural analysis

## CHAPTER 1

# Representation, subjectivity and spectatorship

The argument about the cultural significance of the "new man" imagery that this book sets out is carried through an analysis of visual representations – pre-eminently fashion photography. How I approach textual analysis, then, has been a prominent methodological and conceptual concern. The work of Michel Foucault has been consistently illuminating in this regard. In turning to Foucault, I have wanted explicitly to signal my distance from a model of textual analysis that dominates a good deal of the work on visual representations within cultural studies and the newer forms of media studies. Namely, the semiotic approach to textual analysis. This work foregrounds attention to the construction of meaning through the rules of signification internal to the representations that are at the centre of its analysis. Positively, this emphasis gives due regard to the efficacy of the moment of representation in producing a determinate set of meanings. It usefully insists that these cannot be read-off from either the conditions of the image's production or its consumption. In concrete studies, this close reading is then usually supplemented by a move from the representation itself to a set of contextual factors – most frequently in the shape of a set of assertions about the moment of the representation's consumption. In Barthes's famous reading of the *Paris Match* cover, for example, it was the specific conjunctural context of the Algerian War that Barthes called up to pin down his reading of the connotations of the image (Barthes 1972).

In prioritizing the process of meaning production internal to the representations that it focuses upon, however, this semiotically informed work has some conspicuous limits. Most significantly it produces a dangerously foreshortened account of visual representations. Other determinants of particular representations (including the cultural forms within which they circulate) are relegated to a side event. What is privileged in the analysis, and in practice given an effective autonomy, is the detailed reading of the representation's formal or preferred meanings.[1]

This is where Foucault's work – and specifically his conception of discourse – is key to my account. His conception of discourse has allowed me to hold onto the best insights from semiotics, while developing a broader account of representation.[2] There are four clear ways in which this has shaped the analysis developed in the book. First, Foucault's argument about the discursive characteristics of representation has guided my insistence on charting the way the "new man" imagery was produced across different representational forms. We find this imagery in more than one place, then, organized as a regime of representation and governed by a certain discursive regularity. Secondly, putting together an account of the "new man" imagery as a regime of representation has meant giving a full place in the analysis to the institutional sites within which the "new man" imagery was rooted. I emphasize, then, the imbrication of the "new man" representations in specific institutional practices and centre-stage the forms of knowledge and practice that came into play in their production. Thirdly, Foucault's account of discourse has committed me to analyzing the way such forms of knowledge and practice imply relations of power that operate through the differentiation of the field of representation. This operation of power is markedly productive in relation to the "new man" imagery. It renders masculinity intelligible through specific visual codes and establishes certain injunctions to look, guiding the eye across the space of representation. Power relations are also constitutive of the relations forged in the formation of representational space between – in particular – the subject of the representation and those who look.[3] Fourthly, in opening up for consideration the forms of knowledge and expertise that shape representations, Foucault's account of discourse has directed me towards a consideration of the economic calculations and practices that figure prominently in the production of commercially produced representations like the "new man" imagery. Though Foucault's own work generally sidesteps these economic practices and tends to consign "the economic" to the domain of extradiscursive practices, his conception of discourse has nonetheless prompted me to analyze economic practices discursively. This has, in particular, led me to challenge the tendency within the post-

Althusserian tradition of cultural analysis to play up the "relative autonomy" of cultural processes, while maintaining the epistemological guarantee of economic determination in the last instance. It is this ordering of different social practices that Foucault's work clearly problematizes and that in turn opens up the possibility of another model of determination within cultural analysis.[4]

## Subjectivity and subjectivization

Foucault's conception of discourse also advances a particular account of the relationship between discursive regimes and subjectivity. This is one in which discourses are seen as the bearers of various historically specific subject positions. These positions establish the conditions for agency and identity in relation to discrete social practices. This is a significant formulation for the book in thinking about masculinity and representational regimes. It has not only forced me to emphasize the central role played by the external structures of discourse in producing the attributes and characteristics of masculinity as it is lived by men, but has also made me recognize the specificity of the discursive representations of masculinity that I am dealing with. This has meant being attentive to the particular discursive practices through which the "new man" imagery was produced. These commercial practices, with their emphasis on individual consumption and leisure, will in principle produce a different range of masculinities from those produced within, for example, work and professional discourses (whether that be around middle class notions of career advancement and competencies in technical know-how or working class notions of the dignity of physical labour and the weekly wage packet (Roper 1991, Willis 1979).

This sense of the differentiated production of masculinities across a range of discourses has additional implications for how we conceptualize masculinity as it is lived by men. In Foucault's terms, not only is there not one singular, totalizing version of masculinity, but the masculinity of individual men is itself (potentially) plural. In other words, individual men might be addressed by a range of discursive masculine identifications: as fathers, union officials, Englishmen, northerners, consumers of clothing, as taxpayers, and so on. Lived masculinities, then, are crucially determined by both the co-articulation of these discursive positions and the tensions and fractures between them.

13

Much of the work of identity involves the organization of a more or less coherent sense of self through these identifications and a handling of the various disjunctures that might exist between them. [5]

An emphasis on the plural nature of cultural identities is not, however, the only dimension of Foucault's account of subjectivity that has informed my conceptualization of masculinity. Equally instructive has been Foucault's insistence on the lines of normalization and power that criss-cross discursive regimes. Subject positions, for Foucault, then, are not simply dispersed and unconnected across different discourses – such as those associated with work, public policy, religion, consumption. Rather, they are regulated interdiscursively by what Foucault called "social hegemonies" (Foucault 1978: 93).[6] That is, by common attributes and characteristics or recurrent positionalities. Such a conception forces us to insist on the formation of norms of masculinity that not only establish continuities across different discursive representations, but also rank different masculinities in relation to each other. Foucault's account of subjectivity, in this second sense, then, directs us to the way formations of masculinity are both dependent upon and cut across other structures of power. This attention to the lines of normalization and power regulating masculinities sheds light, notably, on the way – as Tosh & Roper have argued – dominant versions of masculinity are sustained by dominance over other masculinities as much as by the exclusion and dominance over femininity (Tosh & Roper 1991). This suggests a conception of the field of gender relations structured around polyvocal forms of power, rather than one divided along the lines of univocal masculine dominance and feminine subordination. It is within this more pluralized model of the field of gender relations that I understand particular versions of masculinity being inserted (like the "new man") – and relations between different groups of men and women being played out.

Foucault's account of subjectivity is strongly accented, as I have suggested, towards an emphasis on the way external structures of discourse shape subjectivities. This account of subjectivity is allied to a distinctive theorizing of the process whereby discursive subject positions (like the "new man") meet an historical individual on the ground (such as a reader of a magazine). The central mechanism that Foucault posits to understand the formation of historical identities is the operation of power within discourse. For Foucault, this is centrally seen as a question of the government of conduct with power prescribing and shaping conduct according to certain norms. This process structures a limited number of positions within which individuals can establish agency and within which an individuated sense of self is produced. Power can also intensify the pleasures of the body, its posture and movements, constituting the fabric of the individual and its conduct.[7] In this account of subjectivization, then, Foucault places emphasis on the non-ideational quality of the process. That is, he emphasizes the way subjectivization does not require individuals to be interpellated through mechanisms of identification to secure the working of power/knowledge upon them. Power/knowledge works directly on the body, organizing its attributes and characteristics.

Despite the richness of this formulation of subjectivization, however, it has posed problems for my account. First, it is not clear from Foucault's comments whether he completely rules out of court the process of subjectivization working through the production of individuals' own representations within conscious or unconscious identifications. I would want to retain some sense of the usefulness of a concept of identification as a component of subjectivization. Secondly, and more importantly, Foucault's arguments are extremely vulnerable to the charge that he overemphasizes the effectiveness of specific power plays upon individuals and pays insufficient attention to the forms of negotiation that might be possible to specific discursive strategies or their more mundane failure. There is something perfunctory about the mechanism or process of subjectivization in Foucault's work at this point: the subject positions inscribed in discourse are effectively read as being mirrored in the lived forms of subjectivity.[8] The only block to plays of power/knowledge are other discourses and it is, then, the contradictory subject positions inhabited by an individual that set limits on the other subject positions. There is little interest from Foucault, however, in the subjective experience of these potential antagonisms and contradictions. For me these aspects of Foucault's work present a too foreshortened account of subjectivization. Two alternative accounts have more to offer: the account of subjectivization advanced within psychoanalytically informed cultural analysis and the account of subjectivization developed in Foucault's late writings where he turns more adequately to the processes of subject formation.

## Psychoanalysis and spectatorship

Psychoanalytically informed cultural analysis offers a number of suggestive terms for theorizing subjectivization. Pre-eminent amongst these is the concept of identification.[9] It was within film theory in the 1970s that writers most assertively developed the implications of the visual character of the structures of identification described by Freud and Lacan and laid claim to this lineage of psychoanalysis as offering a privileged way into the analysis of visual representations.[10] This work is instructive for my account in a number of ways. Pivotally it addresses the power of the visual for the consumers of visual culture, and offers a gendered account of the processes of looking and identification. Laura Mulvey's 1975 *Screen* essay, "Visual pleasure and narrative cinema", particularly clearly illustrated what a psychoanalytically informed account could deliver regarding the theorizing of the power of representation (reprinted in Mulvey 1989). The analysis of the look – and the organization of the pleasure in looking – is most interesting in Mulvey's essay. Drawing on Freud in particular, Mulvey detailed the way narrative cinema mobilized both the narcissistic aspects of the pleasure in looking (or scopophilic instinct) and its voyeuristic and fetishistic components – essentially those forms of active scopophilia. For Mulvey, however, the mobilization of these pleasures in looking was far from innocent. She asserted a very specific organization of spectatorship in relation to the scopophilic drives. For Mulvey, in her famous conceptualization, the "pleasure in looking has been split between active/male and passive/female" (Mulvey 1989: 19). The interplay of looking, then, is split around a marked imbalance, with the feminine coded as visual spectacle (passive object) and the masculine positioned as the bearer of the look (the active eye). In these formulations, Mulvey suggests that one important element of this gendered imbalance in looking is the careful coding and positioning in the cinematic narrative of the male figures. For Mulvey there is a marked displacement of any erotic, "spectacular" significations in relation to men in narrative film that maintains the power relations between men and women; between the active masculine control of the look and the passive feminine object of the look.

Mulvey's development of Freudian concepts provides a suggestive way of conceptualizing the moment of articulation between individuals and representational forms. It suggests that the positioning of individuals within the codes of a particular visual representation is achieved through the organization of scopophilic drives and the channelling of unconscious identifications. This is also a process that can (depending upon representational conventions) reproduce the positions of sexual difference or gender.

Mulvey's account, however, has not gone unchallenged by other writers working from within the same psychoanalytic problematic. In particular, the singular notion of sexual difference and the assumption of a heterosexual object choice that underlies Mulvey's writing has been problematized (Merck 1987).[11] The writings on fantasy within cultural theory have also attempted to overcome the exclusive emphasis within Mulvey's account of the successful positioning of individuals within particular representational systems. Elizabeth Cowie and James Donald have both underlined the way the concept of fantasy points to a less rigid, gendered positioning through the look (Cowie 1990; Donald 1989).[12] There is a significant sticking point for my account, however, in the appropriation of Freudian and Lacanian psychoanalysis in whatever form by cultural theorists. The problem concerns the universal and reductive account of identity formation advanced in Freud and Lacan's work.[13] For both these writers the psychosexual structures of the oedipal order are given the privileged position in accounting for (almost) all there is to say about the formation of identity. Even in those accounts – like Mulvey's – which explore the articulation of cultural/historical forms with psychic structures, the psychic is privileged in establishing the limit positions of the subject. Thus, in Mulvey's work on the look and the gendered positioning of individuals, there is a search for the positions of looking given by particular visual texts in terms of the fundamental tropes of sexual difference – active/passive; masculine/feminine; mother/son; father/daughter. Subjectivization from this perspective, then, is conceptualized as not only being secured through the reactivation of the fundamental positions of identity that Freud posits, but ultimately always in the terms or in the index of the oedipal order. Historical and cultural determinants of identity are – in the end – reduced to the calculus of psychosexual structures. Thus, while psychoanalysis can give a clear account of the articulation of individuals with fields of representation, and certainly poses some important questions about the unconscious and desire and the look, this is in the end too ahistorical and totalizing.

I have learnt much, however, from this psychoanalytically informed cultural analysis and it has been generative on how I approach

17

the question of subjectivization. Rather than completely reject these arguments, I have held onto the concern with spectatorship and identification but now understood as operating without their precise psychoanalytical underpinnings. In re-situating this account of spectatorship and subjectivization Foucault's later writings have been instructive.

## Practices of the self

In the preface to *The uses of pleasure,* Foucault (1985) refers to his intention – ultimately jettisoned by the change in direction of his project – to produce a study of the specific "modality of relations to the self" through which children, women and "perverts" organize themselves as sexual subjects (Rabinow 1984: 338). This process, he infers, involves a set of practices or technologies of the self. In fleshing out the precise nature of these technologies or practices, Foucault emphasizes his interest in forms of writing such as private diaries. These forms of writing constitute techniques for narrating the self and represent, for Foucault, important elements in characteristically modern "technologies of the self"; that is, techniques or practices of self-formation and individuation.[14]

Foucault's comments on "practices of the self" make it possible to conceptualize the articulation of individuals with particular representations as a performance; a performance in which the formal positions of subjectivity are inhabited through specific practices or techniques. This lays the basis for an account of subjectivization that is historical in nature and circumvents the deployment of the full psychoanalytic connotations of identification, scopophilia or fantasy in order to theorize in a dynamic way the process of subjectivization.[15]

In conceptualizing the way the formal positions inscribed within the regime of "new man" representations might have been inhabited by men, Foucault's comments, then, direct us towards a specific set of practices or techniques of the self. A number of techniques of care, consumption and leisure seem to me pivotal in this respect. The practices of grooming and dressing and the activity of shopping represent practices through which the attributes and characteristics of masculinity coded in relation to the "new man" imagery might be operationalized as an historical identity. At the heart of these techniques or practices of the self, I want to insist, are specific techniques of looking. I am not interested in the ways these techniques of look-ing might have been articulated with scopic drives, but in the way they drew on and cut across an established "technology of looking". In Part II and Part IV I offer some pointers to this "technology of looking" associated with the sites of consumption and leisure across which the "new man" representations emerged. One would need to piece together, of course, a more concrete picture of the moments of looking and their associated practices to make further claims about the articulation of the "new man" imagery with masculinity as it is lived by groups of men. For example, we would need to know more about the way certain practices of looking and the care of the self were regulated by other masculine scripts. We would also need to know how they might have been disrupted by other forms of knowl-edge and practice that shaped particular lived masculinities. A formal account of subjectivization can only take you so far in this regard. One of the contentions regarding representation that I hold is that this limiting of a formal analysis should be acknowledged in a posi-tive spirit. It is important not to cut through the determinancy of the moment of articulation between historical individuals and specific representations.

CHAPTER 2

# Men's markets, consumer sectors and flexible specialization

I suggested in the Introduction that looming large in the story the book sets out to tell are the consumer institutions that played a pivotal role in the formation of the regime of "new man" imagery. My concern with these consumer institutions has stemmed largely from the Foucauldian arguments about the institutional underpinnings of representation delimited in Chapter 1. However, in attending to these consumer institutions, my account has also been brought into an engagement with a body of work coming out of economic and political theory: specifically, the work on post-Fordism or flexible specialization. This work offers an account of structural change within both Western economies and the wider global economy through the 1970s and 1980s. It highlights a number of related processes. These include the increasing globalization of production, the emergence of a new international division of labour and the consolidation of a new financial order. Most prominent in this work, however, is an attention to the establishment within Western economies of new forms of flexible manufacturing. This involves the use of flexible, general-purpose machinery and multi-skilled groups of core workers to produce more differentiated goods for segmented consumer markets. The manufacturing process is strongly marketing-led with a tighter integration of the stages from production through to point of sale. This principle – known as just-in-time – is strongly reliant upon the application of computer technology and the linking of each stage of the production process with design, distribution and retail. This innovation in manufacturing techniques is counterposed to the forms of mass production based upon the principles of economies of scale, standardization and limited product differentiation that dominated key consumer sectors of Western economies in the post-war years.[1]

The emergence through the 1980s of a range of new structures for regulating economic activity across Western economies – particularly within West Germany, Japan and Italy – also forms part of the claims made about the emergence of post-Fordism or flexible specialization as an emergent technological paradigm or well regulated regime of accumulation.[2] The work on these regulatory structures has emphasized the importance of either organizational frameworks associated with industrial districts made up of small or medium sized firms or the establishment of flatter management structures within a more decentralized organizational structure in large firms. Both forms emphasize the importance of subcontracting based on innovation through co-operation and knowledge sharing between firms. At the macroeconomic level, attention has been focused on the way government policy has supported these micro-regulatory structures by overseeing the integrity of regional economies and by underpinning the development of training and the infrastructure. Again, these regulatory structures are seen to be replacing the organizational forms and Keynesian demand management structures and national economic policies associated with the regulation of post-war Fordism or mass production.

The arguments about economic change associated with the work on post-Fordism or flexible specialization have pushed me into locating the shifts in institutional practices that I chart as part and parcel of the restructuring of consumer markets associated with both these new forms of flexible production and economic regulation. Developing this contention, however, requires being specific about the way these markets have been restructured along post-Fordist or flexible specialization lines. This means marshalling some of the empirical evidence relating to the restructuring of the UK economy and, in particular, the consumer sectors associated with the men's markets that concern me in this book. Charting the impact of flexible manufacturing techniques on clothing production – and specifically menswear – is key in this latter respect. This sector represents the principal form of manufacturing associated with the consumer markets that loom large in the story the book sets out to tell.

# The UK economy, mass production and flexible specialization

Perhaps the most striking finding to emerge from the empirical work on the restructuring of the UK national economy is its slow and partial re-organization along flexible specialization or post-Fordist lines.[3] The UK national economy is not, in this sense, the most fruitful economy to look towards for evidence of flexible specialization or post-Fordism. A number of factors have contributed to this. The first is that the UK national economy was only weakly re-organized in the inter-war and post-war years along classic Fordist or mass production lines. This immediately raises questions about how we conceptualize and periodize the transition to flexible specialization or post-Fordism. The weakness of Fordism or mass production was in part the symptom of the small domestic market in the UK. More importantly, the long-standing strength of financial capital within the UK economy and the highly internationalized nature of sections of UK manufacturing (with the basis of their production located outside the UK) that stemmed from the legacy of Empire, were also important.[4] As a result, UK manufacturing based in the national economy suffered from low levels of investment – especially in new machinery – with British capital more often than not concerned to invest overseas. The re-organization of certain sectors along mass production lines from the 1930s – such as consumer electronics, cars, steel, plate glass and rubber – needs to be situated within these broader characteristics of the UK economy and the relative weakness of nationally based manufacturing.

The second point, which is essentially a correlative to the first, is that UK manufacturing has been in decline for a long time. Relative decline began in the period from the 1880s, and has continued with the reduction in the UK's contribution to world output and trade in manufactured goods. Hirst & Zeitlin argue, however, that real decline and a process of de-industrialization begin in the late 1960s – a moment that coincides with the periodizing of the general crisis of Western Fordism or mass production.[5] The crisis of profitability that hit leading mass production sectors – most notably the car industry, consumer electronics and clothing – was compounded, however, by this underlying weakness of the manufacturing sector. Import penetration in these markets through the 1970s on the back of increased world trade was a symptom and further determinant on this reduction of national manufacturing capacity. For the UK economy, then, the crisis of Fordism or mass production has been highly distinctive: a weakly Fordist national economy suffered a profound and rapid crisis of its key Fordist sectors.

Thirdly, the peculiarities of economic restructuring that took place from the late 1970s and through the 1980s have been strongly shaped by the neoliberal economic strategy developed within government policy through this period (Jessop et al. 1988, 1990). This articulated a particular vision of the place of the UK economy in relation to the development of flexible specialization in the West and the reshuffling global economy. Looming large in this have been initiatives to extend the openness of the UK national economy, the encouraging of outward investment (particularly in financial services and producer services (like advertising and design)) and the development of a policy designed to present the UK as a "greenfield" site for foreign manufacturers, with relatively low wages and critically (for Japanese firms) a foothold in the EEC (Jessop 1988, 1990). Government policy has also been concerned to promote the growth of services as part of its attempt to imagine a new alignment of the UK national economy. This overall vision of the UK economy has been notably shaped by the language of enterprise and enterprise culture; that is, by the attempt to "marketize" greater areas of economic and social life. Public services – especially the key institutions of the Keynesian welfare state (KWS) – have been restructured under the influence of this thinking with new commercial criteria and "market testing" replacing older social democratic definitions of collective provision. This new model of the regulation of economic and organizational activity was driven by arguments developed within new wave management theory (Du Gay 1991). Looming large in this theory was an emphasis on the need to focus the organizational structure of the firm and its practices upon the consumer in new ways; that is, to develop what Rodney Fitch of the design company Fitch-RS termed "an end user culture" (Gardner & Sheppard 1989a: 4). It was enterprise discourse that gave political direction to these strategies and that helped to institutionalize this new model of economic activity. As such, the popular currency of enterprise discourse was critical to the process of economic restructuring. It represented the way in which a particular (neoliberal) culture of flexible specialization was established within the regulation of economic processes.

24

Conspicuously absent within this neoliberal strategy, however, have been initiatives to support innovations in manufacturing. In fact, as Hirst & Zeitlin have forcefully argued, government policy set the terms for UK manufacturers' failure to take up flexible manufacturing techniques on a significant scale during the 1980s.[6] Economic restructuring from the late 1970s, then, has not re-invigorated the UK manufacturing base on the back of flexible production, but has rather produced a further reduction in manufacturing capacity (Hirst & Zeitlin 1989, Jessop 1990).

## The UK clothing industry

Within the general weakness of UK manufacturing, however, Zeitlin has argued that innovative developments did take place. Significantly for this account, manufacturers in the clothing sector proved responsive to the potential of new flexible forms of production. Zeitlin identifies the strategies of multiple retailers as pivotal to the introduction of flexible manufacturing techniques. It was their shift from price competition in mass markets towards a greater emphasis on fashion and variety, he argues, that transformed their relationship with their suppliers and drove the implementation of flexible production (Zeitlin 1988: 218). Zeitlin suggests that this shift in retailer strategies was itself a response to the changing nature of clothing markets. These included, he argues, demographic changes (principally, the decline of teenagers) and a perception that consumer demand was "at once more fragmented and more discerning" (ibid.: 216).

The well established power of multiple retailers in relation to manufacturers – a power and degree of leverage that had been strengthened by the severe recession of 1980–81 – enabled them to initiate new relationships with suppliers based on more flexible requirements. Zeitlin highlights increased collaboration between the buyers from large retail chains as a key development in this process. Rather than send out detailed designs to manufacturers on a cut-make-and-trim (CMT) basis, or buy from wholesalers' catalogues, retailers like Marks and Spencer or Next worked more closely with their manufacturers in developing designs (Zeitlin 1988: 215). The aim was to produce a more flexible process of garment design and innovation that could be highly responsive to fairly small shifts in consumer demand. While manufacturers were encouraged to contribute more to the design process of garments, retailers demanded both much shorter runs and much shorter lead times – that is, the time from placing an order to its delivery. Zeitlin quotes a Marks and Spencer supplier who wryly indicated that,

> In the old days . . . Marks and Spencer was buying bulk just to fill the shelves. We would supply 1,000 dozens in one style and that was it. Today they're buying merchandise – styles have to be tried and tested and runs could be as little as 50 or 100 dozen (Zeitlin 1988: 219).

New production technology was important in enabling manufacturers to meet these demands. Computer Aided Design (CAD) and Computer Controlled Cutting (CCC) were the key innovations. Together they principally made possible the easier modification of styles and switches between garments for short batches. CAD, with its ability to store garment patterns and allow their quick modification, meant that production decisions could be delayed until up to date sales information was available (Zeitlin 1988: 222).

The take up of these new manufacturing systems was strongly concentrated amongst suppliers of large retailing multiples. In 1984, for example, 23 of the 39 Gerber cutters (the market leading computer controlled cutting machine) belonged to Marks and Spencer suppliers (Zeitlin 1988: 223). S. R. Gent, a leading Marks and Spencer supplier, was by 1985 deploying the most sophisticated CAD and CCC technology (*Design*, June 1985: 41). Its production was linked to Marks and Spencer's electronic point of sale system (Epos) – the product literally being pulled through the factory as it was required. [7]

Next also encouraged the investment in new technology among the manufacturers that it dealt with, 80 per cent of whom were UK based. As with Marks and Spencer, this was built upon more collaborative relationships. As Next's managing director put it,

> Next does not believe in simply contracting out its own in-house designs to a garment maker. It prefers a two-way process with design input coming from manufacturers as well as its own staff (quoted in Zeitlin 1988: 218).

The strategies of large retailers through the 1980s, then, integrated the historically tight relations between themselves and manufacturers in the UK clothing sector. Emphasis on the design content of garments and flexibility of product ranges gave, as Zeitlin argues, UK producers an advantage over imports from newly industrializing countries.

The formation of flexible specialization had further complicated effects on the UK clothing sector (including the menswear trade) in the 1980s, however. The development of flexible production methods across other EEC clothing industries provided fierce competition in terms of design content and flexibility. For a number of reasons – largely to do with the dominance of large "mass market" retailers (like Marks and Spencer) over UK manufacturers that I have commented on – the upper end of the clothing market, and even the upper end of the middle market (the more expensive elements of Next's range, for example) were increasingly serviced by predominantly Italian and German manufacturers (Zeitlin 1988: 221).[8]

Apart from the sourcing by UK retailers from other EEC manufacturers, a further characteristic of the UK clothing sector remained the large number of small firms. The segmented nature of the industry has remained in place despite the shifts amongst larger manufacturers to flexible production methods.[9]

These caveats about the impact of new flexible manufacturing techniques in relation to UK clothing production need to be set next to earlier comments – drawn in particular from the work of Hirst & Zeitlin – about the weakness of flexible specialization within the UK economy as a whole. Simple-minded notions of the full scale transformation of the UK economy along post-Fordist or flexible specialization lines have no place in a grounded account of the restructuring of the UK economy from the 1970s.[10] However, I do want to continue to insist that it is necessary to locate the shifts in the organization of key UK consumer markets in relation to the implementation of flexible production amongst manufacturers and the wider impact of new macro- and micro-regulatory practices associated with flexible specialization. The empirical evidence drawn from the clothing sector suggests, as we have seen, that the impact of flexible manufacturing on clothing production included both those manufacturers associated with UK multiple retailers and other EEC based producers. Developments in regulatory practices have pointed us towards a wider set of practices that were central to economic restructuring. The account that I offer in the chapters that follow, then, makes it clear that the construction and operationalizing of more segmented consumer markets by retailers, marketers and advertisers in relation to certain male markets is usefully conceptualized in terms of the formation of a culture of flexible specialization within these consumer institutions. I want to turn in Part II to the institutional practices associated with the menswear trade and begin to ground these arguments further in more concrete detail.

# PART II

# Menswear, retailing practices and the "new man"

# Introduction

In the current economic climate it makes sense to manipulate your image for maximum effect and instant respect. Sharp dudes have always known when it comes to a showdown nothing steels the scene as effectively as a well cut whistle, but even hardcore wildboys have started to tumble that "style" does not necessarily equate with excess and outrage. The smart money is suddenly on menswear.

*(I-D*, September 1986: 18)

In charting the formation of the regime of "new man" imagery, developments in and associated with menswear play an important role. Together with the reshaping of the men's toiletries and grooming products markets,[1] developments in menswear markets set some of the big terms for the emergence of the "new man" imagery. Specifically, it is through cultural practices associated with the functioning of these markets that the new visual representations of masculinity emerged. Part II, then, has a number of ambitions. In Chapter 3, I comment upon the formal innovations in menswear garment design. In Chapter 4, I offer an account of one component of the process of retailing – retail design – as this impacted on the selling of menswear. In Chapter 5, I begin to theorize the forms of spectatorship organized in relation to the "new man" representations at the point of sale.

In commenting on the design of menswear garments, I have attempted to steer a path between the burden of presenting a massive inventory of menswear in the 1980s – season by season, collection by collection – and the more banal terms of a very general commentary on garment design. I am probably guilty of erring, in fact, towards the latter mode of commentary. Fashion discourse, however, offers a stubbornly fixed vocabulary for reading clothes as cultural forms. The dangers of fatuousness lurk close to the surface. If at times the commentary veers into the stock-in-trades of fashion journalism ("And this season taupe is back with a vengeance"), it is testimony to the power of such vocabularies.

My concern with menswear design is focused around the way the garment ranges were made to signify within the process of selling, marketing and display. In Parts III and IV I consider the way menswear designs were resignified through the forms of marketing and display associated with press and television advertising and magazine fashion photography. Here, I focus upon the way processes of selling – from catalogues and catwalks, to the marketing of the name-label and the retail environment – have tied the garment designs into a supplementary set of meanings. The coding of shop space and shop display are central to my account in this sense. I argue that retail environments functioned as sites of representation – organizing and shaping the particular meanings of garments. Pivotally this process of representation not only gave rise to meanings and values to do with quality and the exclusivity of the clothes, but also represented specific masculinities in the selling of the garments.

## CHAPTER 3

# New designs on men:
# menswear and the "new man"

My favourite designer at the recent diploma shows, Dean Bright, does menswear. He uses "unmanly" colours like soft lilacs but emphasises shoulders so you feel comfortable wearing it.
> (Joe McKenna, fashion stylist, November 1984)

Menswear is currently the most innovative market in the fashion business. Greater design content, wider choice, and increased consumer awareness has given the industry a buoyancy not enjoyed since the sixties.
> (*Fashion Weekly*, Report on IMBEX 85, 7/12/85)

The seasons of 1984 and 1985 were important for the menswear industry in the UK. In the degree and diploma shows of fashion and art colleges and in the more established trade shows, menswear – as both Joe McKenna's comments and the *Fashion Weekly* editorial testify – was the focus of renewed interest from both designers and buyers.

This represented a marked shift in each of these fashion circuits. The degree and diploma shows presented student work strongly shaped in many of the prominent educational institutions by a fine-art based system of training. This had not traditionally offered a sympathetic arena for menswear design. The attention given to Dean Bright's menswear by fashion journalists in 1984 was symptomatic, then, of the way his designs challenged the established design choices of such students. Bright's interest in menswear did have its precedents, however. He consolidated the success of collections produced in the early 1980s – most notably, Stephen Linard's St Martin's School of Art graduation collection from 1981. This collection

("Reluctant Emigrés"), like Dean Bright's menswear, used the licence given it by the art school context to extend the parameters of menswear by drawing on some of the conventions, colours and fabrics of womenswear. "Reluctant Emigrés" presented, as *I-D* magazine described it, "rugged men with stubble, sideburns and tattoos, modell[ing] see-through organza shirts, flamboyant astrakhan coats and smug grins" (*I-D,* June 1990: 137).

Underlying this attention to menswear from art and fashion school designers was a new sense of the creative possibilities of menswear. Roy Peach, designer and tutor at Trent School of Fashion, commenting in 1984, suggested that "Students are excited about menswear because there's suddenly more scope and a new market in between classic suits and sporty casual clothes" (*The Face,* November 1984: 87).

The designer John Richmond, reflecting on his own work at the same time, made a similar point, though in more extreme terms: "Menswear has become more important because womenswear can't go any further. Menswear is more challenging; there are more barriers to be broken down" (ibid.).

This extended interest in menswear from within the circuits of fashion education was paralleled by different but equally important developments in the conservative institutions of the mainstream menswear industry. IMBEX, the International Men's and Boy's Exhibition, was the mainstream menswear industry's most important showing event. Dominated by manufacturers and wholesalers, however, IMBEX was notorious for the dowdy and conservative menswear it exhibited. The increase in the amount of menswear shown at the exhibition in 1984 and 1985, and in particular its greater design content, represented a watershed for this circuit of the industry. These developments were partly attributable to the initiatives of a group of designers, the English Menswear Design Collective (EMDC), who had been agitating inside the industry since their formation in 1981. Roger Dack and Stephen King, guiding lights of the EMDC, were products of established menswear businesses and well versed in the traditions and conspicuous limitations of the trade. They played a key role in contesting the established tradition of menswear trade shows and in driving into the mainstream trade a concern with new menswear markets, particularly designer menswear.[1]

The developments in the mainstream UK menswear trade, as well as in the avant-garde arena of fashion education, were part and parcel of more extensive transformations affecting menswear in the mid to late 1980s. From the catwalks of European *haute couture* to the consolidation of the designer menswear market in the UK and the expansion of the middle market, there was a significant reworking of the garment ranges associated with menswear. This chapter considers these industry-led transformations of menswear and offers some pointers to the way menswear was constructed across the three key menswear retail markets: the designer menswear market, the middle market and the mass menswear market.

## Designer menswear

In 1984–5, alongside what was happening in fashion education and the mainstream UK trade shows, menswear collections were produced by five high profile designers operating within the couture or high fashion circuits: Wendy Dagworthy, Katherine Hamnett, Jasper Conran, the French designer Jean Paul Gaultier and the Japanese designer Yohji Yamamato. In addition, the group of designers associated with the EMDC produced a new collection. Gaultier is most noteworthy for this account. Along with three further designers – Giorgio Armani, Paul Smith and Comme des Garcons – his designs had a significant impact on designer menswear in the UK.

Gaultier's professional skills were formed by the established Parisian institutions of French couture. He trained with Pierre Cardin and Thierry Mugler, and was fortunate to benefit early on in his solo years from the backing of the Japanese manufacturer Kashiyama and the Italian manufacturer Gipo. (*The Face*, February 1983: 22–6). His first menswear lines were produced in 1983 and signalled what *Arena* later called "his radical designs on men" (*Arena*, Summer 1987: 63). This work explicitly disrupted many of the traditional tenets of menswear. For example, the backless T-shirt – "a striped yatching T-shirt with cut-away back and elasticated waist" – formed part of his "The Man Object" collection (*The Face*, February 1983: 22). Gaultier explained the motivation behind this collection as follows:

> Walking around London and New York, I got the feeling that the era of the sexy male had arrived. In London people had swapped the normal grey trousers for exotic pirate culottes. In New York the Americans were in the throes of a body building craze. There

35

was no question for me of copying the pirate look, nor of getting into sportswear, so I asked myself: what would erotic clothes for men look like? (ibid.: 27).

A further answer to that question for Gaultier was to put men into skirts. These designs, from his 1984 collection, worked with the familiar fabrics of respectable menswear – such as pinstripes – to further scramble the conventions of male dress.

A distinctive feature of Gaultier's designs was the way they quite self-consciously drew upon the developments associated with London "street style". Thus, Gaultier appropriated cycling shorts, motor-cycle trousers, cotton leggings, hooded sports tops, trainers, the MA–1 flying jacket and the denim jacket that had first been re-worked in the dress of young urban *bricoleurs*. In this sense, Gaultier was representative of a more general shift in fashion in which it was increasingly difficult to clearly oppose, as Angela McRobbie has suggested, the world of "street" or second-hand style to the arena of high fashion (or even the High Street) (McRobbie 1989: 27). Traditional fashion hierarchies, in which the couture houses established the parameters of fashion in popular dress, were destabilized: it was "street style" that innovated and couture that followed. Gaultier was more explicit and direct than most couture designers in displaying these influences.

Gaultier's couture menswear design received considerable praise from the fashion establishment, as well as from the style press with whom he shared a close relationship (magazines like *The Face* and *I-D*).[2] Part of Gaultier's critical success derived not only from his innovative designs, but also from the careful presentation and marketing that accompanied their production. Both his catwalk presentations and the press advertising established a strong identity for the clothes. Prominent was a strong repertoire of casting. Early press adverts, for example, featured boyish black models. Subsequent promotions were more extravagant, using white models and mixing bald heads, strong, heavy features (lots of mouth, chin and cheek-bones) and "vulgar" facial gestures exaggerated by make-up.

Gaultier's marketing was not restricted to the catwalk extravaganzas or the press advertising. The launch of the Junior Gaultier diffusion range in 1988–9 was an initiative to reach a wider customer base for his clothes through the controlled use of the name label. The buying policy of a number of "high fashion" retailers was also important to the influence of Gaultier on the British menswear market. Prominent here was Browns, the retailers in South Molton Street run by Sidney and Joan Burnsten and Joseph, the stores owned by Joseph Ettedgui.[3]

A well practised integration of marketing and design was the hallmark of Giorgio Armani's success on the fashion scene. From the inception of the Giorgio Armani label in 1975, Armani, like Gaultier, developed the currency of the name label. Based in Milan in the Via Borgonouva, at the heart of an international operation that ranged from Tokyo to Los Angeles, Armani's fashion was antithetical to Gaultier's "radical designs on men" and the Frenchman's plundering of London "street style". In place of camp outrage and Gaultier's pursuit of a new relationship between the body under the clothing and the fit and cut of the garment in menswear, Armani offered crafted sobriety and minimal elegance. Armani saw his approach to design as involving a process of purification: "I design by taking the world and filtering out all the things I don't like. I hate things that shout. I don't say that vulgarity is not creative, but it's not positive" (*Arena*, Autumn/Winter 1987: 31).

The result was a repertoire of styles based on, as Deyan Sudjic suggested, a "refined, understated, updated Englishness" (ibid.: 30). Central to the Armani "look" was a reworking of the blazer and a strongly gendered but contemporary approach. The reworking of the blazer was important to Armani's success, particularly in America where he was "King of the blazer" (ibid.: 31). The cut of Armani suits was strong and characteristicly "loose"; the cut suggested that the material was heavy, sumptuous and roomy. These were wide but not aggressive profiles with shoulders that fell slightly on long, deep jackets. Shirts were casual and loose with large, creamy buttons or formal in wine and white stripes. The collections – from the Giorgio Armani range to the Emporio Armani lines – suggested, as Deyan Sudjic neatly put it, that the wearing of an Armani label was "like driving a BMW . . . discreetly modern, discreetly affluent" (ibid.: 30).[4]

The deployment of the name label on the clothing and in its marketing mixed established assumptions about quality and taste with the rubric of corporate identity. The careful use of the name label across the different Armani products – from the black on white label Giorgio Armani collections to the white on black label of the Emporio Armani products, the Armani "Eau pour Homme" parfums and accessories lines – was part of a form of presentation that

37

spanned the press advertising, the shop design and merchandise packaging. The light sepia-washed press adverts that formed the basis of the campaigns by the late 1980s powerfully evoked a "moody", coolly controlled version of 1940s Italian-American.

The sobriety and "noiselessness" of Armani's designs and the tightly controlled marketing of these qualities was shared by the Japanese company Comme des Garcons. Comme des Garcons, under the direction of Rei Kawabuko, in fact went further than Armani in its attention to an almost obsessive minimalism and to a tightly marshalled corporate philosophy. This was articulated in such a way that it seemed – if you listened to Kawabuko – that the clothes were merely ways of following the abstraction of form.[5] As Kawabuko put it, "I try and reflect my approach not just in the clothes, but in the accessories, the shows, the shop, even in my office. You have to see it as a total impression" (Sudjic 1990: 48).

Kawabuko came to prominence on the international fashion scene in 1981 with Comme des Garcons' radically asymetrical womenswear. In this work seams were left exposed, hems were cut at extravagant angles and the clothing swathed rather than "fitted" the body.[6] In these designs Kawabuko established a foregrounded concern with the texture of clothes that remained an abiding focus.[7] The early collections also established Comme des Garcons' trademark use of monochrome. As Kawabuko later said, "I design in three shades of black."

The "Homme" menswear line was launched in 1978. Peter Popham saw this menswear as developing into – by the mid 1980s – "a recognizable style that's classic and slightly avant garde" (*Sunday Times*, "Menswear Extra", 1989: 13). Roomy suits, shirts and waistcoats with the quirky details were its trademark: a white shirt with red, blue and yellow button holes, for example.

The assertive minimalism of Comme des Garcons' menswear was carried through, as I have already noted, into the overall presentation of the clothes. From the Helvetica typeface of the name label to the packaging of the goods and the fitting of the shops, Comme des Garcons articulated a disciplined economy.

Comme des Garcons' emphasis on the interconnection of the clothing design with the symbolic rendering of shop space and marketing was highly influential, and in particular the "look" of the shops shaped the retail design vocabularies on offer across the "designer" and middle market menswear outlets. I consider in the next chapter these design vocabularies and their place in menswear retailing.

If the exploration of design (in its multiple forms) was central to Rei Kawabuko's presentation of Comme des Garcons, then the identity of the shopkeeper was uppermost in Paul Smith's self-representation. Although he celebrated the local qualities of the English shopkeeper, his status was, like Kawabuko, that of an international fashion designer with shops in Tokyo and New York, as well as London and Nottingham. Smith's designs from the early 1980s revolved around a particular definition of "classics". His trademark repertoire consisted of jackets, shirts, suits and knitwear. Smith passed these elements through a subtle transformation. As Steve Taylor suggested, "Taking elements of classic English men's style [he] added a quirky individual twist, whether in the cut, colour, choice of material or the way the garments [were] combined" (*Arena*, Autumn/Winter 1987: 26). Under Smith's attention, then, a houndstooth jacket – traditionally finished in sombre colours – was turned out in blue Italian linen, while a chambray shirt would be discreetly inscribed with a pattern on the yoke (ibid.). Smith's knitwear lines used a wide range of colours. Polo-shirts, V-neck sweaters, cardigans and sweaters were produced in solid blocks of lime, lilac and lemon. This all added up to a carefully reworked version of classic English menswear, which also referenced the cut and immaculate neatness of mod style.

## The middle market on the move: Next for Men

The mid 1980s saw important developments taking place within the menswear middle market. These developments were pivotally shaped by the menswear produced by Next. Next was formed as a line of womenswear shops in 1982 following the acquisition of Kendalls by the men's outfitters Hepworths in May 1981. Central to the expansion of Next into menswear – which came with the launch of Next for Men in August 1984 – was the application of the concept of "affordable collectables" first deployed in the development of the original womenswear concept (Davies 1989: 64).[8] This approach to menswear put a premium on a relatively restricted range of clothes, while organizing these into loose collections.[9] The marketing ethos here, which I expand on in the next chapter, was about presenting a fairly tightly integrated "lifestyle" package. These "collections" were quite explicitly pitched between established menswear chains and upmarket menswear. George Davies, Next chairman and chief executive until the end of 1988, and architect of the Next strategy, put this approach as follows:

> I'd looked at a variety of menswear chains – Dunns, Fentons, Colliers as well as Hepworths – and I'd seen that everyone was turning out the same drab and uninspiring merchandise. The clothes were very traditional and without any of the stylishness the Italians, say, were producing. In London there were one or two expensive shops like Paul Smith and Woodhouse where stylish garments were being sold. But elsewhere, there was nothing other than Top Man, which catered only for the young, and besides wasn't an upmarket operation (Davies 1989: 74).

For Davies, then, these were upmarket clothes at affordable prices. In his account of the Next story, he emphasizes – and it is a theme reiterated throughout his account – that considerable effort was made to provide a "look" that was "fashionable and stylish, and the prices accessible" (ibid.: 59).

In targeting a middle market in ways that attempted to signal stylishness, a certain exclusivity and quality, the Next design team went for a range of menswear that aimed to "combine the contemporary with the traditional" (ibid.: 83). Central to this was the mixing of casualwear and classics. A promotional spread run in *Vogue* in August 1984 set the tone for Next's (early) range. It presented two looks: a grey/brown flecked wool single-breasted jacket combined with green herringbone trousers and an abstract patterned shirt, as a casual ensemble; and, as a more formal arrangement, a navy/grey striped single-breasted suit worn with a blue/white striped shirt and silk tie (*Vogue*, August 1984).

Subsequent Next menswear extended this general approach. For example, the shop catalogue for Autumn/Winter 1987 and the *Next Directory* of 1989 give ample illustrations of what became a well established and successful repertoire.

The 1987 catalogue was organized around three thematic identities: what were called, "TransEuropean", "Baltic Defectors", and "Watching the Detectives". "TransEuropean" brought together formal double-breasted check suits – in cream and brown or black and white Prince of Wales check – with striped shirts and patterned ties,

together with more casual single-breasted Prince of Wales window-
pane check suits with chambray shirts or turtleneck sweaters. "Baltic
Defectors", on the other hand, combined chunky casualwear – lots
of patterned knitwear, including thick Aran, corduroy jackets, and
"survival jackets".

The 1989 *Next Directory* expanded the repertoire of "identities"
offered in both casualwear and formal wear. Here were, "Tycoon",
"Portrait of a gentleman", "Long Island weekend", "Gym", "Holly-
wood", "Zuma beach", and "Fast pack". The written text that accompanied the "Tycoon" section of the directory affirmed the underlying Next principles of modernity and tradition:

> Maximise your image. Personalised dressing with the new pro-
> portioned suits. A witty approach to accessories. The small
> details that make all the difference. Mix colour and tie patterns
> . . . Maximise tie and handkerchief combination . . . the precise
> elements of detail . . . braces, the pins and cufflinks . . . Maxim-
> ise style with confidence (*Next Directory*, 1989: 178).

The place of accessories within this presentation of menswear was
significant, and characteristic of the attention to detail that established the "classic with a twist" offered by Paul Smith within the
range of the middle market. The Next repertoire was styled with
considerable confidence in the spreads that followed this commentary: "classic" trenchcoats in stone; beige single-breasted raincoats;
button-down Oxford shirts; pointed long collar shirts; paisley or
other patterned ties; flannel suits in navy or charcoal; Prince of Wales
check in polyester and wool worsted; chambray shirts; corduroy
trousers; gabardine trousers; three-quarter length casual coats in
suede or beige cotton; linen trousers ("chinos"); wool patterned zip-
up tops, cardigans and crew neck sweaters . . . and so on.

The range of suits developed by Next was particularly important to
its merchandising mix. By 1989 it offered two distinct "body fits"
across its suit range: the "Classic suit" – "traditionally tailored to give
a smart, sharp appearance while still being easy and comfortable to
wear"; or "New Mood in Tailoring" – "a modern and relaxed attitude to tailoring, these suits are more softly constructed and have
larger proportions. The shoulder line is wider and more natural"
(*Next Directory*, 1989: 160–61). These latter suits, predominantly
available in a double-breasted style, echoed the "look" of Armani's

trademark suits and reaffirmed the status of the suit as smart casual-wear (worn with roll-neck sweaters or polo shirts). These wide-pro-filed suits underlined one of the strong themes played out in the Next lines: the connotations of "European style" that drew particularly on selected elements of Italian apparel and presentation. Central to these connotations was the invocation of an easy, restrained but assertively stylish aura to the clothes. Also jostling amid these conno-tations were allusions to 1940s/50s gangster chic, reworked – follow-ing films like Oliver Stone's *Wall Street* – as the modern masculine iconography of business.

Two versions of "America" also informed the Next collections: a distinctively "retro" version of (North East) American "college" casualwear and styles drawn from the "Great American Outdoors". The latter "look" delivered fringed suede jackets, sleeveless "puffa" jackets, lumberjack shirts, ribbed sweaters, red/black-check lined denim jackets, and so on. This was a version of outerwear echoing the ruggedness of the Rocky Mountains (as a headline put it) for an urban context. The "college" look – checked jackets, corduroy or gabardine trousers, chambray shirts and ties – conjured a world of privilege and modern sophistication through playing off the cues of a 1950s Eisenhower America.

Next's collections, finally, also played on appeals to "classic" English tailoring. This element in the merchandise was strongly confirmed by references to the warm "English" colourings of the wood of the gentlemen's outfitters in aspects of the design of the shop interiors.

## Mass market menswear

Some of the innovations in middle market menswear – especially the appropriation of classic English menswear – were taken up by mass market menswear retailers. The two dominant retailing players in this market – the Burton Group and Marks and Spencer – played a key role in this process. Both companies re-organized their menswear in the 1980s following quite clear calculations about who their target customers were and what they were looking for in menswear. The Burton Group was quickest to transform its menswear, and it did so within a framework established by a rethink in its approach to cloth-ing markets that dated back to the early 1970s.

The group had been established as Burton in 1900 by Montague Burton and had gained a reputation between the wars and into the 1950s as a popular gentlemen's outfitters. The self-proclaimed "tailor of taste" reached a position of prominence on the High Street that reached a peak in the 1950s. By the early 1970s, however, the still family controlled enterprise – combining the retail outlets and significant manufacturing holdings – was in serious decline. The source of the group's problems derived significantly from a general decline in the sale of suits and the expansion of casualwear markets, together with the strong showing of imported menswear.[10] Burton was also suffering from an ageing customer profile. The group's response was to set in motion a process that would fundamentally redefine its retailing operations. Central here was the decision in 1970 to launch a womenswear boutique called Top Shop, under a team headed by Ralph Halpern. Top Shop broke with Burton's established approach in a number of ways. First, it represented the movement of their operations into the womenswear market. Secondly, Top Shop was set up as a boutique; that is, along the lines of what had been the most innovative form of clothing retailing of the 1960s.[11] This represented, quite dramatically, a different mode of selling clothes than that practised by Burton's main outlets. Top Shop also focused Burton towards a more self-consciously fashionable audience. Thirdly, Top Shop represented a move into a younger market – women aged between 16 and 25 – and set the scene for Burton's ambition to cover more effectively these younger markets through the 1970s and into the 1980s.

The approach to new clothing markets tested out with Top Shop was applied to the young menswear market, as Burton continued to segment its operations across a range of markets. Top Man – "aimed at the 15–24 year old market with high fashion menswear" (Burton Group, 1985: 18) – was launched in 1977 and increasingly took a larger share of Burton's menswear operations: from 44 branches in 1978 and 50 in 1980 to 177 in 1985 (Burton Group, 1989: 228). Nineteen eighty-five was an important year for Top Man. A flagship store was opened in Oxford Street in London and significant new merchandise lines were introduced. Important here was the introduction of the "Portfolio" range aimed at "older and more affluent customers (25–30)" (Burton Group, 1985: 18). This tilting of Top Man upwards in terms of the age of its target audience was a feature that ran through the Burton Group's menswear outlets as it refocused its business into the late 1980s. I look in the next chapter at the specific retailing ethos this fitted into. For the moment, however, we only need note that this rejigging of the relative balance between the different menswear markets serviced by the Burton Group – an emphasis away from the younger markets (16–25) towards older markets (25–45) – led in 1985 to the launch of the Principles for Men chain. The Principles for Men outlets were first rolled out in August 1985 and aimed to offer "an understated fashionability, the look of top European couture, without having to pay the top-of-the-market prices" (ibid. 1985: 22). This was a different market from that serviced by Burton, the group's mainstream stores. Aimed at customers aged between 20 and 40, Burton offered mainstream smart, casual clothing. Principles for Men was directly pitched at the market opened up by Next. Further garment ranges were developed between 1985 and 1989, including the introduction of more expensive ranges. For the Burton Group there was a "gap for quality, high design in the context of the High street" (Burton Group Information, on *The clothes show*, BBC TV, 1/10/89). The introduction of three discreet ranges produced for Top Man by the independent design company Identikit in 1989 fitted into this strategy. They consisted of "Sharp City", "Biker Style" and an English Country look.

Each of these store formats contributed to the profitability of a group that had been struggling in the 1970s, and were part of the transformation of Burton Group from what the *Independent on Sunday* called "a threadbare manufacturer of working men's suitings to the largest specialist fashion group in Britain" (*Independent on Sunday*, 22/7/90: 10).[12]

Marks and Spencer's menswear merchandising underwent significant changes in the period 1984–9. The most pronounced shifts were in relation to the ready-to-wear suits offered by Marks and Spencer. The company had first entered this market in the early 1970s. Through the 1970s this had become an important and highly successful market for the company, and it effectively dominated the ready-to-wear market in men's suits. The suits, like all the Marks and Spencer range produced under its St. Michael trademark, gained a reputation for reliability and value for money. They were also, as Roger Tredre put it, "stiff, predictable, and plain boring" (*Independent*, 22/9/90: 32). An important, if not dramatic, process of change was brought to bear on the range of suits offered under the St. Michael label from the team in charge of the menswear department.

This took the form of offering more expensive and fashionable suits alongside the bottom-of-the-range vented (so called) Classic Cut made from a mixture of polyester and wool. New suits included lightweight wool double-breasted versions in the ventless contemporary cut, or wool two-button single-breasted suits in a looser, less waisted cut. The variations in cut were complimented by the introduction of new colours. In addition to the traditional navy and grey, suits were available, for example, in a rich olive textured fabric (ibid.).

The redesign of men's suits was complimented by the introduction of new ranges of shirts, ties and knitwear. As with the extension of the suit range, Marks and Spencer's new garment ranges made available more expensive, quality products. The introduction of Brooks Brothers shirts and silk ties, following the acquisition of the long-established USA menswear company in May 1988, was one example of this trend.

The casualwear and leisurewear ranges were also expanded: cotton polo-shirts, chambray shirts, lambswool sweaters, pure new wool blazers, turtle-neck wool jumpers in bottle-green and cotton "chinos" offered more fashionable garments for Marks and Spencer's core 35–54 year old men (Marks and Spencer 1989).

## Summary

What has this survey of some of the defining features of menswear design in the mid to late 1980s delivered? I have argued that in relation to the sort of garments produced for the three key menswear markets, the "look" of menswear was subject to a number of developments. The seasons of 1984–5, I argued, were pivotal moments. They condensed in particularly clear fashion the renewed interest in menswear in a number of regions of the fashion industry: the avant-garde circuits of fashion education, the mainstream trade shows and the *haute couture* shows. The new designs that emerged from fashion education and the designer shows (like Gaultier's designs) established a space for high-fashion menswear and signified menswear as a dynamic and contemporary design area. These circuits brought together two dominant approaches to menswear. On the one hand, menswear was constructed around body-conscious styles that drew on "street style" and its appropriation of elements from sportswear.

These valorized "tough" outerwear elements (like the MA–1 flight jacket) and figure-hugging lines. On the other hand, there was a rediscovery of classics, especially in suit design. These harked back to the broad-shouldered jackets and looser trousers of 1940s and 1950s suit styles. Finally, colours in shirts and knitwear were bolder. Both approaches to menswear took up the currency of the name-label, often worn – in the case of Gaultier's sportswear-inspired tops – on the outside of the garment.

These broad trends in high-fashion menswear were paralleled in the middle and mass markets. Next, in both its choice of cuts and fabrics, consolidated a version of classic menswear, particularly around the suit and in its strong outerwear and casualwear. The Burton Group and Marks and Spencer offered menswear ranges that drew on these design innovations for the mass market. The sportswear influence on menswear – from hooded tops, tracksuit bottoms, the strength of name-label sportswear and footwear – was particularly influential on the garment ranges sold in Top Man.

CHAPTER 4

# Menswear and retailing practices: the case of retail design

An underlying thread in the previous chapter was that the formal design innovations in menswear produced for each of the three key retail markets were shaped and accented by their insertion within a set of practices of selling. I referred to the importance of the marketing of the name-label in the designer markets and the attempt to articulate through this marketing a clear set of meanings and values associated with the clothes. I also begin to gesture towards the specific forms of retailing practised by the Burton Group and Next. In this chapter, I want to consider in more detail a component of retailing that was centre-staged by many retailers through the 1980s and which had a significant impact on the retailing of menswear across the markets I have focused on: that is, retail design and the whole organization of shop design and display techniques. Paying attention to retail design is central to my larger argument about the formation of the regime of "new man" imagery. It was through these shop design and display techniques that specific masculinities were represented at the point of sale.

## Retail design and retailing strategy

Retail designing was one of the ascendent professional identities of the 1980s. As specialist design businesses like Fitch-RS (formerly Fitch and Co.), Michael Peters Group, David Davies Associates, Allied International Design, Peter Saville Associates, Pentagram and Din Associates grew through the decade – accelerating a process of corporatization in the design industry – retail design contributed strongly to the public profile and success of many of these businesses.[1]

The rise in professional status of retail designers stemmed from a number of developments. Gardner & Sheppard identify the progressive centralization and more systematic organization of shop display and shop design by High Street multiples – such as Marks and Spencer – from the late 1950s and into the 1960s as a key development (Gardner & Sheppard 1989b: 79). They suggest that this set the terms on which multiple retailers begin to buy in retail design services and in turn provided a market for specialist retail designers through the 1970s and into the 1980s. More importantly, as we will see shortly, the ascendency of retail designers was rooted in the decision of retailing strategists to privilege retail design as the single most important selling technique within retailing. It was this decision that gave retail designers a new higher public profile.

The development of a distinctive set of retail design practices in the 1950s and 1960s was a key part of the genealogy of retail design in the 1980s. Gardner & Sheppard, correctly I think, pick out Terence Conran's design for his Habitat shops as a significant turning point in the development of a deliberately design-led approach to selling. It is worth briefly identifying the elements of Habitat's approach that have informed more recent practice.

Conran started up Habitat with a shop in the Fulham Road, London in 1964. Two prime motivations shaped the launch of Habitat. On a very practical level Conran – essentially a furniture designer – had been frustrated by the way retailers were selling his designs (Gardner, *New Statesman & Society*, 9/3/90: 9). Habitat, in this sense, was an attempt by Conran to present his designs more effectively at the point of sale. In addition, Habitat was driven by Conran's mission to bring "good design" to a discerning public and to educate consumers in the appreciation of "good design".[2] Both these elements fused in Habitat's approach to design-led selling. Conran brought together a set of domestic objects – furniture, furnishings and homewares – in a strongly co-ordinated range of materials and colours; lots of "natural finishes, timber, earthenware, rush matting, basketware, wool and cotton" (Gardner & Sheppard 1989b: 78). Importantly, these domestic objects were displayed in a warehouse-like shop and arranged either as piled up "stock" or set out in room displays. The room displays were particularly innovative as an approach to selling. Gardner & Shepherd quote a long-standing associate of Conran's, Oliver Gregory, who signalled the break marked by this mode of display. Gregory suggested, "twenty years ago furniture wasn't displayed, there were no surprises – all you saw was a sea of cubes three feet high" (ibid.: 78).

The setting out of room displays made very visible the co-ordinated nature of Habitat's range. Here were the clean simple lines of "modernist" design combined with the reclaimed rusticity of Conran's beloved Provence. Conran was, in addition, very clear that this product range was aimed at a specific set of consumers; as he put it: "[I] don't try to satisfy every taste" (ibid.: 77). Gardner & Sheppard suggest that Habitat was principally aimed at "consumers in the 20–30 years old age group, who were relatively affluent, probably professional or white collar, and living away from their parents or recently married" (ibid.: 79).

For this account these are the seminal elements of Habitat's innovation: the "lifestyle" organization of products co-ordinated through selling techniques and addressed to a specific group of consumers. Conran's skill, in fact, was to put more rigorously into practice elements that had been emerging in fashion retailing from the mid 1950s and into the 1960s, most prominently through the development of boutiques. Mary Quant had opened Bazaar in 1955, while in Carnaby Street John Stephen had established His Clothes in 1959. Stephen's boutique concept for His Clothes reworked the look of the shop in order to speak to particular consumers – conceived very loosely within the rubric of fashionableness. Nik Cohn, reflecting on his sojourns through Carnaby Street in the 1960s, caught the new exuberance of fashion retailing (and specifically menswear retailing) that His Clothes embodied:

[He] made his shops like amusement arcades. He had records blaring as loud as they could go, kaleidoscope window displays, garments hung around the open doorways and spilling out across the pavements . . . Inside there was more infinite brightness and newness and glamour (Cohn 1971: 66).

Harrods' Way In, designed by architects Zogolovitch and Gough, marked an intensification of these presentation techniques: purple walls and purple carpets lined its cave-like space (Woudhuysen 1988: 39–40). Granny Takes a Trip in the Portobello road and Barbara Hulanicki's Biba similarly created retail spaces for loosely defined consumer constituencies in which the interior look of the shop was central.[3]

By the mid 1970s the experimentations of small, metropolitan fashion boutiques and Conran's more systematized approach through Habitat, were registering in wider design discourse. James Pilditch, writing in *Retail and Distribution Management* in January 1974, attempted to synthesize the lessons of these experiments in retail design into a more generalizable approach. For Pilditch retail design was the central solution to the "problem" of retailing. That is, it was a way to "improve sales and profitability" (Pilditch 1974: 26). Two linked themes – echoing some of Conran's ambitions – concerned Pilditch. First, he suggested that retail design could play the role of "helping define and create a personality for a retail outlet" (ibid.). In a nice phrase Pilditch saw this as involving the need to "find a corner of the [public's] imagination" (ibid.: 27). Retailers then, and especially multiple retailers, could differentiate themselves from competitors not only through "price cum quality", but through establishing an "emotional" response from the consumer through the shop design. Secondly, "the more fundamental work design can do for retailing is to help it first into the changing consumer-dominated world. We can forecast that shopping will become more specialised – not by product but by type of consumer" (ibid.: 28). Or, more bluntly, "different people – different needs" (ibid.). Retail design, then, functioned to represent the shop's "identity" and to address that "identity" to a specific segmented set of consumers.

Pilditch's comments were specifically addressed to mass market retailers or what he termed "the generalist who aims for a particular audience" (ibid.). In his polemical assertion of the pivotal role retail design should play in solving the "problem" of retailing, Pilditch identified Burton as a mainstream retailer which was receptive to this design-led approach to selling.

The Burton Group's long term designers, Fitch-RS, were assertive advocates of retail design as a powerful marketing tool. Rodney Fitch, founder, chairman and joint managing director, started his career – like a number of other high profile designers of the 1980s[4] – with Conran Design, before establishing Fitch and Co. in 1974. The company grew rapidly over a ten year period servicing a range of clients: Midland Bank, Heathrow Airport, Asda, Esprit du Vin, for example. Fitch, together with Fitch-RS's director of information, James Woudhuysen, were articulate in putting forward in a range of forums a developed conceptualization of design strategy in retailing. They argued that design was fundamentally a "strategic business resource" (Fitch & Woudhuysen 1988: 15); a strategic resource that could be used by retailers in four principal ways. First, to differentiate; secondly, to focus or segment operations; thirdly, to reposition stores; fourthly, to represent stores as brands, fixing their image. (ibid.: 19). They cited the work Fitch and Co. had undertaken for Midland Bank as an example of differentiation. Here the bank used a major overhaul of its interior design to set itself apart from other banks and building societies following changes in the regulation of financial services. The redesign emphasized the bank as a more customer-friendly retail outlet against the austere traditions of bank design. Fitch's work for Debenhams, on the other hand, aimed to reposition the store through the redesign of the shop interior. Starting with the flagship store in Oxford Street, London, the redesign aimed to shift, in Carl Gardner's words, "[Debenham's] dull and worthy image" (Gardner 1987), and to counter falling sales and an ageing customer profile. The overall effect of the work was to produce a glitzy, brightly lit store – "Busby Berkely meets Norman Foster at the disco", to quote Gardner's apt, if somewhat awestruck, description (ibid.). The design represented a 1980s rehash of the department store in its heyday; shopping defined as overblown spectacle, playing off all the right cues about luxury, glamour and status.

What most interests me, however, are Fitch & Woudhuysen's comments on the practice of focusing or segmenting through design. They were very direct about design's role: "Design is a key weapon with which to implement the basic strategy of market segmentation" (Fitch & Woudhuysen 1988: 19). To produce the desired segmentation, Fitch & Woudhuysen emphasized the dialogical ambitions of retail design:

> Design is about capturing the consumer's imagination ... Designing is about needs and desires, about social circumstances; it is about touching people in their hearts as well as their pockets ... We should be concerned with what people want rather than with what we can sell them. A good designer, therefore, will conduct a continuous ... enquiry into the consumer's visual, tactile and spatial consciousness (ibid.: 15).

It is the concern with the cultural values at work within the realms of the "visual, tactile and spatial", signalled in this quote, that gives retail designers a set of co-ordinates through which to segment consumers. In this sense, Fitch & Woudhuysen's comments were a much more rigorous formulation of some of the already established concerns with retail design addressed above. The quote is telling in a further important sense, however. It demonstrates very clearly the concern of designers to organize identities through the coding of shop space. In other words, Fitch & Woudhuysen explicitly understand retail design as working through the organization and incitement of identity. This design practice amounts to the construction of shops as sites of representation in a very deliberate way. This is important for the argument I am making about the representation of specific masculinities through these practices of selling. The coding of retail environments and the articulation of the cultural values represented by this signification of space with the meanings of the garment design, produced specific representations of masculinity. What, though, were the particular cultural values that these retail designs attempted to connote around the menswear merchandise? How was this merchandise accented by the retail design? What were the masculinities represented through the coding of shop space? To answer these questions we need to look in more detail at the design vocabularies mobilized in the retailing of menswear.

## Design vocabularies and menswear

In putting together an account of the design vocabularies deployed by menswear retailers, it is appropriate to begin with one of the most successful practitioners of a design-led, segmented mode of retailing in the 1980s: Next.

Next's retailing strategy was focused around the presentation, as I signalled in the previous chapter, of a limited and co-ordinated garment collection; what George Davies called a "tightly edited range" (Davies 1989: 108). This garment range was targeted to a specific group of consumers – 25 year old plus ABC1 consumers or, more specifically (and initially), "young working women who were weary of the fast fashion in the High Street boutiques but not weary enough for the staider styles of the Department stores" (*Direction*, 23/9/88). The menswear range was merchandised effectively to address and shape an "upmarket" but affordable middle market in menswear. Next, then, in their terms, identified an underserviced segment of the clothing market and based their retailing strategies on effectively servicing this segment. The development of Next – through a proliferation of its retailing forms (Next Too, Next Essentials, Next Accessories, Next Café, Department X, Next Directory, Next Interiors, Next, Next for Men, Next Lingerie) – aimed for a "complete" Next store (in Davies's phrase) that would extend and maintain the "exclusivity" of Next into a wider range of goods and services (Davies 1989: 94). Absolutely pivotal to both the initial formulation and the expansion of the business was the construction and careful regulation of Next's "image". Davies outlined the basis of this concern as follows:

> One of the things that had struck me was the lack of image among the retailers I'd visited. I would visit ten stores in an afternoon, and when I'd finished I'd have real trouble distinguishing one from another in my memory – all of them were quite lacking in any identity . . . Image was uppermost in my mind at the outset, and I knew that image must start with the shop fitments (ibid.: 49–50).

In setting in motion the process of producing what was to become a highly influential shop design, Davies drew inspiration from the early Benetton stores in London. He was impressed by the way Benetton broke with established conventions of display: "Unlike everyone else, they weren't using window dummies to display the merchandise – they simply draped it over black plastic fittings" (ibid.: 48).

Next followed this innovation as part of its approach to the retail interior; an approach that aimed to be – in Davies's favourite phrase – "upmarket from the shop fittings to the sales girls, who were dressed in Next merchandise and looked wonderful" (ibid.: 64). The design formats of the stores varied across the different retailing formats, whilst retaining a strong corporate coherence. Two young design companies were important in the development of this design: David Davies Associates (DDA) and Din Associates. DDA was responsible for the formative designs, while Din Associates worked on later shops – most significantly, the Kensington High Street Next department store and Department X, in Oxford Street, London. These stores marked an important evolution of Next's retail design in the late 1980s.

The formative designs were very distinctive. Central to the design of the Next menswear interiors (including the point of sale materials and packaging) was the use of space and materials. The frontage of the stores gave the first indication of this: a large window set in a dark matt-grey frame beneath the trademark signage – Next – in lowercase lettering. The window displays – framed by this frontage – were similarly uncluttered. A combination of garments was displayed on abstract mannequins, often backed by large display or show cards that gave written accounts of the merchandise range. The display cards – featuring details of the clothes being worn as well as the accompanying copy – played off the themes of space, colour and line in the shop through their layout and lettering. Inside, the lighting, colouring and organization of space were distinctive. Here were the features that formed a coherent design vocabulary: bleached-wood pigeon-holes and dresser units; downlighting spotlights; gently spiralled staircases with matt-black bannisters. The "edited" collection of clothes was displayed in various ways. Around the sides of the shop slatted wooden units displayed a few folded jumpers next to hangers with three jackets; socks were folded in pigeon-holes or individual shoes perched on bleached-wood units. A dresser unit commanded the central space of the shop, placed upon a classic woven carpet. Such features acted as centripetal counterpoints to the displays of clothes set against the walls and encouraged customers to circulate around the shop. The overall feel of these shops was of spaciousness and a cool modernity that invited echoes of cruise-liner aesthetics, together with strong references to traditional gentlemen's outfitters.

The connotations of "upmarketness" and exclusivity that DDA's formats established were rooted, in part, in the quality of the materials used. The polished woods and solid metal chosen were materials conventionally ruled out of court in mass and middle market retail following the developments in synthetic materials (such as moulded plastics) in the 1960s and 1970s.

The choice of these fine quality materials for the shop fittings drew upon an influential vocabulary which had emerged within design practice in the late 1970s. Mark Landini, then of Fitch-RS, and Rasheid Din of Din Associates, whom I spoke to in 1989, both identified the consolidation of minimalism in architecture and product design as formative to this design practice. Landini spoke of the importance of the German electrical goods manufacturer Braun, and their early 1970s designs in matt black and chrome, in establishing certain precepts in the "look" of design materials for a generation of young designers finding their professional feet in the 1980s. More significantly both men – talking about the importance to their work of materials like granite, polished wood, distressed metals and very subdued colours – identified the design emerging from Japan in the early 1980s as seminal.

Rei Kawabuko and the Comme des Garcons' design loomed large here. The interior design of the Comme des Garcons' shops, which I mentioned in the previous chapter, were dramatic in their austerity and "stillness". Typically, the shops were harshly lit with a minimum of clothes displayed on units stripped of detailing or sculpting. Kawabuko, as I suggested earlier, saw this as part of a "new understanding that the shop as much as the clothes should carry the designer's message" (Sudjic 1990: 111).

Rasheid Din underlined the importance of these elements:

> It was the Japanese influence . . . that was the main visual image of the early 80s and that was obviously to do with the minimalism, with the lack of references to any particular period or style or colour and that had very much to do with the strength of designers like Comme des Garcons . . . and about a kind of translation of interiors from Japan to this country. That's where everyone was looking for inspiration. It was incredibly shocking when that came out (interview with Rasheid Din, 1989).

A less austere – but equally influential – minimalism was developed by the Czech-born architect Eva Jiricna. Her work also shaped the parameters of retail design vocabulary in "high fashion" outlets in the early 1980s. Jiricna's design came to prominence through her close collaboration with Joseph Ettedgui for his Joseph shops. The shops featured an identifiable set of carefully controlled colours and materials: pale plaster walls, light marble or stone floors, lots of glass cabinets, matt metal fittings and spot-light brackets, and large-windowed frontage.[5]

The minimalism of Kawabuko and Jiricna was not the only influence, however, on the design vocabularies of menswear retail interiors. A further important design idiom – and this was clear from my comments on Next – was drawn from the fittings and fixtures of traditional gentlemen's outfitters. One retailer was particularly important in "rediscovering" this design vocabulary at the beginning of the 1980s and in establishing its importance: this was Paul Smith. Smith celebrated a nostalgic image of the shopkeeper in his whole retailing ethos and in the design of his retail outlets. As he put it,

> I prefer the individuality and oddness of corner shops or food shops, or shops where old and modern utilitarian items are sold together . . . I enjoy seeing how people sell things, whether its pots or pans in Greece or fruit and vegetables in Marrakesh (Blackwell & Burney 1990: 99).

This enthusiasm for the detail of selling was applied to the collection of objects that embellished the Paul Smith shops: "old cameras, glass soda siphons; plastic radios, old stamp albums . . . train sets", and toy robots (*Arena*, Summer 1992: 154). These curios added to the mahogany fittings, the polished wood and glass cabinets, and the woven rugs that fitted out his shops. All these elements evoked the feel of an English gentlemen's outfitters in the inter-war years, mixed with references to more recent (1950s) childhoods.

World Service Limited, the designer menswear shop in Covent Garden, London, drew on some of the same "retro" menswear out-fitters elements in its retail design; wooden pigeon-holes and glass-fronted cabinets as well as props such as leather-bound suitcases. These design elements were mobilized to capture what its owners and designers, O'Reilly and Prendergast, saw as "the spirit of the well-travelled man" (*Arena*, Spring 1988: 133). Davies, in Great Newport Street, London, went even further in evoking the lost environments of Edwardian England: old-fashioned cricket bats; an ancient-looking canoe; authentic cigarette cases and lighters set out in glass-topped cabinets; and an antique dressing mirror. Here was a set of objects that most directly connoted the visual style and ambi-ence of Merchant and Ivory's film adaptations of Forster's novels: clothes and accessories for your "room with a view".

The influence of minimalism and of references to gentlemen's outfitters wasn't restricted, however, to the retail design of the designer and middle market menswear retailers. It also crossed over into the mass market, most clearly in the retail design of the Burton Group's Top Man.

The Burton Group's interest in retail design grew from their attempts through the 1970s to refocus their business through the segmentation of their retail operations. The launch of Top Shop in 1970, as I noted earlier, marked the beginning of this process. By 1980 this segmentation of their portfolio was quite well established. The 1980 annual report, however, was undemonstrative on the subject: "The Burton Group consists of a number of retailing chains and each with a distinctive face to the public" (Burton Group, 1980: 1). By 1985, the language of segmentation was altogether more confident. Gone was the reference to "the public" – and its implied sense of a limited differentiation within a mass market. Speaking of its menswear concerns, the report suggested,

> the market is fragmenting strongly. Within mainstream purchasers of menswear . . . three principal classes of customer have been identified. This type of market stratification, not by socio-economic class alone, but by consumer preferences and lifestyles, is fundamental to the Group's approach to the marketplace (Burton Group, 1985: 7).

The 1987 annual report went further still in justifying the process of segmentation:

> The British shopper, wishing to express individuality and a sense of style, continues to demand a wider and increasingly specialised range of products and services. The Burton Group has built its success on meeting the specialised needs of the largest and most profitable sectors by developing a widespread but integrated portfolio of national and small space retail chains . . . Everyone knows the standard age, sex and socio-economic categories [can] be used to segment markets. But things aren't that easy. Rather than squeeze people into boxes that don't fit, we have thrown away the boxes and now use more creative and flexible ways of grouping customers. We look at their attitudes to living, how they want to live and express themselves. What their aspirations are . . . What sort of shopping experience are they seeking . . . For each group we develop a shopping experience that meets their requirements (Burton Group, 1987: 1 and 10).

In segmenting their portfolio – which consisted of Burton Retail, Alias, Top Man, Radius, Champion Sport, Principles for Men, Principles for Women, Dorothy Perkins, Secrets, Top Shop, Evans, Harvey Nichols and Debenhams by 1987 – and in developing the appropriate "shopping experiences", the Burton Group emphasized the value of retail design: "We constantly consider and innovate new ideas for shop formats . . . related to customer needs" (ibid.: 10).

The Burton Group's concern to innovate in shop formats impacted very clearly on the fitting out of Top Man. It moved away from its boutique-inspired interiors towards a more restrained mode of presentation by the late 1980s. Fitch-RS's redesign in 1989 broke with the earlier, dominant "look" of Top Man. Introduced with the launch of the chain in 1977/8, and developed through the 1980s, this format emphasized the quantity and diversity of the merchandise on offer: lots of clothes bulging from hangers on floor-standing displays, lit under high voltage lighting. The shop frontage and graphics, as well as the fittings, evoked what Landidni aptly described as the feel of the disco or *Top of the pops*. These elements drew from the visual style of 1960s boutiques. In particular the Top Man signage and logo proclaimed a brusque exuberance through its bright, plastic chunkiness. Fitch-RS attempted to rework this retail design so that it spoke to a slightly older consumer. In came – not surprisingly – bleached wooden floors, slatted wooden units and a less "busy" organization of space. Significantly the typography of the Top Man logo moved towards a more restrained format.

The Top Man redesign – and its selected appropriation of the design vocabulary developed in "high fashion" menswear retailing – is testimony to the ironies of the drive to segment through retail design. One outcome by the end of the decade was to produce some strong continuities across the different menswear markets. The signification of these design elements across the markets consolidated two dominant repertoires of cultural values: a sense of "modernity" and a sense of "tradition" in the presentation of menswear. From the stark, austere minimalism of Comme des Garcons to the softer dark-wood interiors of Paul Smith, menswear outlets mixed – to varying degrees – the aesthetics of non-reference and placelessness of an aggressive modernity with the nostalgia of a particular re-imagined Edwardian past. In this sense, as I have suggested, the coding of shop space added a set of meanings and values to the garments to produce specific representations of masculinities at the site of retail. From Next's new service-class professional and Armani's cool, understated Italian macho to Paul Smith's quirky English gent and Top Man's stylishly casual lad, the shop design and techniques of display, in articulation with the garment designs, coded a number of new or reworked masculinities. In addition, internal to each retailer, were further distinctions. Next's garment range was co-ordinated explicitly, as we have seen, into a range of related but distinct identities. Armani's multiple labels similarly organized a number of Armani "looks": from the conservatism of the blazer to the Emporio Armani jeans and outerwear. Top Man also accented its garment range to make available a number of looks.

The organization of a very deliberate address to certain male consumers through retail design was particularly significant in relation to mass and middle market menswear retailers. This use of retail design was part of the representation by these retailers of a more differentiated construction of the staple blocks of the menswear market; differentiations based on loosely conceived "lifestyle" distinctions. In this sense, retail design was critical to the formation of what, in Part I, I called a culture of flexible specialization in retailing. Together with the targeting and co-ordination of merchandise and close and flexible relations with suppliers, it was through shop display and design that retailers like Next and the Burton Group drove the implementation of a logic of flexible specialization. The representation of a set of masculinities at the point of sale – the representation of a number of "new men" – was part of the cultural languages produced in this formation of a culture of flexible specialization at the point of sale.

## CHAPTER 5

# Menswear and the spectacle of shopping

In the previous chapters, I advanced an argument about the shifts that took place in menswear design through the 1980s and the developments in shop design and display techniques that impacted on the retail of menswear in the same period. I argued that through the articulation of both these elements – the meaning of specific garment designs and the signification of shop space – menswear shops were sites at which new masculinities were represented. Underlying this argument was an attention to the organization of the visual within retail environments. The elements of shop interiors which I detailed – the polished wood, solid-metal fittings, large plate-glass windows, dressing mirrors, show cards, props, spotlighting and so on – addressed shoppers primarily in visual terms. The representation of masculinities at retail sites, then, was imbricated with the construction of visual allures and visual spectacle. The visuality of this process of representation is significant. It formally organized ways of looking for consumers in relation to the selling of menswear. That is, it organized ways of visually apprehending the clothes and the shop space. In this chapter, I want to reflect on the ways of looking associated with menswear retail in the 1980s. At the heart of these reflections is the ambition to develop one of the central concerns of the book: an account of the forms of spectatorship established for men in relation to the "new man" representations and, from that, a concern to float the larger questions about masculinities and sexual identity posed by these ways of looking.

## Technologies of looking: retailing and the visual

As a way of getting to grips with the forms of spectatorship constructed within the retail environments of shops like Next or Top Man, I want to turn to accounts of an earlier period of consumption. Specifically, accounts of the formation of characteristically modern forms of consumption through the nineteenth century and the early twentieth century. I contend that the essential characteristics of the forms of spectatorship associated with menswear retailing in the 1980s can be found, already in place, in this period. Turning to accounts of the formative period of modern consumption, and what I argue was a distinctive technology of looking rooted in these developments, then, sheds considerable light on contemporary forms of consumer spectatorship.

Modern forms of consumption occupy a central part of Rachel Bowlby's book, *Just looking* (Bowlby 1985). The book is concerned to chart the way consumer culture in the period between 1880–1920 was represented in the naturalist fiction of Zola, Gissing and Dreiser and, in particular, the way that the double register of the development of modern forms of consumption preoccupied naturalist fiction. As Bowlby suggests, on the one hand retailing was subject to an intense rationalization and systematic organization as an industry through the nineteenth century. The department store, the great institution of turn of the century urban life, exemplified this process: They were "factories" of selling. On the other hand, however, the developments in selling were characterized by an aesthetisization of the process. As Bowlby puts it "The grand magasins . . . appear as places of culture, fantasy, divertissement, which the customer visits more for pleasure than necessity" (ibid.: 6).

At the root of this organization of pleasure, for Bowlby, was the pleasure of – in her phrase – "just looking"; of enjoying the visual spectacle of goods presented for display. Bowlby, drawing on the accounts of consumption in the work of the naturalist writers, highlighted the distinctiveness of consumer culture in terms of its visual impact – from de luxe goods to plate-glass windows – on the everyday experience of urban life.

Nicholas Green, in his account of the cultural formation of the French bourgeoisie through the nineteenth century, also sheds light on the visuality of the expanding new consumer culture (Green 1990). While Green raises some significant questions of periodization concerning the take-off of consumer culture, locating modern forms of consumption as early as the mid 1770s in Paris, his account similarly emphasizes the importance of visual display to the new forms of selling and consumption. Quoting an anonymous writer – the so-called hermit of Chaussée-d'Antin – Green recounts the way tourists and foreigners were encouraged to try establishments like Vèry's near the Tuileries, "whose 'brilliant salons' were exquisitely arranged for the 'pleasure of the eyes' " (ibid.: 23).

Walter Benjamin, however, has offered perhaps the most celebrated account of the "spectacular" qualities of the expanding consumer culture and his commentary is a point of departure for both Bowlby's and Green's accounts. Benjamin's reading of these developments forms part of what David Frisby has called his "pre-history" of Parisian modernity. This "pre-history" was constructed around a reading of the lyric poetry of Charles Baudelaire and Baudelaire's own critical reflections on modernity. For Benjamin, Baudelaire stood on the cusp of the full-blown process of modernization and its particular impact on the status of the writer. In this sense, Baudelaire illuminated for Benjamin the distinctiveness of modernity, and in particular the consequences of the increased commodification brought by modernization.

Baudelaire provided both the precepts of, and the inspiration for, the exemplary figure of Benjamin's narrative: the *flâneur*. Together with the prostitute, the thief, the ragpicker, the lesbian and the gambler, it was the *flâneur*, the male stroller in the city, who, above all, condensed the quintessentially new in modern life for Benjamin. Significantly, it was through his proximity to the new signs of modern consumption that the modernity of the *flâneur* was shaped. As Benjamin put it,

> he [the *flâneur*] is at much at home among the facades of houses as a citizen is in his four walls. To him the shiny, enamelled signs of businesses are at least as good a wall ornament as an oil painting is to a bourgeois in his salon. The walls are the desks against which he presses his notebooks; news-stands are his libraries and the terraces of cafés are the balconies from which he looks down on his household after his work is done (Benjamin 1973: 37).

In particular it was in the arcades that the *flâneur* was at home. They provided the perfect space for strolling and looking. Benjamin quotes from a contemporary illustrated guide to Paris in invoking the arcades:

> The arcades . . . are glass-covered, marble-panelled passageways through entire complexes of houses whose proprietors have combined for such speculations. Both sides of these passageways, which are lighted from above, are lined with the most elegant shops, so that such an arcade is a city, even a world, in miniature (ibid.: 36–7).

This is a gushing advertisement for the arcades. Nevertheless, it both testifies to their spectacular qualities and gives us a clue to their importance in establishing the basis for a new style of consumption. Underlying the development of the arcades were new production technologies and materials: advances in plate-glass manufacture, iron-working techniques, gas lighting, bitumen and, later, electricity. These made possible features such as the smooth street surfaces for promenading and the display windows and interiors of the arcades. These technologies also underpinned the development of the department store and consumer spectacles like the Grandeville or world exhibitions in Paris and the Great Exhibition of 1851 in London.

Benjamin saw in these retail spectacles (the arcades, the department stores, the world exhibitions) a new staging of the commodity, and in the *flâneur* an allegorical representation of the new relationship between the display of commodities and consumers.[1] The way Benjamin conceptualized this new commodity culture is significant for my account. Centrally, Benjamin's description of the *flâneur* suggested the construction of a new spectatorial consumer subjectivity in relation (initially) to the arcades and its window displays of de luxe goods and expensive trifles. In other words, it suggests the formation of a distinct way of looking at "beautiful and expensive things" (ibid.: 55). In addition, Benjamin emphasized the way this consumer subjectivity not only established a series of looks at the displays of goods and the detail of the shop interiors, but also invited the consumer to look at themselves amidst this spectacle – often literally, through catching sight of their reflection in a mirror or shop window. A self-monitoring look was implicit, then, in these ways of looking. The self-consciousness of the *flâneur* in Benjamin's account underlined this.[2]

Benjamin's account of the *flâneur* also hints at other determinants on the spectatorial consumer subjectivity. Together with the display techniques used in the arcades, the immediate context of the city – and in particular the crowds that filled a city like Paris – shaped specific ways of looking in Benjamin's account. What was produced were a series of interrupted looks or glances. Baudelaire's description of the *flâneur* captured this way of looking well:

> For the perfect flaneur, for the passionate spectator, it is an immense joy to set up house in the heart of the multitude, amid the ebb and flow of movement, in the midst of the fugitive and the infinite. To be away from home and yet to feel oneself everywhere at home; to see the world, to be a centre of the world, and yet to remain hidden to the world. The spectator is a prince who everywhere rejoices in his incognito (Frisby 1985: 17).

Modern life for the *flâneur* – the life of the arcades and the crowds of Paris – is here visually apprehended through such "transitory, fugitive elements, whose metamorphoses are so rapid" (ibid.: 18).

Baudelaire's sonnet, "To a passer-by", which Benjamin comments on, further underlines the formation of new ways of looking conditioned by the urban environment. In the sonnet, the male narrator catches sight of, and is fascinated by, a woman who passes by in the crowd. In the moment of his desire being aroused, however, the woman is already lost again in the crowd. For Benjamin this representation of masculine desire in the city is significant. It is, he suggests, a representation "not so much of love at first sight, as love at last sight". In other words, the desire experienced by the narrator in seeing the woman is the product of the fleeting quality of his look and the transitory nature of the encounter. It is a representation of the frisson of the passing stranger.

Benjamin's commentary on the *flâneur* points us towards the formation of specific ways of looking that were shaped by the new techniques of consumer display and the increasingly differentiated space of the wider city context (such as the distinctions between industrial districts and largely retail and leisure based areas) (Green 1990: 23–42). The sonnet, "To a passer-by", also alerts us to a further dimension of these ways of looking. That is, the way in which these ways of looking were implicated in a set of gendered power relations of looking.

Janet Wolff and Griselda Pollock, as Elizabeth Wilson has shown, have emphasized in quite similar terms the dominance of specifically masculine pleasures in looking associated with modern city space and its consumer display. Wolff goes so far as to suggest that "the possibility of unmolested strolling and observation first seen by Baudelaire, and then analysed by Walter Benjamin were entirely the experiences of men" (Wolff, quoted in Wilson 1992: 99).

Pollock cites the career of the painter Berthe Morisot and her focus on domestic scenes and interiors, to make the same point. Thus for Pollock, "the gaze of the flaneur articulates and produces a masculine sexuality which in the modern sexual economy enjoys the freedom to look, appraise and possess" (Pollock, quoted in Wilson 1992: 101). This was a look, importantly, in which women shoppers were as much the object of masculine visual enquiry as the shop displays. Quite deliberate slippages were often made, in fact, in consumerist commentaries between decorative consumer trifles and women's appearances.[3] Rachel Bowlby quotes an emphatic representation of these relations of looking. The illustration from *La Vie de Londres* (1890), titled, "Shopping dans Regent Street", put it succinctly: "Shopping is checking out the stores – for ladies; for gentlemen, it's checking out the lady shoppers! Shop qui peut!" (Bowlby 1985: 80–81).

This latter commentary, however, also hints at a more complex picture of the gender ascribed to forms of consumer spectatorship in the nineteenth century than the totalizing conceptualization advocated by Pollock and Wolff. Elizabeth Wilson, in her essay, "The invisible flaneur", takes to task Wolff and Pollock for underestimating the ability of groups of women to participate actively in the new consumer subjectivity and its associated forms of spectatorship. Noting the growth of white-collar occupations for women towards the end of the nineteenth century, Wilson argues that this constituency of women were explicitly courted by commercial entrepreneurs and also participated in the pleasures of "just looking" associated with consumption. As she says,

> the number of eating establishments grew rapidly, with railway station buffets, refreshment rooms at exhibitions, ladies-only dining rooms, and the opening of West End establishments such as the Criterion (1874), which specifically catered for women. At the end of the century Lyons, the ABC tearooms, Fullers

tearooms .... the rest rooms and refreshment rooms in department stores had all transformed the middle- and lower-middle
class woman's experience of public life (Wilson 1992: 101).

Nicholas Green also argues that certain groups of women were visible
as promenaders and active shopping voyeurs around the emergent
sites of consumption. An important constituent in this respect was
what he calls "fashionable women" (Green 1990: 41); namely,
wealthy women often involved in fashion or part of the new breed of
society hostesses. These women had the necessary economic power
to consume and were able to negotiate, Green suggests, the uninvited
looks of men in the pursuit of the visual and materials pleasures of
consumption. These women had a privileged and respectable place
in the fashionable boulevards of Paris quite different from that of
other women who moved across the urban topography. These were
"immoral" women like street prostitutes, lorettes and courtesans,
themselves part of the modern phantasmagoria of the city and part of
another arena of masculine consumption.

Green's and Wilson's accounts suggest that women of all classes
were a much more significant presence within the modern city and
around its new sites of consumption than either Wolff or Pollock
suggest, and, more than that, were able to enjoy the pleasures of
shopping spectacle – albeit within more tightly controlled boun-
daries than leisured men. It is also important to re-assert – in contradistinction to Pollock – that these ways of looking were shaped by the
predominance of an interrupted or broken series of looks (including
those that involved forms of self-visualization) rather than by a fixed
gaze. What remains clear from these accounts, however, is the
specific link that was forged in the formative periods of consumer
culture between certain public masculine identities (and the *flâneur*
is, of course, exemplary) and the new modes of spectatorial consumer subjectivity.

The modes of leisurely looking – at the spectacle of displayed goods
and the visual delights of other shoppers – through which the
spectatorial subjectivity of the *flâneur* was produced, were determined by more, though, than the spatial configuration of shop display
and the built form of the city. My argument is that these ways of looking formed part of a larger "technology of looking" associated with
consumption and leisure. The forms of representation associated

67

with a new style of journalism linked to the expansion of the popular press and popular periodicals, and subsequently (and critically) the circulation of photographic images through these same forms, were the other key components of this technology of looking. Benjamin, again, provides some pointers to these processes and their cultural significance.

A whole popular literature devoted to representing the culture of the metropolis and the new delights of consumption was associated with the development of modern forms of consumption. Benjamin singled out the genre of popular publications called *physiologies*, pocket-sized volumes which detailed Paris and the figures who popu-lated the new districts. These were immensely popular publications, with, as Benjamin details, 76 new *physiologies* appearing in 1841. In addition, other styles of brochure and pamphlet appeared that detailed salon culture and were often tied in with the expansion of art dealing and the trade in contemporary pictures and other *objects de luxe*.[4] What is important for my argument is that these publi-cations represented the city and the new forms of consumption in highly visual terms. In Benjamin's memorable phrase, "the leisurely quality of these descriptions [of Paris life in the *physiologies*] fits the style of the *flâneur* who goes botanizing on the asphalt" (Benjamin 1973: 36). I think this can be put more firmly. The spectatorial sub-jectivity of the *flâneur* had conditions of existence in the visual apprehension of the city represented in these literatures; the *flâneur's* ways of looking were shaped by the organization of particular looks or ways of seeing within popular publications. The widespread circu-lation of photographic images of the city and consumer goods that followed the introduction of half-tone plates in the 1880s extended this process through another representational form. Half-tone plates made possible the cheap reproduction of photographic images in newspapers, periodicals, in books and advertisements (Tagg 1988: 55–6). In practical terms this massively extended what John Tagg calls the "democracy of the image", undercutting the previous luxury status of the photograph and turning it into an everyday, throwaway object. Culturally, this photography set the terms for new forms of perception. For Benjamin, at the heart of this process were tech-niques like the close-up and juxtaposition. The practices of photog-raphy associated with the new "democracy of the image", then, visually represented modern life in new and distinctive ways. As such, they formed an important part of the "technology of looking" that structured the experience of consumption in the period around the turn of the century. This was a technology of looking whose precepts went back, as we have seen, as early perhaps as the 1770s and which linked an intertextual set of looks from the interiors of retail environments and the surrounding streets to the written and pictorial representations of city life and consumption in paperbacks, magazines and newspapers. The spectatorial consumer subjectivity associated with the characteristically modern forms of consumption was produced across these constructions of ways of looking or seeing.

## Shopping spectacle and the "new man"

It has been important to set out in some detail the forms of spectatorship inscribed within the technology of looking associated with the emergent period of consumer culture, because these forms of spectatorship illuminate the ways of looking associated with a more contemporary shopping spectacle. My argument, as I suggested at the beginning of this chapter, is that there were strong continuities between the spectatorial consumer subjectivity shaped in the formation of modern forms of consumption and the ways of looking organized for consumers by menswear retailers like Next or Top Man through their shop designs and display techniques in the 1980s. The allegorical figure of the *flâneur*, in this sense, continues to throw light on how we can conceptualize the ways of looking organized within these menswear shops. Mirrors, large plate-glass windows, artificial lighting, and the displays of garments and accessories in shops like Next, Top Man or Comme des Garcons, combined to organize precisely the forms of spectatorship that I elaborated on in relation to Benjamin's description of the arcades of Paris in the 1840s.

Asserting the continuities in these forms of spectatorship, however, cannot in itself deliver a sufficient account of the ways of looking associated with more contemporary menswear retailing. Specifically, what is underdeveloped in the account so far is a consideration of the central question I posed earlier on. What was the nature of the relations of looking established between the male consumers addressed by retailers like Next, Top Man or Comme des Garcons and the masculinities represented at these sites of retail?

I suggested, above, that the forms of spectatorship produced within the technology of looking associated with characteristically modern forms of consumption, privileged certain public masculinities as the subject of the look. Women were, in Nicholas Green's phrase, "partially disenfranchised" from this visual apprehension of the city and its forms of consumption. They appeared more often themselves, as we saw, as part of the spectacle of consumption, as *objects de luxe* viewed through the eyes of a masculine spectator in accounts and representations of the city. This conceptualization of consumer spectatorship, however, foregrounded (for good reason) one set of looking relations (between men and women), at the expense of other relations of looking in play at consumption sites. Problematically, it cannot help us conceptualize the forms of masculine–masculine looking written into shopping spectacle. These are particularly important in the selling of menswear, given the kinds of address to male consumers made by the shops (detailed in the previous chapter) and the nature of the other shoppers circulating within and around these shops.

Getting to grips with these ways of looking means developing the implications of the contention I have made throughout this chapter. Namely, that the ways of looking which characterize the experience of shopping are shaped not only by the organization of ways of looking through the coding of shop space, but also by the construction of ways of looking within cultural forms associated with this consumption, be that brochures, consumer guides, catalogues, adverts or periodicals.

What cultural forms of the 1980s constructed such intertextual ways of looking? My argument is that the advertising representations that signified the developments in menswear and the two types of popular magazines at the heart of the book – the "style press" and the men's general interest magazines – did precisely that. The magazines, in particular, represented a privileged site in the construction of forms of looking. Through the styling and presentation of menswear, the magazines framed specific ways of looking between the male models in the text and the male readers of the magazines. Both the codings of masculinities within the magazines and the ways in which the reader's eye was guided in the construction of these representations, were determinants on the spectatorship associated with shopping for clothes. The particular configuration of the masculine–masculine relations of looking within menswear shops was largely set, then, by these forms of representation. Fully developing an account of the masculine–masculine ways of looking organized within the shop space of retailers like Next or Comme des Garcons, requires, then, an account of these magazines. In Part IV, I set out in detail the dominant ways of looking constructed within the fashion pages of both the "style press" and men's magazines. It is in this context that I advance an argument about the forms of masculine–masculine looking coded in relation to the new representations of masculinities across the regime of representation.

## Conclusion

It is appropriate to take stock of the arguments I have set out in this chapter, as they operate in a slightly different register to the arguments I made in the previous two chapters of Part II. Let me repeat. I have argued that the construction of forms of visual spectacle and visual allures were important to the selling of menswear in the 1980s across the three retail markets. This coding of shop space set the formal conditions for ways of looking at the menswear garments and accessories. I argued that these ways of looking were not new, however, but rather reproduced ways of looking associated with the emergence of characteristically modern forms of consumption. Turning to accounts of the formation of the technology of looking associated with early consumer culture provided ways of conceptualizing the consumer spectatorship organized in the menswear shops that concerned us. Benjamin's commentary on the *flâneur*, in particular, pointed us towards the formation of specific ways of looking shaped by the new techniques of consumer display and the increasingly differentiated space of the wider city context (such as the distinctions between industrial districts and largely retail and leisure based areas) and the representation of the city and consumption in visual terms within cultural forms like periodicals. At the heart of this, was the construction of a spectatorial consumer subjectivity; that is, a consumer subjectivity shaped through ways of looking at the consumption spectacle. These ways of looking were allegorically represented in Benjamin's description of the *flâneur*. In addition, I suggested, these ways of looking were dominated by glances or an interrupted series of looks, rather than a fixed gaze. Within this interrupted series of looks, a self-visualization by consumers was also

71

important. These ways of looking opened up a narcissistic dimension to spectatorship.

A final additional point needs emphasizing. It is important to underline that I have been reflecting on the formal construction of ways of looking. It would be dangerous to read from these conceptualizations the actual visual investment made by real shoppers. I have argued in Part I that it is necessary to hold out against temptations to cut through the moment of the articulation between real individuals and the formal positions of subjectivity produced within systems of representations – in this case the coding of shop space and popular representations and their associated ways of looking. An adequate account of the exchange of looks that took place in shops like Top Man or Next would need to reconstruct the actual investments made by shoppers. This would include piecing together the organization of looking as part of a number of practices: walking, handling the garments, the social relations of shopping (individually and with male and female friends), and even the conventions of service practised by shop staff. Such an account would also need to insist that the formally constructed ways of looking have themselves to be operationalized as techniques of looking. The injunctions to look organized as part of the experience of shopping, then, have to be learnt and performed.

# PART III

# Advertising, market research and the "new man"

# Introduction

It is funny how women do not appear in any of these splash and smell ads for men anymore. I am not complaining, but the latest in the genre is all hiss and puff noises and lots of New Man preening.
(Robert Ashton, *Campaign Choice*, 18/11/88: 7)

If developments in the design and selling of menswear set some of the big terms for the formation of the "new man" imagery, advertising practices played an equally important role in underpinning the new representations of masculinity. The two institutional sites, as we have already seen, were not unconnected. Advertising practices intersected very directly with the marketing and selling of menswear and associated accessories. Press advertising – usually produced "in-house" by designers or retailers – was particularly important in the designer menswear market. For Gaultier or Armani – to take the two most prolific advertisers – it was central to the marketing of the name-label.

The signification of the developments in menswear design was not restricted, however, to representations associated with menswear advertising. The appropriation of elements of the new designs in menswear was a *leitmotif* across a number of advertising markets in which the "new man" imagery was mobilized in the mid to late 1980s: grooming and toiletries advertising, as well as financial services, alcohol and consumer electronics advertising.

The production of the new codings of masculinity in advertising representations was dependent on specific institutional practices. Looming large in Part III, then, is an argument about the nature of these institutional practices and a specific reading of developments in UK advertising that bore upon the production of the representations.

In the account developed over the next three chapters, I put together a picture of the specific forms of knowledge and practice that intersected in the production of adverts and the development of campaigns. In putting together this picture, I foreground the work of certain groups of advertising practitioners. These were the practitioners associated with the so-called "creative revolution" within UK advertising. From the end of the 1970s, these practitioners problematized the established priorities of advertising production. The changes they brought about were significant. They shifted the underlying problematics of what constituted an effective advert; how advertisers addressed consumers within campaigns; and the image of the market place which underpinned campaign development.

In Chapters 7 and 8, I focus upon three seminal elements of these new formations of advertising production: account planning, media buying and the classification systems used to segment consumers within advertising research. It was the alignment of these elements within the rubric of "creative advertising" which was central to the construction of a distinctive style of "image-led" advertising. This form of advertising – which intensified the aesthetisization of advertising representations – was absolutely central to the representation of the "new man" within television and press advertising.

These shifts in the process of advertising production had larger institutional or organizational dimensions to them. In particular, they were often linked to questions about how advertising agencies should be managed and structured as businesses. I begin Part III, then, by sketching out some important institutional developments within UK advertising within which the shifts in advertising practice that primarily concern me were located. An account of these institutional shifts is important because, during the 1980s, the UK advertising industry experienced its most expansive period of growth in the post-war period. Underpinning this in part was a marked increase in advertising expenditure.[1] If the expansion of the industry in the 1960s, however, had been driven by the growth in the consumer sectors of the economy under the impact of mass production, the institutional expansion of the industry in the 1980s was tied in with the increasing globalization of production and the construction of new global markets. It is to these developments and how they impacted on UK advertising, that I now want to turn.

## CHAPTER 6

# Acquisition, the stock market, diversification and globalization: institutional developments in UK advertising

Two rather different January events point us towards the important institutional changes that occurred within the UK advertising industry during the 1980s. In its first issue of the decade, on 4 January 1980, *Campaign*, the advertising trade journal, reported the replacement of J.Walter Thompson, the American owned multinational and so-called "University of Advertising", at number one in the rankings of advertising agencies in the UK, by the ten year old British agency, Saatchi and Saatchi. Seven years later, on another January day, the advertising industry's own share listing sector – the *Financial Times* Actuaries All-Share Index, Classification 75 – was established.

Saatchi and Saatchi's ascendancy to the top of the rankings on the cusp of the decade presaged their dominance of the agency rankings through the rest of the 1980s, and their enormous impact on UK advertising and the international industry. As we will see, Saatchi and Saatchi's strategy for expansion and institutional development set the terms for one influential version of what an advertising agency ought to be like as an organization. Their eventual fall from grace in 1989, largely under the weight of debts accrued in the course of their massive expansion, signalled, significantly, the gearing up of what was to be a severe recession in the industry. In an almost oedipal narrative, however, in the final months of the decade Saatchi and Saatchi's place in the agency rankings was taken by WPP – the "super-acquisitive" company headed by Saatchi and Saatchi's former finance director, Martin Sorrell.

The establishment of Classification 75 came at the height of the City's "love affair" – to use the language of *Campaign* – with the advertising industry. Traditionally, City brokers had been sceptical of advertising agencies as investment opportunities because of their low net-asset values. To City eyes, then, agencies had looked like insecure investments because they lacked the underpinning of valuable assets. Conversely, few UK owned agencies had historically gone down the road of public flotation. Brunnings had been the first UK owned agency to request stock market listing in 1961. The late 1960s saw a further group of agencies going public. Their fortunes were generally poor, however, with only Geers Gross (floated in 1969) remaining public by the mid 1980s.[1] Much of the reluctance of agencies to float on the stock market stemmed from a perception by them of the constraints imposed on running an agency by the responsibility to shareholders – especially institutional investors – which came with being a public company. The establishment of Classification 75 was part of a new, positive (and at times celebratory) view of advertising agencies by City investors and also registered moves by a number of agencies towards a rethink of the value of stock market status.

What lay between these two January events, in fact, was a period of expansion and re-organization for the UK industry; expansion and re-organization shaped in institutional terms by advertising agencies' relationships not only to the stock market, but also, relatedly, to acquisition and globalization. Both Saatchi and Saatchi and financial institutions loom large in this story.

## Agencies and financial institutions

In 1984, the accountants Spicer and Pegler produced their first annual profitability study of British advertising agencies. The publication of the study, from a prestigious firm, was part of the new approach to advertising agencies from within the financial sector. Underlying the interest in agencies, and informing the publication of the Spicer and Pegler reports, were two factors. First, as the second survey from Spicer and Pegler in 1985 evidenced, profits among the top 50 agencies were increasing at a rapid rate. Secondly, and more importantly, however, investors' criteria for assessing agencies had changed with the introduction of the price–earnings index. The introduction of the index signified a shift away from market capitalization assesments of companies towards a performance-based assessments of shares. Within these new criteria, a publically floated agency looked less like a flimsy, low-asset company and, if its shares performed well within the price–earnings index, more like a good investment opportunity. A further important dimension of City–advertising agency relations followed from the adoption of the price–earnings index. New accountancy regulations in the City transformed the relationships between agencies and City institutions. As Peter York has argued, these new forms of accountancy enabled financial institutions to help finance the acquisitions of publicly floated agencies well above the real capital asset values of the agencies. As York (*Campaign*, 24/2/89: 42–3) noted, while the agencies' price–earnings ratios remained good the City turned a blind eye to what was the increasing accumulation of debt in the agency sector through the 1980s and to the slow pace of managerial restructuring in the emerging international agency networks.

Investment institutions' renewed interest in advertising agencies was complimented by agencies' own turn to the City, as I have already noted. Since the merger of Saatchi and Saatchi with Compton Partners in 1975, no agencies had gone public. However, Wight Collins Rutherford Scott's entry onto the stock market in 1983 signalled the beginning of a new phase. Nineteen eighty-six marked the high-water mark of this trend, with six agencies and one media independent going public in the course of the year (*Campaign*, 20/6/86: 40). The change in attitude of agencies to acquiring a stockmarket listing requires some unpacking. Although they had gone public at an earlier moment, Saatchi and Saatchi's development sheds light on this shift in business practice. Their expansion articulated important dimensions of the strategic thinking that informed agencies' ambitions to go public.

## Saatchi and Saatchi

Saatchi and Saatchi's relationship to the City was based upon a clear strategy of expansion and acquisition. This strategy was built around two interlinked aims: to diversify their business and globalize their operations. Saatchi and Saatchi saw advertising agencies as increasingly becoming global multinational organizations capable, through their international networks, of fully servicing international clients. In addition, through being what Saatchi and Saatchi management called – in an important phrase – a "one stop shop", agencies would be able to offer a complete range of advertising and marketing services to these clients. The status of Saatchi and Saatchi as a public company was fundamental to these long term ambitions. Only with the ability to finance expansion against the value of its shares could the agency contemplate acquisition and its global goals.

Two features of Saatchi and Saatchi's programme of acquisition and restructuring through the 1980s are worth reflecting on. These were the buying up of foreign advertising agencies and communication businesses, and, associated with this, the centralization by Saatchi and Saatchi's management of its media buying operations. A balance sheet of the Saatchi and Saatchi "empire" in April 1986 – prior to its acquisition in the latter part of that year of the USA agency, Ted Bates, which led to its emergence as the world's biggest advertising agency – reveals the extent of these developments. The company was organized around seven communications and consultancy services: advertising (the core operations); direct marketing; public relations; sales promotion; design; market research; and management consultancy (*Campaign*, 25/4/86: 31). This aggregation formed part of the strategy of globalization. In its core area of advertising, for example, the parent company, Saatchi and Saatchi Compton (UK), was accompanied by seven UK agencies, seven USA agencies, one UK/USA international agency, one USA international agency, and one Hong Kong agency; while in the fields of direct marketing, public relations, design, market research and management consultancy, a similar mix of UK and USA companies was evident, together with a small number of European companies.

The commitment to the development of a "global one stop shop" was underlined by Saatchi and Saatchi's centralization of their media buying services. The strategy was a logical development within the processes of globalization and diversification, and the concomitant spreading of the agency's networks. The acquisition of Ray Morgan and Partners (RMP) in August 1988 provided the vehicle for this process of media buying concentration. RMP, as *Campaign* noted, formed the nucleus of a centralized media buying unit which included the media buying operations of its three key UK agencies – Saatchi and Saatchi itself, BSB Dorland and KHBB. Saatchi and Saatchi had established their capacity to enter the league of serious global media buyers eight months earlier, with their co-ordination of the media buying for British Airways' "Club Class" service campaign. Rather than the Saatchi and Saatchi-owned agencies in each individual country buying the media space, space was booked in eight international magazines and newspapers through a central office. This represented the end goal of global advertising: the simultaneous targeting of different national markets (*Campaign*, 11/12/87: 21). Saatchi and Saatchi also used the centralization of their media buying to improve the terms of their dealings with media owners, most notably the ITV companies in the UK (*Campaign*, 12/8/88: 12).

How Saatchi and Saatchi managed their polyglot networks became the litmus test of their particular organizational vision of advertising for many trade commentators. *Marketing*, in applauding the agency's acquisition programme, suggested that their goal should be "'quality networks', with developed commonality between clients of each agency and a cross-feeding between New York and Europe" (*Marketing*, 23/7/87: 12). Saatchi and Saatchi attempted to deal with organizational questions of this kind in the summer of 1987 through a major restructuring programme of their business. The restructuring involved the merging of Saatchi and Saatchi's two worldwide networks – Saatchi and Saatchi Compton Worldwide and Ted Bates Worldwide – with two New York based USA agencies they owned – Damer Fitzgerald Sample (DFS) and Baker and Spielugel (ibid). The restructuring attempted to improve the communication within the Saatchi and Saatchi empire, in particular in relation to their USA markets.

In a *Campaign* debate in 1988, Terry Bannister and Ray Warman, joint managing directors of Saatchi and Saatchi, defended the reorganization and its strategic consequences. Significantly, despite the enormous creative reputation of the advertising produced by Saatchi and Saatchi's London agency, Bannister and Warman had to begin their defence of the global model of expansion chosen by Saatchi and Saatchi against the charge that (what tended to be called) "multinational companies produced "multinational art". That is, bland, predictable and unstylish advertising. This was a recurrent theme in contemporary trade debates.

Bannister and Warman organized their argument around, in part, a telling plea for the issue of agency development to be grounded in the recognition of the many possible pathways open to agencies. They were staunch, however, in their defence of the global route:

> Across a wide selection of industries . . . size and an organised multinational capability has become a prerequisite for success . . . In these cases it is often beneficial to have the management and coordination of communications carried out by an agency with both the experience and infrastructure in place (*Campaign*, 1/4/88: 38–9).

In addition, the services offered by a global agency like Saatchi and Saatchi could produce a coherent global marketing strategy – and from that a clear global identity – for the client company across different national markets. Global agencies functioned, then, in Bannister and Warman's words, as a "totem pole around which the national managers dance" (ibid.).

The success of global advertising in the Saatchi and Saatchi model was not based, however, on the classic form of global marketing best represented by Coca Cola through the 1970s.[2] For Bannister and Warman, to be good globally meant being good locally. Thus,

> Getting it right from a Saatchi and Saatchi point of view means recognising that you cannot be good globally without being good locally. Even centralised multi-national clients have the right to expect creative work to compete effectively in the context of local markets in which they sell (ibid.).

Underlying this "local" approach to global markets were new forms of consumer research. Saatchi and Saatchi could both aggregate an advertising campaign across different national markets, and yet register local differences, because they had identified new global consumer groups. These were groups of consumers who shared similar values and lifestyles, despite their national differences. Saatchi and Saatchi's annual report for 1985 succinctly articulated this thinking:

> sophisticated marketers are recognising that there are probably more social differences between midtown Manhattan and the Bronx, two sectors of the same city, than between midtown Manhattan and the 7th Arondissement of Paris . . . [consumers] bond horizontally across international borders more strongly than they do vertically within a country (Saatchi and Saatchi 1985; *Campaign*, 24/4/87: 49).

Bannister and Warman's article was counterposed in the same issue of *Campaign* to an article by John Bartle, joint managing director of the agency Bartle Bogle Hegarty (BBH). The juxtaposition of these two articles dramatized fractures within the industry on the issue of agency development; namely around questions of acquiring a stock-market listing, acquisition and globalization. Bartle set out BBH's alternative strategy of a defiantly "local" solution to global

advertising, challenging Saatchi and Saatchi's ability to really produce an effective service within what he called – pointedly – the
rubric of a "Napoleonic Complex". It is important to consider BBH's
organizational strategies because they were read, by many trade
commentators and by the key protagonists, as signifying a different
philosophy of advertising. A philosophy of advertising borne out, it
was claimed, in the type of advertising produced by BBH.

## Bartle Bogle Hegarty

BBH began life in 1982, formed by a breakaway split of three of the
senior partners at the Paris owned network TBWA – creative director, John Hegarty, and joint managing directors John Bartle and
Nigel Bogle. The trio had gained strong reputations for their development of TBWA's London office (founded in 1973), establishing
in particular recognition as producers of what *Campaign* called,
"creative work and solid service" (*Campaign*, 19/3/82: 29). Hegarty,
especially, was gaining a reputation as "London's most acclaimed art-
director" (ibid.). The statements made at the time of BBH's formation by its founding partners echoed those of other so-called
"second wave" agencies formed in the late 1970s and early 1980s.[3] It
is worth underlining here a couple of points from these statements.

First, BBH saw its founders as having a high profile involvement in
the advertising process, rather than retreating within a distancing
management structure. As a built-in element of the agency's pro-
jected development, and as an indicator of the agency workplace
culture, this represented a clear attempt to run an agency on "small
shop" lines: to maintain the agency's key assets – the skills of their
founders – at the forefront of the agency's work. The ambition to
involve the agency's principles in the day to day running of the
agency, as a matter of principle, was complemented by a stated infor-
mality of office life:

> What we'll be doing is making the agency more informal. We'll
> be quite happy if we have people at BBH who walk in and the
> clients can't tell whether it is a creative person, an account per-
> son or a planner (*Campaign*, 23/4/82: 15).

Secondly, an important founding principle of BBH was the refusal
to do creative pitches for work. This bucked an axiomatic practice.

Advertisers would discuss their advertising requirements with a number of agencies who – usually once shortlisted – would competitively bid or pitch for the work through submitting a rough outline of a possible campaign. Accounts were won in this way, and often had to be defended in periodic reviews by the client. These reviews, in turn, would also usually include a pitch. The rationale behind the no-pitches principle, however, was continually defended by BBH. As Hegarty put it, "By asking for a pitch a client is denying himself his role in the production of advertising" (*Campaign*, 23/4/82: 15).

Liz Watts, account planner at BBH, elaborated on the same argument to me in July 1989. She argued that the work done on creative pitches was usually wasted (even if the agency won the account) because it rarely ran, and that the refusal to enter pitches ultimately benefited the client because it allowed them to buy the full value of the agency's time.

This "no pitch" policy proved controversial in the industry. Other agencies criticized it publically either for its naïvety or else contested the honesty of the claim. As Winston Fletcher pointedly suggested, John Hegarty's ability to knock up a quick sketch on the back of a napkin for the client effectively amounted to a pitch. The policy, however, underscored BBH's reputation as an agency committed in an uncompromising way to innovative and stylish advertising. As a business practice the insistence on this policy appeared to bear out BBH's ardent defence of it. In the mid 1980s, BBH was winning over 50 per cent of those accounts it was in contention for. This compared with average figures for account gains amongst agencies of 25 per cent.[4]

BBH's "no pitch" policy and its concern to retain the company's founders in the day to day production side of the business, were central to the service offered by the agency. The institutional development of the agency was constructed around these core service principles. In 1986, for example, on the back of impressive account gains,[5] the agency established a media department and also diversified into design with the formation of the design consultancy, Tango. A "below-the-line" business, Lexington Street Group (LSG), was also set up by the agency (*Marketing Week*, 3/3/89: 45).[6] Unlike the approach exemplified by Saatchi and Saatchi, however, BBH's diversification was managed within a very different set of organizational arrangements. Thus, although Tango and LSG worked with BBH's clients, they were essentially affiliated groups with free-standing operations, rather than part of an integrated service package. In other words, they did not form part of a "one stop shop".

A second line management structure was also established by BBH in early 1989. This was a response to further account gains and to the agency's general growth. The organizational rationale behind this move was both to maintain the agency's youthful image and to continue to include the presence of the founders in the servicing of client accounts (*Marketing Week*, 3/3/89: 46).

BBH's organizational set up also remained assertively opposed to public flotation and expansion through acquisition into other national markets. The founding partners continued to feel that if the agency became a public company, it would be compromised in the production of its work by having to be attentive to the demands of shareholders (interview with Liz Watts, 1989). In addition there was a sense that the organizational restructuring that being a public company would impose on the agency would counter its "small shop" ethos. More straightforwardly, there was the sense of "why rock the boat when its already going full steam ahead?" (Bartle, *Campaign*, 9/1/87: 32).

The strategy *vis-à-vis* globalization was equally clear. In contradistinction to Saatchi and Saatchi's vision of globalization as providing the basis for improved service provision, BBH continually asserted the "creative" execution of adverts and their appropriate placement against globalization. As Bartle put it,

> For people who want the convenience of an international network we are not the agency. For people who want effective international advertising there's no reason why we shouldn't be on the list (*Marketing Week*, 3/3/89: 45).

These concerns were re-emphasized in Bartle's head-to-head in *Campaign* with Saatchi and Saatchi's joint managing directors, Warman and Bannister, which I have already commented on. For Bartle, the issue of globalization and the development of international networks came down to a significant philosophical divide. His comments are worth quoting at length:

> [Is] the best way of providing client service providing the best work you can? If it is . . . then being multinational strews your path with almost every possible obstacle. It opens you up to the

"multi-national creative solution" (otherwise known as the low-est common-denominator, except in the rarest cases). Someone said that multinational solutions were pursued by those more interested in saving money from advertising than making money through it. I agree (*Campaign*, 1/4/88: 38–9).

Next to this rubbishing of global advertising, Bartle went on to outline BBH's alternative approach. Commenting on BBH's work which had run in countries outside the UK for clients like Audi, Levi-Strauss, Dunlop and Pepsi he said,

(These campaigns were) all created in one office primarily to meet the needs of a local market [UK]. It has been evaluated for elsewhere, passed the test and run. And, believe me, that is very different from creating work "internationally" somewhere in a network for some generalised audience and then evaluating it. At least this way you start with the best work you can do (ibid.).

Bartle's comments seem to me, however, to miss their mark badly. As we have seen, Saatchi and Saatchi's version of global advertising was much closer to BBH's notion of "local" advertising than Bartle was prepared to acknowledge. His comments, in this sense, were indicative of slippages made in trade commentaries between the organizational development pursued by different groups of agencies in the 1980s and the nature and quality of the advertising they produced. Saatchi and Saatchi certainly confounded the easy equivalences that were often made between, on the one hand, highly diversified global agencies and wooden and unimaginative advertising and, on the other, small entrepreneurial agencies and highly innovative and stylish advertising.

This is not to suggest, however, that there was nothing in these arguments. The institutional developments in advertising and the competing models of expansion did refract shifts going on within the professional culture of the industry and the alignment of different formations of practitioners. One of the concerns at stake in these shifts was the advocacy of "creative" advertising by groups of practitioners. For John Hegarty, whose work with BBH was closely associated with this approach to advertising, creative strategy was centrally based upon the construction for consumers of "a vision they can aspire to" (*Campaign*, 3/3/89: 42). BBH's company maxim underlined this commitment to a creative style of advertising: "We don't sell," it claimed, "we make people want to buy" (*Marketing Week*, 3/3/89: 44). It was about, in other words, constructing an advert around the "emotional selling point" of the product (ibid.; interview with Liz Watts, 1989).

This concern to construct for consumers an elaborated imaginary landscape within which the "emotional" values of the product were signified, took issue with the styles of (particularly television) advertising which had been enshrined in the textbooks of advertising practitioners in the post-war years. One figure had best articulated this established form of advertising practice and was the implicit target of the new formation of practitioners: Rosser Reeves. Reeves, the Chairman of Ted Bates through the 1960s, had expounded what he termed the "USP" method of advertising in his highly influential book, *Reality in advertising*, published in 1961. For Reeves, good advertising sprang from the effective identification of a product's unique selling proposition. That is, the product's distinctive features or qualities – usually features and qualities associated with what the product could do – which distinguished it from competing products. Once these had been identified, they could be hammered home in the campaign. This technique underlay the classic genre of fast moving consumer goods advertising, which included products like foods and household products. The immortal piece of copy – "this product washes whiter" – said it all.

The USP form of advertising centre-staged the written copy or verbal statements in delivering the message in the advert. It was the perceived decline of the centrality of such a copy-led advertising that concerned some practitioners. A series of articles in *Campaign* through the mid to late 1980s gave a glimpse of the tensions being played out between the advocates of this kind of advertising and practitioners committed to "creative advertising". The article headlines caught the terms of what was at stake: "Words vs images: who wins?" (*Campaign*, 27/3/87: 17); or, "Communications irony which is killing-off the copywriters" (*Campaign*, 24/4/87: 48–9). For Stuart Bull, the new priorities in advertising production took the form of an increased "reliance on aural and visual ideas that tap emotion, rather than written propositions, spoken and logical claims which appeal to the head" (ibid.). Against the trend of image-led advertising, commentators like Bull defended the craft and rigour of copywriting skills and copy-driven advertising. The cry was consistently put:

"[We are seeing] the decline of copywriters in creative departments at the advantage of the art director" (*Campaign*, 19/7/85: 33).

Amidst sentences littered with admonishments like "style over content" or "a disproportionate emphasis on visual over copy", the work of BBH for Levi's 501 jeans, GGT for Holsten Pils and Saatchi and Saatchi for Lanson were damned as anathema. In their place, what was evoked as the exemplar of quality advertising was Collett Dickenson Pearce's work for Heineken in the 1970s. This was work characterized by the sharpness of the idea behind the advert and its copy ("Heineken refreshes the parts . . . "), rather than its visual style.

Different kinds of acumen were set against each other in these articles: the written competences and forms of wit associated with a copy-led practice versus a much more visually literate practice which drew upon a range of representational – especially aesthetic – traditions. The creative ambitions of advertising associated with the so-called creative agencies in the 1980s (like Yellowhammer, Publicis, Gold Greenlees Trott, Saatchi and Saatchi and Bartle Bogle Hegarty) were not, however, entirely new. They had precedents as far back as the forms of advertising associated with early consumer culture. Pears Soap's classic advertising, for example, quite clearly marketed the product through the construction of "emotional" qualities and attributes by linking it with a powerful visual representation of an angelic child. Closer to home, television advertising – where USP styles were most aggressively mobilized – had from the early to mid 1960s begun to use musical scores in favour of jingles and a more dynamic combination of picture editing and sound to signify a particular "way of life", mood or emotional feel in relation to the product. The London Press Exchange's two 1963 television campaigns for Super National Benzole – "Beach" and "The Getaway People" – for example, offered an exhilarating vision of the freedom of motoring to sell the corporate name within the competitive petrol and motor oil market.[7]

This is not to suggest, however, that the advertising practices of "creative agencies" did nothing new. What was distinctive about many of the adverts associated with the "creative" advertising of the 1980s was the specific representational techniques and conventions mobilized in the making of adverts based upon an "emotional selling point" or ESP strategy. The turn to forms of pastiche in appropriating retro-imagery, the self-conscious use of black and white film stock, cinematic forms of lighting, very fast editing and jump cuts, and the use of new typefaces for the accompanying copy on television advertising were just some of the shifts in the construction of representations which extended the ambition of ESP advertising in the work of BBH, Yellowhammer, GGT and others.

The turn to these representational techniques was dependent on a number of factors. What interests me here are some of the institutional reasons for these shifts. First, they were underpinned in part by the change in the relative mix of clients serviced by agencies. In the 1980s, a marked feature of advertising expenditure was the relative decline of fast moving consumer goods advertising and the expansion of financial services advertising, corporate advertising, government advertising and car advertising (Jordans 1989). These clients and product fields were not only less rooted in the tradition of copy-based USP advertising, but also more open to new approaches. In particular, the marketing managers of these clients tended to be free of the legendary conservatism which characterized the marketing managers of companies like Unilever and Procter & Gamble, the big spending fast moving consumer goods advertisers.

Secondly, there was some shift within the advertising profession away from the recruitment within creative departments of university educated humanities graduates in favour of art school trained practitioners. These practitioners brought with them a set of competences in visual representation rather than written and literary skills. This again laid the basis for a shift in creative practices (interview with O'Donahugue, 1989).

Thirdly, and more importantly, three related elements impacted upon the drive towards creative advertising in the 1980s. These were the influence of new forms of consumer research, the rise to prominence of account planning and the perception by advertising practitioners of media pluralization and a concomitant fragmentation of mass audiences and readerships. These were crucial dependencies within which the arguments advanced by groups of practitioners about "creative" advertising were rooted. They laid the institutional basis for the deployment of new representational languages within "creative" advertising.

I want to turn to the developments in consumer research first, and then move on, in Chapter 8, to account planning and the trade representations of media pluralization. The aim is to put together a picture of the way these three elements were aligned within the practice of advertising production associated with the "creative" style of advertising. Before I do that, though, it is appropriate to take stock of what this chapter has delivered.

## Summary

I have suggested that the 1980s was a significant decade for UK advertising in terms of the institutional restructuring that occurred in the industry. I dramatized the nature of these institutional developments by focusing on the three key components of this process: acquisition, diversification and globalization. These processes were largely driven, I suggested, by the ambitions of agencies to gain competitive advantage in relation to the increasing globalization of production and the imperatives of global markets. As we saw, however, there were competing organizational solutions advanced by different agencies in the face of these pressures. Saatchi and Saatchi and Bartle Bogle Hegarty pursued very different organizational strategies, and both were assertive in articulating their particular vision of agency development.

The question of organizational development, as I argued, was highly charged in the industry. Sensitive professional arguments about creative strategy were often displaced onto them. I suggested, however, that these arguments about creative strategy did not neatly mirror the organizational differences between agencies. Rather, they pointed to different professional formations which cut across the multinational/small shop divide. It was in these arguments about creative strategy that the practitioners who loom large in my account were highly visible – as objects of vilification, if not enunciators of their own vision of advertising creative strategy. These were the advocates of "creative advertising".

## CHAPTER 7

# "Who are we talking to?" Representations of the consumer in advertising research

> People nowadays feel they need to be treated as an individual . . .
> The old, large categories were like herds of people. Now you are
> talking about lots of smaller little wolf packs all searching for
> their own style.
>
> (*Campaign*, 11/8/87: 10)

The production of advertising representations and the orchestration
of campaigns requires – as a *sine qua non* – a working sense on the
part of advertising practitioners of the consumers they are addressing. Specifying the target consumer, then, is a constitutive element
within the process of making adverts. In the 1980s, advertising practitioners had two dominant paradigms of consumer segmentation
to draw on in formally describing their target consumers. These were
demographics and attitudinal or motivational segmentations. Both
traditions of classifying consumers were already established within
advertising-directed research prior to the 1980s, though demographics had the longer history. The social class component of
demographic segmentations – segmentations by "age, sex and class"
– were derived from the classification of social class first produced
in 1911 by government departments. It is the attitudinal and motivational segmentations, however, that are of most interest to my
argument in this chapter. There was a proliferation of these
segmentations in the 1980s, and they threw up a number of new
representations of consumer markets and a new set of consumer
types. Amongst these were segmentations of male consumers. These
segmentations foregrounded changes in groups of men's values, attitudes and lifestyles, and defined a number of new male consumer

types. These segmentations were one important determinant of advertising representations of the "new man". I advance an argument in the next chapter about the way these consumer segmentations impacted on the production of "new man" imagery. In this chapter, however, I want to detail the way consumers were segmented within these forms of advertising-directed market research, and in particular consider the new segmentations of male consumers.

## Demographics and the rise of qualitative research

Demographics was the central segmentation system used by advertising practitioners in the post-war period and remained the most important segmentation system through the 1980s. Social class was the key factor in demographic segmentations. JICNARS, the Joint Industry Commission on National Audience and Readership Surveys, the industry body responsible during the 1980s for regulating these segmentations, identified six social classes. These were defined by the occupation of the head of the household. *The Economist* (12/8/89: 5) summarized them as follows:

A    Higher managerial, administrative or professional;
B    Intermediate managerial, administrative or professional;
C1   Supervisory or clerical;
C2   Skilled manual workers;
D    Semi- or unskilled workers;
E    Casual workers, labourers, those on benefit.

Conventionally, in research documents produced either by agencies or by market research companies, these class classifications were clustered to produce more meaningful target groups of consumers. In addition, they were supplemented by the factors of "age and sex". Thus, for example, a classic demographic segmentation was "ABC1 Housewives with kids" (*Admap*, May 1987: 10).

From the mid 1950s in the USA, and from the mid 1960s in the UK, research institutions began to supplement demographics with further segmentation factors. These involved the mobilization of psychological distinctions between consumers. This shift in advertising research was famously charted by Vance Packard in *The hidden persuaders* (Packard 1981 [1957]), his assault upon what he perceived as the insidious techniques of market research and advertising. Along with the development of "scientific" quantitative testing of consumers, forms of behavioural psychology were applied to the anticipation and influencing of consumer responses. A key figure here was Ernest Dichter, president of The Institute for Motivational Research, Inc. Dichter's work offered a limited motivational analysis of consumer behaviour, identifying and targeting consumers in terms of motivational distinctions. Packard gave a celebrated example in *The hidden persuaders* of this technique at work. Dichter, Packard recounts, was called in by an airline to improve its turnover of leisure passengers. A previous piece of research had suggested that many potential male customers were put off by a fear of the plane crashing. The airline had initially responded to this through a campaign that foregrounded questions of safety in its service. The consumer response had been poor, however. Dichter was brought in to try and resolve this apparent paradox. Taking a group of potential male travellers, Dichter attempted to lay open the motivational dimensions of the reluctance to fly. He came up with the following (ingenious) analysis: the men who were concerned about flying were not frightened of crashing *per se*, he argued, but of the imagined embarrassment and guilt produced by their wives' reactions. As Packard put it, the men were embarrassed by the thought of their wives saying "The dammed fool, he should have gone by train" (Packard 1981 [1957]: 60). A new campaign was then produced which emphasized family flying. As Dichter put it, "the man was taken off the spot through the symbols of family approval of flying" (ibid.: 60). We are not told whether the airline was more successful after this campaign.

Dichter's deployment of behavioural psychology stopped short of producing the psychological equivalent of demographics. His work was more a consultancy, problem-solving service. It was also closely associated, as I noted, with quantitative research methodologies. These included laboratory techniques for pre-testing adverts and gauging consumer responses. They involved technologies like "tachistoscopes, pupil dilators, and blink rate calculators" (*Campaign*, 9/3/ 79: 21). What these techniques and technologies tested were simple behavioural changes in the sample consumers during exposure to adverts. These included apparently insignificant changes such as pupil dilation and blinks.

More significant developments occurred in the late 1960s and early 1970s. Three events are particularly important for my account. These were the establishment of the Yankelovich Clancy Shulman's Monitor and the publication of William Wells's early research in the

USA, together with the formation of the Target Group Index in 1968 in the UK.

The Yankelovich Monitor was a prestigious research programme which charted social trends. It went about this by deploying a novel set of psychographic (as opposed to demographic) segmentations. The Monitor isolated seven pyschographic consumer types. What it called: self-explorer; social resister; experimentalist; conspicuous consumer; belonger; survivor; and aimless (IPA 1989: 8). These seven consumer types were, in fact, subdivisions of a threefold psychographic segmentation derived from the work of the social psychologist Abraham Maslow and his notion of a "hierarchy of needs" (interview with Liz Nelson, 1989). Liz Nelson, who had been involved in the development of the Monitor and who brought it to the UK in 1973, defined these three core psychographic types in the following terms:

> "the sustenance motivated" are those concerned mainly with getting by; "the outer directed" are concerned with status, prosperity and getting ahead; the "inner-directed" are concerned with self-fulfilment and self-esteem (*Marketing*, 2/6/86: 12).

William Wells's work in the late 1960s was based less on the appropriation of theories of motivation from psychology, as on descriptive accounts of observable or "actionable" behaviour. As such it lacked the intellectual pretensions of the Yankelovich Monitor. As Liz Nelson put it to me, Wells was concerned with "attitudes, opinions and beliefs and behaviour" (interview with Liz Nelson, 1989). Wells called this set of factors, collectively, a lifestyle.

The Target Group Index (TGI) had even less grand conceptual ambitions. Based on door to door research, the TGI built up a picture of preferred brands and set these alongside the preferred media consumption of consumers, clustering the resulting interrelationships into groups. The TGI, in this sense, shared the concern of both the Yankelovich Monitor and Wells with bringing into consumer research factors other than "age, sex and class".

The research practitioners involved in the development of these segmentations were quite clear about what drove their interest in establishing new forms of consumer research. For them the impetus came from events outside the walls of the market research institutions. Liz Nelson was emphatic about the driving force for change:

> Undoubtedly . . . in the States and Europe and here . . . there was a social revolution taking place . . . absolutely unbeknown to parents and professors there was a revolution, a permissive revolution taking place. Nobody understood it . . . I mean it was the dawn of post-industrial society. At the time it was just a break from traditional norms, developing new norms (interview with Liz Nelson, 1989).

Research companies, she suggested, were quick to attempt to understand the changes in society and to formulate those changes in terms of changing consumer attitudes and lifestyles. Advertising agencies responded cautiously to these new forms of consumer research. In 1972, however, Leo Burnett produced the first major UK "lifestyle" segmentation. William Wells was a key player in its production (*Campaign*, 29/9/72: 24). The segmentation was derived from an extensive questionnaire based on the interests, reading and buying habits of the selected consumers (clustered by age and social class). From this, 235 different attitude statements were produced. The results were condensed into 13 "population types", and a "face" was put to each group. Among the 13 groups, for example, there was "Andy". "Andy" was, as the report put it, "in a high social grade and is left-wing. He has few hang-ups to restrict the enjoyment that as a young person he feels is his of right" (ibid.).

Leo Burnett were convinced of the value of lifestyle types like "Andy". Simon Broadbent, director at Leo Burnett defended the turn to these sorts of segmentations in the following way:

> The trouble with normal social grades is that they are often poor descriptions of the real targets that interest advertisers. Maybe they worked 40 years ago, but now society is more fluid and rigid classifications based on social class or income just don't work. There are more working women, more independent teenagers, more men in the home – none of whom are satisfactorily identified under the ABC1 system (*Campaign*, 29/9/72: 24).

Broadbent's assessment of the interpretative value of lifestyles shared much common ground with Nelson's comments on the impetus behind the Yankelovich Monitor. The critique of demographics as an effective discriminator between groups of consumers was the most important dimension of Broadbent's advocacy of lifestyles. It remained, as we will see shortly, the formative injunction to lifestyle and psychographic segmentations through the 1980s.

Leo Burnett's early lead in lifestyles was not, however, followed in any significant way by other agencies. Leo Burnett themselves produced one further lifestyle segmentation in the 1970s before ceasing production of them. "Lifestyles" research, as Liz Nelson recalled, stopped in the mid 1970s. Making sense of this interregnum means looking beyond the immediate context of the market research companies. It means, in particular, considering the relations between consumer research and key practices associated with advertising production within advertising agencies. In this sense, it was clear that the entrenchment of demographic segmentations in the way advertising space on television and in the press was bought and sold, in particular, was an important block to the take-up of attitudinal or motivational research by agencies during the 1970s.

## Lifestyles and psychographics in the 1980s

The production of the ACORN segmentation in 1979 marked the beginning of a renewed interest in attitudinal and motivational consumer classifications. The launch of SAGACITY followed in 1981, and through the 1980s a range of general psychographic or lifestyles segmentations were produced by market research institutions (*Campaign*, 10/7/81: 45). In addition to ACORN and SAGACITY, there was VALS, OUTLOOK, ACE (RISC), and the ongoing development and application of the Yankelovitch Monitor and the TGI. A number of advertising agencies also produced their own segmentations. Most important in this respect were McCann-Erikson's 1984 "Man Study" and 1985 "Woman Study", McCormick's 1987 "Womantrack", and Grey's 1990 "About Men".

These initiatives were underpinned by discussion and debate within the trade press and at industry conferences about attitudinal and motivational segmentations. Two conferences held under the auspices of *Admap* were particularly significant. In November 1981, the conference "Reclassifying People" was organized, while in April 1987 *Admap*, in association with *Campaign*, organized the "Classifying People" conference. In 1989, The Institute of Practitioners in Advertising (IPA), acknowledging the renewed interest in lifestyles and psychographic research, produced a guide for its members on the developments that had taken place in these forms of consumer research.[1]

The market research company Taylor-Nelson, was a key player in the expansion of psychographic research in the 1980s. Their research represented very clearly the ambitions of the renewed appropriation of motivational research. It was based upon the development of the Yankelovich Monitor and was concerned with tracking changing attitudes.

Taylor-Nelson put together research documents which detailed the relative balance between the three core psychographic segments used in the Monitor. Namely, the "inner-directeds", the "outer-directeds" and the "sustenance motivated". Taylor-Nelson's research on changing attitudes charted the shifts in motivational categories relative to each other across a pan-European market. This formed part of a research project co-ordinated with the French based International Research Institute on Social Change (RISC) through their Anticipating Change in Europe (ACE). Taylor-Nelson was concerned to isolate those individuals or groups they termed as being "at the forefront of social trends", and to explore the motivations of these groups. The research charted the movement of values along a graph from "traditional norms and roots" to "new values".

Taylor-Nelson identified the following as key motivations among the groups at the forefront of social trends: "networking, polysensuality, hedonism, desire for emotional experience, risk-taking, and exploring new mental frontiers". "Polysensuality", for example, referred to the increasing importance to the consumer of "smelling, tasting, touching, as well as seeing and hearing and being in touch with his affectivity . . . To the consumer this means the joy of smelling fresh bread and newly ground coffee, feeling silk next to one's skin or the texture of ripe brie." "Desire for emotional experience" homed in on the way, "people have the need to feel their body in new and different, intensive ways, the desire for frequent emotional experiences and the enjoyment of doing something which is just a little dangerous or forbidden" (interview with Liz Nelson, 1989).

These "personal motives and drives" were mapped – in the ACE/ RISC studies – onto a grid of European countries, with France, Italy and Norway located towards the "new values" axis and the UK towards the "traditional values" axis.

What emerged from this, for Taylor-Nelson, was an increasingly diverse and fast moving consumer market place, but one which also exhibited strong lines of connection across European markets in terms of psychographic types. This information was used by Taylor-Nelson with clients like Volvo, in marketing across different European markets.

The social trends dimension to Taylor-Nelson's research, and its concern with the relative balance between "new" and "traditional" values, "inner-directeds", "outer-directeds" and "sustenance motivated", was echoed in the SRI-VALS research. Like the Taylor-Nelson segmentations, SRI-VALS was a general classification of consumers based upon psychographics. Four "value" groups figured in the classification: need-driven; outer-directed; inner-directed; integrated-personalities (IPA 1989: 11). Nine subdivisions were then produced from this: integrated (approximately 2% of the population); societally conscious (4%); experiential (8%); I-am-me (3%); achievers (28%); emulators (10%); belongers (32%); sustainers (10%); and survivors (6%).[2] This classification was taken up by the advertising agency Young and Rubican, and reformulated as the 4Cs (cross-cultural consumer classifications). This research, again, was mainly directed at clients targeting different pan-European markets like Ford and Kodak.

The Taylor-Nelson research and Young and Rubican's 4Cs/ SRI-VALS research were, as I have suggested, psychographic segmentations. They offered, then (in their terms), a picture of the underlying motivations that distinguished different consumer types. As such, psychographics claimed an interpretive reach into any advertising market. The same psychographic types, its advocates claimed, were as present among consumers of clothing as they were among consumers of food.

Lifestyle segmentations were deliberately more descriptive forms of segmentation. OUTLOOK, produced in 1987 by Baker and Fletcher, was based upon a cluster analysis of the 1985–6 TGI survey. It classified six lifestyle groups: "Trendies" (15%); "Pleasure seekers" (15%); "The Indifferent" (18%); "Working class puritans" (15%); "Sociable spenders" (14%); and "Moralists" (16%) (*Admap*, 3/1987: 23).

SAGACITY was developed by Research Services in 1981, and marketed as the "new tool to help admen accurately define target audiences" (*Campaign*, 10/7/81: 45). It combined standard demographic classification (derived from the National Readership Survey) with a life-cycle index. These were: dependent; pre-family; family; and post-family (*Admap*, 7/1983: 386–91).

ACORN was a geodemographic classification producd in 1979 and was the most commercially successful of these three lifestyle segmentations. ACORN segmented by neighbourhood. Working on the assumption – and this was a maxim for the advocates of geodemographics – that "birds of a feather flock together" (*Admap*, 6/1987: 23), ACORN was an 11-group classification of neighbourhoods. These ranged from "A – agricultural areas" to "K – better off retirement areas".

ACORN, SAGACITY and OUTLOOK were all commercially available segmentations. Advertising agencies, as noted earlier, also produced their own "in-house" lifestyle segmentations. Three are worth detailing. McCormick's "Womentrack" and McCann-Erickson's "Man Study" and "Woman Study".

The McCormicks study segmented women by lifestyle within three key "life-stages": pre-children; women with children; and post-children. These life-stages were subdivided by lifestyle: the "pre-children" into individualists, romantics, and Thatcher's daughters; the "with children" into optimums Oxo-man, devoted mums, frustrated mums; the "post children" into second honeymooners, and homebody (IPA 1989: 10).

McCann-Erikson's studies segmented men and women into eight roughly equal groups. In the "Man Study" these were: avant guardians; pontificators; chameleons; self-admirers; self-exploiters; token triers; sleepwalkers; passive endurers.

"Avant guardians", the study suggested, were "concerned with change and the well being of others, rather than possessions. They are well educated, prone to self-righteousness" (*Marketing*, 12/6/86: 24). "Chameleons", on the other hand "want to be contemporary to win approval. They act like barometers of social change, but copiers not leaders" (ibid.). "Self-exploiters" were "the doers and "self-starters", competitive but always under pressure and often pessimistic. Possessions are important" (ibid.).

McCann-Erickson's "Man Study" was typical of the majority of lifestyle segmentations produced in this period, in that it was a general segmentation. That is, "Man Study" was not a product specific segmentation. Peter York, of the consultancy SRU Ltd, was one of a number of vociferous critics within the industry who were concerned with this tendency to produce general segmentations. He made a plea for segmentations to be made specific to particular markets. One size, as he put it, did not fit all (*Admap*, 5/1987: 48).

York's criticisms, however, went further than suggesting a qualification of lifestyle segmentations. He argued that these segmentations were only useful if they were used to supplement demographics. As he put it,

> I see "lifestyles" as a method of discriminating within the demographic grid rather than as an alternative to it. It is a way of answering the question, "What kinds of older middle class people are they that, say, read the *Sunday Telegraph*, rather than starting from scratch" (*Admap*, 5/1987: 47).

These were significant criticisms. They also challenged the premises of attitudinal and motivational segmentations. Simon Broadbent's comments on Leo Burnett's decision to develop a lifestyle segmentation in 1972, which we noted earlier, centre-staged the break with demographics. Liz Nelson, of Taylor-Nelson, was even more doctrinaire in her distaste for demographics (and by implications York's recommendations for a "middle way"). She argued that psychographic segmentations delivered a complex picture of consumer markets, which made demographics redundant. She said,

> I mean social class is just so . . . We do a tremendous amount of interviews among doctors. They are all the same demographic group but – crumbs! – you can differentiate between them perfectly in their attitudes towards technology, patients, their attitude to their profession. You can actually have a perfect way of discriminating (interview with Liz Nelson, 1989).

What is significant for my account is the way these arguments about the most appropriate system for classifying consumers illuminated the very different representations of consumers formalized within both paradigms. Psychographics and lifestyles signified a new set of consumer identities which cut across and often pluralized demographic segmentations. Two consequences followed from this. First, lifestyles and psychographics produced a more intensive individualization of consumers. Thus, in McCann-Erickson's "Woman Study", five lifestyle types – the avant guardian, lady righteous, hopeful seekers, lively lady and new unromantic – were classified. These were groups of consumers who, within a demographic segmentation, were likely to have been grouped together within a clustering like "ABC1 females". The lifestyle segmentations also, secondly, explicitly foregrounded cultural distinctions between different groups of consumers. Thus differences between "lively lady" and "avant guardian", for example, were represented in terms of the latter's preference for healthy food in relation to food purchases, and the former's emphasis on the sensuality of food and the pleasure in eating.

The difference between these paradigms of consumer segmentation was also evident in the way each form of segmentation charted the relations between different groups of consumers over time. Demographics tended to emphasize the stability of consumer markets. Lifestyles and psychographic segmentations, on the other hand, centre-staged the changing nature of consumer markets by focusing on new values, opinions, beliefs and motivations. This emphasis on the changing nature of consumer markets underwrote the logic of lifestyles and psychographics. This was to represent ever more differentiated markets.

What needs underlining is the way this differentiation of consumers within lifestyle and psychographic segmentations impacted on the segmentation of male consumers. McCann-Erickson's "Man Study" was important in this respect. Two of the male consumer types represented in the study are particularly interesting for us. These were the "avant guardians" and "self-exploiters". Both segments, for McCann-Erickson, represented shifts in groups of men's "values and lifestyles". "Avant guardians", for example, were characterized by a strongly contemporary view of masculinity. "Self-exploiters" were seen to be at the forefront of social trends. For trade commentators, these characteristics were most clearly expressed through both groups of men's concern with fashion and grooming (*Campaign*, 26/7/85: 37–9; *Campaign*, 24/3/89: 51–2).

A further segmentation was also significant in these developments in marketing to men. They were a category of consumers called "innovators". "Innovators" were the product of a segmentation derived from the three fold psychographic segmentation appropriated from Maslow combined with elements of social trends research. Thus, "innovators" resided at the apex of a pyramid. Below them were a segment called "early adopters", while making up the base of the pyramid were the "late adopters". The segmentation rested on the assumption that the consumption preferences of "innovators" represented significant new trends in values and lifestyles. These, in turn, it was assumed, would influence "early adopters" and ultimately "late adopters".

"Innovators", like "avant guardians" and "self-exploiters", were identified by agencies as having a contemporary view of masculinity which they evidenced through their developed interest in clothing and grooming products. More specifically, "innovators" were described by agencies as being the "style-leaders" in fashion. These research findings were significant for agencies and advertisers of men's clothing and grooming products in particular. As we will see in the next chapter, they laid the basis for a turn to a particular set of codings of masculinity to deliver this advertising in these markets. The identification of these consumer segments also, as we will see in Part IV, gave considerable impetus to the publishing and advertising debates about a new kind of magazine for men in the mid 1980s.

## CHAPTER 8

# Advertising and the "new man": creative practices, account planning and media buying

> [agencies] know that the fashionable young man is out there, but they don't know how to address him. You can't address all men; there's been no one image specific to all men.
>
> (Lucy Purdy, Research Bureau Limited,
> *Arena*, Summer 1988: 24)

Lucy Purdy's comments captured the dilemma faced by advertising practitioners in the early to mid 1980s in advertising to men. Consumer research, as I have argued, was producing a picture of shifts in the values and lifestyles of groups of male consumers. These shifts were represented in consumer types like the "avant guardian", the "self exploiter" or the "innovator". Advertising practitioners were confronted with the problem of making decisions about the significance of these findings and with assessing whether they were appropriate for the specific male markets they were producing adverts for.

Two practices within the process of making adverts shaped the way certain groups of practitioners responded to the evidence from consumer research. They were account planning and media buying. Both practices were important because it was through them that research findings – like that about new groups of male consumers – were incorporated into the advertising process and ultimately impacted on the decisions made in the production of adverts by art directors and writers.

## "The voice of the consumer in advertising": account planning

Account planning or planning, as it was usually abbreviated to, had a history within UK advertising which extended beyond the emergence of the "creative agencies" towards the end of the 1970s. Two individuals – Stephen King at J. Walter Thompson and Stanley Pollitt at BMP – were generally credited with having formulated the principles of planning in the late 1960s. Behind both men's formulation of planning, was a concern to improve the way market research information fed into and – in their terms – helped improve the production of adverts and the running of campaigns. Pollitt cogently spelled out these ambitions in an article published in *Campaign*, just before his death in 1979. Recalling the establishment of planning at BMP he said,

> I decided . . . that a trained researcher should be put alongside the account man [or handler, the person with overall responsibility for the campaign] on every account. He should be there as of right, with equal status as a working partner. He was charged with ensuring that all the data relevant to key advertising decisions should be properly analysed, complemented with new research, and brought to bear on judgements of the creative strategy and how the campaign should be appraised . . . This new researcher – or account man's "conscience" – was to be called the planner.
> . . . In addition to the development of advertising strategy and campaign appraisal we started to involve planners more closely in the development of creative ideas (*Campaign*, 21/12/89: 49).

As *Campaign* noted, however, these principles – and planning as a recognized practice – were marginal within the industry at the time of Pollitt's death. (*Campaign*, 21/12/89: 11). The expansion of planning in the early 1980s changed this situation. By the time planning celebrated its twentieth anniversary in 1988, 25 of the top 30 agencies claimed to have account planning departments. More significantly, in a number of high profile agencies – BBH, Butterfield Day Devito Hockney, Woolams Moira Gaskin O'Malley, Howell Henry Chaldecott Lury – what *Campaign* called "star planners" were among the founding partners.[1]

The formation of the Account Planning Group (APG) in 1979 played an important role in this process of expansion. Formed by a group of respected practitioners, the APG ran an influential series of seminars and conferences in the early 1980s. These both raised the profile of planning in the industry and contributed to the new status of planning practice.[2]

Listening to what the APG had to say about planning – in particular how it developed on Pollitt and King's founding premises – gives us a way of opening out how planning shaped the process of making adverts within the agencies that appropriated it in the 1980s and, more specifically, how it shaped the production of "new man" imagery within advertising.

Kay Scorah, one of the APG's sharper intellectuals, identified three dimensions to the way planning intervened in the process of advertising production. These were the planner's relationship to clients, the planner's relationship to consumers, and the planner's relationship to art directors and writers within the agency creative department. Scorah began her account of these relationships, in a piece published by the APG, by commenting on the relationship between planners and the client. She said,

> The account handler must ensure that the planner has sufficient access to the client to both receive information in the form of market research data (produced by the client), sales data, product information, even company gossip, and to impart information (Cowley 1987: 3).

What is important for Scorah, then, in dealing with the client, is the formulation by the planner of a clear sense of the product and a sense of the client's own marketing ideas. This included the planner being attentive, as she suggested, to informal knowledge about the product which could reveal fresh information about the product and would contribute to an innovative campaign.[3]

The planner's relationship to the consumer was the second key relationship that structured the planning process. Scorah saw this relationship as being built up through a number of procedures. First, it involved a clear specification of the target consumers. As Scorah put it, "Who is the target audience, and what are they like?"(ibid.). From this specification of the target consumer, the planner had to consider a number of questions: "How does the target audience feel about the product field? How does this target audience feel about our brand in relation to others? How does the target audience feel about advertising in this product field, and in particular our advertising?" (ibid.).

Scorah's schema, in fact, condensed a number of different moments in the relationship between planners and consumers. These were different moments in which the planner moved from a representation of the consumer drawn from consumer research to extended discussions with concrete consumers. In the early stage of this process – when the planning focused on representations of the target consumer – the kinds of attitudinal or motivational consumer research detailed in the previous chapters were important for planners like Scorah. They delivered the appropriate vocabularies for specifying target consumers. Scorah made clear in her article the importance of this type of consumer research. At root, she suggested, planners had to have or produce knowledge about the target consumer's values and motivations in relation to the clients products and the associated product field. As she suggested, "More important than reflecting the way people are, or the way they think they are, is to reflect their aspirations, feelings and ideas" (ibid.: 4). From this planners could formulate a strategy that "presents those aspects of [the] product or service most motivating or appealing to our target audience, and in a way which is both interesting and sympathetic" (ibid.: 9).

The third dimension of planning's input into the development of advertising, for Scorah, was the relationship between planners and advertising creatives. This was a crucial relationship, since advocates of planning (as was clear in Pollitt's comments) made significant claims for planning in improving creative execution. Scorah outlined the process as follows:

> The creative team should see the planner as a source of clear briefs, telling them exactly what aspect of the product is most motivating to the target audience and why. They should also see the planner as an objective sounding board for ideas, representing the likely consumer response but also going beyond that to analyse and develop embryonic creative routes" (ibid.: 5).

The relationship between planners and creatives – as Scorah articulated it – was organized through a number of briefings. These included early strategy formulation and further conversations between creatives and planners which followed the planner-led consumer discussions of the proposed adverts. The creative brief was a key document in this process.

The creative brief was a succinct document, usually only one side in length. It consisted of a number of elements. First, the brief contained a characterization of the target consumers. Secondly, the brief listed the explicit objectives of the advertising and its role in the marketing process. Thirdly, it consisted of a "proposition" or "positioning statement". Fourthly, the brief detailed supporting reasons for the proposition. Fifthly, creative guidelines or, what was generally called "tone of voice" were listed. And finally, any mandatory requirements or practical considerations were set out.[4]

We can get a better sense of these elements of the creative brief if we consider the brief produced by the planner Sue Oriel, at the agency FCO, for the press campaign produced in 1987–8 for the hi-fi manufacturer, Technics. A version of the brief looked like this (courtesy of Sue Oriel):

- Who are we talking to? Principally men aged 18–34, upmarket, but with a recognition that the brand is purchased by older users, too.
- Why are we advertising? To increase awareness of Technics as the brand that distinguishes premium quality, slightly "clever" audio equipment.
- What do we want to say? Another innovative piece of equipment from Technics.
- Why should the consumer believe us? Heritage of the Technics brand image as the finest quality mass market brand.
- What is the tone of voice? Quirky, intriguing.
- What are the practical considerations? How can we make our ads stand out from the mass of technologically intensive, boring "black box" ads.

Oriel's brief represented the final version of a creative brief. It was from this that the press adverts that ran in 1987–8 were produced. As Scorah's account suggested, however, a whole series of procedures went into the production of such a polished brief – including the pretesting of creative ideas. Liz Watt's account of the work she undertook as a planner at BBH on the K-shoes account sheds light on these procedures.

Watts, like Scorah, begin by emphasizing the importance of the dialogue between planner and client as the first stage in the formulation of a creative brief. One starting point in this sense for Watts was to draw out from the client a working sense of the company philosophy and the company's feelings towards the specific product – in this case, K-shoes' new range of women's shoes. Besides revealing a general commitment to quality on the part of the client, this dialogue gave Watts a clearer impression of K-shoes' sense of the target market for the new range of shoes. K-shoes, in fact, saw this new range as targeting slightly younger and more fashion concious women than they traditionally aimed at.

Watts took this loose consumer definition and began to work up a tighter specification of the target consumers. As a first stage – and as a segmentation device for the selection of research groups – the following specification was produced: "women aged between 35 and 40 years old, moderately well off and who respond positively to a set of attitude statements such as, "I really enjoy shopping for clothes" (interview with Liz Watts).

Following the first group discussions with consumers based on these segmentations, Watts then produced an even more specific segmentation. The key distinctions now revolved around the acknowledged role models of the women in the discussion group. In this segmentation, the women were selected on the basis of displaying a more "contemporary" set of role aspirations. A preference, in this example, for Sue Lawley and Joan Collins rather than the Princess of Wales. This attitudinal group, then, formed the core research group, with the process of research becoming more elaborate. The women were interviewed in their homes and the discussion was steered around how they felt about clothes. They were encouraged to comment on the feel of clothes they particularly liked, and then try on these clothes with the K-shoes.

For Watts, the aim was to produce from these raw comments a picture of how the K-shoes might fit into the lives of the (target) women. And this formed the basis of the brief that was passed on to the agency's art directors and writers.[5]

Both Watts's and Scorah's accounts of the planning process and the way planning shaped the production of advertising, came from the perspective of planners. Art directors and writers – the agency creatives – often presented rather different accounts of the way planning impacted on advertising production. In fact, the relationship between planners and creatives produced some very public displays of conflict. The creative briefing was often cast as a moment of high drama and theatrical excess, as the imperatives of the planner rubbed up against the creative ambitions and often self-consciously artistic egos of art directors. McCann-Erickson's decision to do away with its planning department in 1989 dramatized in a particularly clear way both the local tensions within a particular agency between planners and creatives, and the deeper questions raised within the industry about planning's role.

*Campaign* reported McCann-Erickson's controversial decision as its leading story with the headline, "McCann's drops planning to focus on ads" (*Campaign*, 8/9/89: 1). The implication of the headline gave a sense of the very negative view of planning held by certain agency art directors. There was the sense that planning, rather than assisting the creative execution of adverts, had come to dominate the process and impose on art directors and writers overly rigid guidelines. Jerry Green, McCann's creative director, suggested that planning got in the way of the creative process and that it had accrued to itself "a star status out of all proportion to its value" (*Campaign*, 15/9/89: 19). McCann-Erickson's decision and the public attacks on planning,[6] however, drew some robust defences of planning from its supporters within the industry. Bob Roscoe, planning director at Saatchi and Saatchi, was representative of the advocates of planning when he argued, "This is a very serious set back. Getting the strategy right is very important and you have to put the resources behind it" (*Campaign*, 15/9/89: 19).

In the wake of the McCann-Erickson planning controversy, however, a different sort of critique of the forms of planning practised within many agencies was voiced. Adam Lury, of Howell Henry Chaldecott Lury (HHCL), took issue both with the hostile attacks on planning and with the more doctrinaire defenders of planning orthodoxy. While endorsing the value of planning, Lury argued that many planners were too uncritical of consumer's responses in group discussions and needed to reflect in a more sophisticated way on what consumers' comments meant. He argued that consumers often tended to rehearse in group discussions a response to adverts which they thought the planner expected. In commenting on HHCL's work for Molson beer, Lury revealed that many of the target group of young men involved in the discussions continually emphasized to Lury the importance of showing young men in the ads. He was unhappy with these responses, precisely because he felt the consumers were playing the role of account planner themselves and offering back to Lury what they thought he was looking for. Acting too literally as "the voice of the consumer", in this sense, he argued was the road to advertising cliché – and hence – uncompetitive advertising.

Lury emphasized the need, then, for planners to develop a more "predictive" approach to consumers' attitudes and motivations; what he wryly called "forward planning". For Lury, planning needed to avoid "becoming backward looking, obsessed both with the consumer and with using consumer research as a 'rear-view mirror'" (*Media Week*, 22/9/89: 23). Lury's comments shared a good deal of common ground with John Bartle's defence of planning. Bartle, planning director and partner at BBH, offered a careful defence of planning, stressing – along with its usefulness – its limits. He said,

> Account planners have confused the use of group discussion with what planning was about. People started to put planning forward as the way of making great ads and it was put on a pedestal – inevitably there was a backlash. Planning has improved the average of commercials but it cannot be credited with the breakthroughs which are always the product of great creative people . . . Planning was becoming a mechanical process (*Marketing*, 13/7/89: 23).

Bartle, however, suggested that – when used effectively – planning had become increasingly important through the 1980s to the advertising process. What underpinned this, he claimed, was the fragmentation of television and press audiences. The effectiveness of campaigns and the style of advertising used depended more and more, in this sense, on the media chosen. Planning was the point within the advertising process, for Bartle, where the consequences for the running of campaigns and the production of advertising representations which followed from these developments in advertising media, could – literally – be planned.

## Media buying and advertising development

Developments in advertising media had been registering in advertising discourse through the 1980s. Gary Betts, writing in *Campaign* in 1982, conjured a picture of a sea-change in media. For Betts, this sea-change was evidenced in the waning of – in his phrase – the omnipotence of the mass media. As he put it,

Today's mass circulation newspapers face increasing competition from a plethora of mini-circulation weeklies, shoppers guides and local government newsheets . . . the growth of regional radio (is a further manifestation of this trend) . . . The development of alternative TV channels, satellites, video recorders, personal computers, TV games and fibre optic cable systems will accelerate the demassification of the media (*Campaign*, 23/7/82: 19).

A *Campaign* special on media services earlier in 1982 similarly pointed to the technology-led dimensions to media pluralization and what it saw as the concomitant fragmentation of audiences. As the report put it, "the security of mass audiences is disappearing" (*Campaign*, 29/1/82: 51–3). Richard Eyre, media director of Aspect Advertising, also identified the erosion of mass audiences as the key to characterizing the shifts that were taking place in advertising media. As he said, "The media environment has changed. Society has shown a shift away from homogeneity . . . towards greater individualism" (*Campaign*, 15/2/85: 47). Eyre periodized these developments in media from the end of the 1960s – the high-water mark, for him, was when "the media was genuinely mass" (ibid.).

For media buyers like Eyre these developments had implications for the practice of media buying; that is, for the kinds of knowledge and practice mobilized in the purchasing of media space for adverts. It was in relation to direct marketing that media buyers began to construct a response to these shifts.

Direct marketing was the term applied to marketing through direct mail or telephone marketing. As such it formed part of what was known in the trade as "below-the-line" services. These also included point-of-sale displays (like in-store literature), press inserts, public relations, and design. Below-the-line services expanded strongly through the 1980s, and many agencies saw the acquisition of these services as key to their development. What had traditionally been seen by many agencies as the "grubby, cardboard end of the business" underwent a transformation in its image. (*Campaign* 13/12/86: 51).[7]

The interest in direct marketing from the large full-service agencies, came out of the sense that direct marketing was seen to offer an effective way of targeting consumers. In a recurrent phrase, direct marketing was cast as "the sniper's bullet compared with the blunderbuss" approach to marketing (*Campaign*, 13/2/86: 51). Brian Thomas, managing director of Treneas-Harvey Bird and Watson, expanded on this logic; a logic soon given a name: "narrowcasting". Thomas said,

> If a product is right, the only problem is to offer it to the right people. When you have sophisticated segmentation procedures, you can offer the product only to the right people – and therefore get a better response rate (*Campaign*, 14/12/84: 49).

Segmentation by choice of media, however, depended on appropriate knowledge of the audiences and readerships associated with different media. The development of narrowcasting, then, was interlinked with the appropriation of new kinds of consumer research into the practice of media buying. These developments set the terms for a break with established forms of media buying.

A strong tradition within the practice of media buying was the so-called quantitative approach. In press advertising, for example, the quantitative practice of media buying – what was sometimes pejoratively called "number crunching" – was based upon two criteria for selecting advertising media. These were the National Readership Survey (NRS) circulation figures and a criterion called "cost per thousand" (CPT). Cost per thousand referred to how much it cost to place an advert in – for example – a magazine, for every thousand readers the advert formally reached. CPT took the form of price lists supplied by media owners. They were derived in part from the NRS audits of the circulation figures. NRS circulation figures included – for the larger readership publications – a demographic profile as well. The media buyer's job in assessing where to buy media space for a press advert using the quantitative method, was to look essentially for the best CPT available in relation to the target demographic group of consumers.

It was this approach to media buying which was challenged under the demands of more segmented media. "Qualitative" audience and readership research became more important for media buyers because it could deliver more useful information about readerships in addition to the bottom line of CPT and circulation figures. Referring to magazines, Richard Eyre put the case well:

> Though age, and to a lesser extent class, may be a discriminator of sorts in identifying the readership of a particular magazine, attitude is always going to be vital when it comes to the actual

business of identifying those people who are most likely to buy (*Campaign*, 15/2/85: 46).

Marketing to attitudinally segmented media audiences or readerships had a further effect. As Kay Scorah argued "As media choices become more diverse and target audiences more tightly defined and precisely targeted, media arguments begin to move away from cost and towards value and environment" (Cowley 1987: 5). In other words, getting value for money in buying advertising space was not simply about buying the cheapest media or the one (in the case of press and television) with the largest viewing or circulation figures. It was rather about ensuring that the advert was appropriately placed so that it could reach the maximum number of the target audience. The critical distinctions that were mobilized in the buying of advertising media, then, were based upon information about the attitudinal nature of their audiences and readerships. Demographic descriptions of audiences and readerships certainly persisted in media buying alongside these developments, partly because many media owners continued to describe their readerships or audiences in those terms. Quantitative assessments (such as CPT's in relation to press and magazines) also remained important given that media buying was constrained within finite budgets. As we will see in Part IV, however, the shifts in media buying practice were very important for new, declining or relatively small media sectors. This was certainly the case in relation to the youth and the men's general interest magazine sectors.

There were important consequences for the creative execution of adverts pursued by art directors and writers in these shifts in the priorities of media buying. Advertising to more segmented media audiences and readerships meant that not only was the choice of media important in terms of targeting, but also advertising representations had to be appropriate for the media space selected. Putting it bluntly, the advert had not only to be in the right place, it had also to look right in that place to the target consumers. It was in relation to this question that planning was again put forward by its advocates as germane to producing an appropriate creative strategy. This concern lay behind John Bartle's re-assertion of the importance of planning that we encountered above. For Bartle, planners could not only furnish the creative team with information about the target consumers' attitudes towards the product and its associated product field, they could also provide information on the media consumption of these consumers and the nature of that media. The relationship between the planner and the media buyer, then, was the fourth key relationship through which planning intervened in the process of making adverts and running campaigns. As such, attitudinal information about consumers made available by media buyers impacted on the production of the creative brief and, from that, the practices of representation of art directors and writers.

## Summary

It is appropriate to take stock of what I have argued so far. I have advanced an account of the way a number of forms of knowledge and practice intersected in the production of a creative strategy within those agencies which gave account planning a central role in the advertising process. Centrally, I suggested that planning in these agencies was the practice through which consumer research – relating both to the product field and to media consumption – was appropriated into the formation of a creative strategy. It was through the planning process, in other words, that knowledge of the target consumer in the form of consumer segmentations, group discussions and research on media consumption was brought to bear upon the production of advertising representations.

A word of warning here, however. In putting together this account I have emphasized the way the practitioners involved in the process (particularly planners) reflected in more or less formal terms on their own practice. It would be wrong to take their descriptions as sufficient for understanding advertising production and especially the planning process. Not only – as we saw earlier – did different professional priorities rub up against each other in the formation of creative strategy, clearly informal knowledge about the consumer and the cultural identifications of the practitioners both intervened in the construction of a creative strategy.

These sort of influences upon strategy were most clearly at work when agency art directors and writers translated the brief into storyboards and a script or a draught press advert. The decisions involved in these translations implicated other determinants upon advertising representations: the training of the practitioners, the kinds of cultural languages and representational practices in circulation, and so on. By pointing to these factors, however, I do not intend to pull back from my argument regarding the specific determinants of advertising representations.

There is an important pay-off from considering the forms of knowledge and practice associated with planning, consumer research and media buying. Paying attention to these processes, gives us a glimpse of the interplay of economic and cultural determinants upon commercially produced cultural forms like advertising representations. What emerges from the above account of advertising production is not only the way practitioners had to make, continually, both economic and cultural calculations concerning the production of advertising, but the imbricated nature of those calculations. Questions associated with consumer targeting, for example, were fundamentally economic questions for agencies. Getting the specification of the target consumer wrong, scaring-off the target consumer through an inappropriate campaign or failing adequately to reach the target consumer through poorly conceived media buying, had real consequences for agencies and clients. Not only could agencies lose the account, but the consumer perception of the product or service could be damaged, and clients could lose sales and market share. Economic calculations, then, were implicit in the formation of the creative strategy. The planner, in particular, brought to bear these determinants on the representational practices of art directors and writers. The production of advertising representations was regulated by these economic calculations.

Conversely, however, the account I put together also points to the way economic determinants on advertising representations were much less autonomous than economic theory conventionally assumes. For example, relations between clients and consumers (which agencies mediated in the marketing of the product or service) were not purely economic. The process of specifying target consumers was, in this sense, a key cultural determinant of the establishment of these (economic) relations. Consumer markets, and the consumers who made them up, had to be pictured or represented in some form. The question that I considered in Chapter 7, "Who are we talking to?", then, was not secondary to the happy functioning of an economic relation already established in an autonomous economic sphere; it was a determinant of its existence. Product markets and their associated economic relations between "producers" and consumers, in this sense, were dependent on cultural practices for their production and reproduction.

This picture of the interplay of economic and cultural determinants of advertising representations, points to an underlying argument of the book. Namely, that cultural analysis needs to move away from a model of "relative autonomy" in conceptualizing determinants on the production of cultural forms. I want to come back to these arguments about the economic and cultural dynamics of cultural production in Part IV. As we will see, they loom large in how I read the formation of a new sector of magazines for men in the 1980s.

## "Creative advertising" and the "new man"

It is my contention that changes in the advertising industry detailed in this part of the book underpin in institutional terms the formation of the "new man" imagery within advertising. I want to draw together Part III by focusing on two campaigns that exemplify these developments. They are Bartle Bogle Hegarty's work for Levi-Strauss's "Levi's 501 jeans" and Grey advertising's work for Beechams Healthcare and Toiletries' "Brylcreem". Both campaigns are significant because they were key to establishing a successful style of advertising to new male markets in the mid 1980s. As such, they provided a positive answer to the question posed by Lucy Purdy at the beginning of this chapter. As we saw, she argued that agencies and their clients were uncertain about how to address the "fashionable young man". BBH and Grey found the appropriate imagery to successfully do just that.

### Levi's 501s

I have already signalled in the Introduction the significance of BBH's two television adverts for Levi-Strauss which ran from the end of 1985 and through 1986. These adverts formed part of a campaign which aimed to turn around Levi-Strauss's fortunes. These had been declining since the end of the 1970s and most rapidly during the early 1980s. They had reached a particularly low point in 1984. That year saw the year on year sales of jeans in the UK market as a whole down by 13 per cent, and Levi-Strauss's sales were hit particularly badly. The company themselves identified part of the reason for this decline in the failure of a marketing strategy which had been introduced at the end of the 1970s with the first signs of shifts in the jeans market. Levi-Strauss had diversified from its core business of jeans into menswear, womenswear and youthwear. In particular, it had more intensively targeted the 25 to 35 year old mainstream male market with a range of leisurewear. These included Levi's sweatshirts and trousers like the Levi's "Action Slacks". This strategy under-mined, however, Levi-Strauss's core product area (the jeans) and what the company saw as their essential values (quality, durability, Americanness, tradition). Research by Levi-Strauss showed, in par-ticular, that the credibility for young consumers of the Levi's name had slipped amidst the proliferation of leisure wear for older mar-kets. As Peter Skilland, Levi-Strauss's marketing services manager at the time acknowledged, "Putting the Levi's name on polyester trousers meant nothing to the polyester trouser buyer and left the jeans buyer totally unimpressed" (*Campaign*, 23/6/86: 50).

The company initiated a major rethink of its strategy. It decided upon what it called a "back to basics" policy. In other words, the product diversification was reversed, and Levi-Strauss refocused its manufacturing and marketing on the jean market. The aim was to re-establish the association of the Levi's name with tradition, Americanness, durability and quality. Three strands of this policy were significant. First, a decision was made to move away from an emphasis on volume sales and instead concentrate on profitability per unit. What this meant for the product range was the relaunch of the company's longest-standing line – the 501 jean – as a quality fashion trouser at a higher price. Secondly, Levi-Strauss was con-cerned to refocus its marketing upon what it saw as the crucial jeans market – the 15 to 19 year old youth market, and especially 15 to 19 year old males. Thirdly, the new marketing of the relaunched Levi's 501 was to be co-ordinated across Levi-Strauss's European markets and be – in this sense – genuinely pan-European.

BBH, who had won the UK account in 1982, satisfied Levi-Strauss that they could co-ordinate the new pan-European strategy. In re-searching the creative strategy for the campaign, BBH discovered a significant trend:

> we uncovered a fascination, almost a reverence, for a mythical America of the past – the America that had produced Dean and Presley, the 57 Chevrolet, Sam Cooke, the Misfits and a host of other heroes and "cult objects". Clothes and shoes featured

strongly in this, and the "fifties" look, suitably processed for the mid-1980s, was current . . . 501s featured heavily in this trend, and were being adopted by opinion-leading "cognescenti" in small but interesting numbers in London, Paris, Hamburg, Berlin, Rome and Milan (Broadbent 1990: 184).

The appropriation of the "fifties" look in "street style" and the valorization of a particular repertoire of "classic" objects (like Zippo lighters and Ray Ban sunglasses) offered a potentially neat fit with Levi-Strauss's "back to basics" strategy. BBH's brief, however, was to establish the Levi's 501 jeans in the arena of mass fashion. That is, it had not only to address opinion-leaders (or what BBH elsewhere termed "innovators"), but – in BBH's terms – "early adopters". As the agency themselves put it,

> We wanted to make 501s compulsory equipment for anyone who cared about the way they looked. We wished to persuade the 15–20 year old males who represent the core jeans market that 501 were the right look, and the only label: the right look because "anti-fit" [the 501 cut] was the way jeans were being worn by those in the know; the only label, because only Levi's 501 had laid genuine claim to the heady jeans heritage that was rooted in the fifties (ibid.: 185).

A more detailed formulation of the brief followed from this specification of the target consumers. Using group discussions with consumers in London and Frankfurt based around video screenings of film footage and collages of magazine photos, BBH confirmed that – in their terms – the "evocation of a mythical America was a motivating route . . . We also deepened our understanding of the role of great pop classics in underlying the status of the product and learned that casting was absolutely crucial" (ibid.: 185).

The final creative brief was produced from these findings and the adverts were art directed by John Hegarty and written by Barbara Noakes. "Bath" and "Launderette" went on the air in the UK on Boxing Day 1985 on both ITV and Channel 4, together with a cinema run of the adverts. In addition, the marketing strategy included a press campaign, the development of extensive point-of-sale materials (to support the new campaign within retail outlets), the design of a 501 logo, coordination with record companies of the release of the two soundtrack songs, and – in 1987 – a second phase of marketing. I come back to the press campaign in Part IV. Importantly, as we will see, it was aimed not at the mass market of early-adopters targeted through television, but at a segmented market of "innovators".

"Bath" and "Launderette" were immediately successful. Sales of the 501s expanded rapidly; so rapidly in fact that in March and April of 1986 the adverts were withdrawn from television because Levi's factories were unable to keep up with demand. Importantly for Levi-Strauss, sales of the 501s markedly improved the profits per units of the company. The adverts also prompted extended press and television commentary, and picked up a number of industry awards.

It was the codings of masculinity put together in the adverts which really concerns us. I have already commented in the Introduction on "Launderette". I want to underline here five characteristics of the masculinity signified in "Bath" and "Launderette". First, the appropriation and glamorization of 1950s style was important. It set the terms for the signification of an assertive masculinity. Secondly, the surface of the models' bodies – and specifically developed muscles – were displayed. Thirdly, the assertive masculinity of both the "fifties" style and the models' physiques, were signified together with the coding of softness and sensuality. Both Nick Kamen and James Mardle had smooth, clear skins, full pouting lips, shiny eyes and glossy, highly groomed hair. Fourthly, the display of these bodies was presented to the viewer in highly distinctive ways. Cuts to arms, chest, face, bottom and thighs, together with a focus on the unbuttoning of the jeans and (in the case of "Bath") a cut of the water seeping over the model's jean-clad crotch, undermined more conventional significations of power and aggression associated with displayed masculine bodies. Fifthly, the male hero was represented as self-contained and on his own.

What these characteristics established was a coherent grammar for addressing new male consumers in the mid to late 1980s. Not all the codings necessarily appeared in every advert, but a combination of them was characteristically present in a series of adverts for clothing and accessories, grooming and toiletries, financial services and electrical goods.[8] This repertoire of codings was central to Grey Advertising's work with Brylcreem.

## Brylcreem

If Levi-Strauss was suffering from a decline in its fortunes prior to its strategic rethink and BBH's campaign for the Levi's 501s, then Beechams's Brylcreem was in near terminal decline. From a peak in the early 1960s when Brylcreem sold one hundred million pots in the UK, by 1984 sales were down to five million because of longer hair and styles requiring blow-drying among men. This dramatic decline was aggravated by the nature of Brylcreem's remaining customer base, which was an ageing group of long-term male users. Beechams saw little opportunity in expanding sales within this market, and no advertising of the brand had been run since the "Brylcreem bounce" campaign of the early 1970s. A general re-appraisal by Beechams of its key brands, however, changed this. Suffering from what industry analysts termed "lack of executive direction" in the early 1980s, Beechams set in motion initiatives to reposition and re-establish brands like Lucozade, Horlicks, Ribena and (what Beechams saw as the most difficult task) Brylcreem. Underpinning this strategy was new product development and marketing. Grey Advertising, which won the new account in 1985, set about researching the creative strategy. A key finding for Grey was that among a younger generation of men, shorter hair and traditionally smart hairstyles were being worn in preference for what Grey called the "'scruffy' styles of the last twenty years" (*Campaign*, 4/10/85: 15). These were, specifically, a highly fashion conscious group of male consumers whom Grey termed "stylepreneurs" (ibid.). Formulating a creative strategy for these target consumers was a problem, however, for the creatives at Grey. Art director Su Sareem and writer Jan Heron described how they came up with the final version.

> Jan and I were despairing – we knew that there was a solution there somewhere but we just couldn't seem to find it. For inspiration, we went through the old Brylcreem commercials and were watching the sixties reel in my flat. Suddenly the phone rang. I put the video on "hold" and the image started to shake. We both realised that with good music, it would be perfect (*Campaign*, 4/10/85: 15).

Three new commercials were cut and re-edited from the old commercials using video-editing techniques and a contemporary soundtrack was added. Beechams was not fully convinced by this creative strategy, and initially allocated only £1 million to test the campaign. Grey used all this budget for a television campaign in London. Both the agency and client were happy with the initial consumer response, and so in February 1986 a second campaign – using similar footage – was launched, together with an extensive press and poster campaign. The press and poster work extended the pastiche of the 1960s advertising using contemporary models. These included Nick Kamen's brother, Barry. This was accompanied by the design of a new tub style. In 1987, further product development was initiated and a range of 13 products (including mousse, gel and aftershave) was launched in black packaging and with a new typeface for the brand name. In 1988, this product range was backed by a new television commercial which – still focusing on the appropriation of 1950s style short hair by young men – extended the repositioning of the brand as an essential purchase for stylish young men (*Campaign*, 11/11/88: 3). The creative team at Grey, like their counterparts at BBH, identified casting as crucial to establishing the credibility of the advert among its target audience. In casting the 26 year old Corsican, Jean-Ange Chiapinini, the team "were looking for the definitive modern man. A cross between Mickey Rourke and Matt Dillon, more of a man on the street than a pretty-boy model type like Nick Kamen" (ibid.: 12).

The advert was set in a barber's shop, amid the traditional paraphernalia of masculine grooming. The narrative of the advert was based around the model being wet shaved by the barber. In dramatically lit gloom we see the shaving cream being applied, the razor being used and the barber massaging the model's temples and then pulling a hot flannel over his face to complete the grooming. Throughout this ritual, which is shot in rapid close-ups, the model is narcissistically absorbed in the care he is receiving. His self-absorption is highlighted by the fact that the process of shaving is shot in such quick edits to a thunderous soundtrack. We glimpse a flame, the razor against his face, a razor being sharpened on leather and the steaming flannel being pulled across his face. The model remains self-absorbed amid these movements around him. In all of this there was more than a hint at sado-masochism connoted through the ritual of grooming between the barber and the model.

The masculine imagery of the campaigns echoed many of the codings at work in the Levi's 501 adverts, despite the self-conscious attempt (through casting in particular) to encode a different masculinity. The appropriation of the iconography of the neat and smart style of respectable 1950s masculinity was key to the first television campaigns, the press and poster campaign and the 1988 television commercial (even if, in the early television campaigns, the imagery was in fact from the early 1960s). The glamorization and – most clearly in the re-cut and re-edited adverts – playful quality of this appropriation was again important. The casting of the models was also significant. Chiapinini's "look", in the 1988 advert, was certainly harder than Kamen's. More important, though, were the continuities in both this advert and the press and poster adverts: the combination of an assertively masculine "look", which also contained elements of softness or sensuality connoted through the gloss of the hair and skin and the fullness of the lips. The television advert of 1988 for Brylcreem also explicitly displayed, like the Levi's 501 adverts, the narcissistic pleasures of grooming and adornment.

These codings of masculinity are at the heart of my contentions about the distinctiveness of the 1980s "new man" imagery. In order to develop my argument about the break they represented in popular representations of masculinity and the forms of spectatorship associated with them, I want to turn to another institutional site in the regime of "new man" imagery. This was the new magazine culture of the "style press" and men's general interest magazines. These magazines are particularly important because the codings of masculinity represented in the Levi's 501 and Brylcreem adverts drew upon codings established within the "style" magazines in the mid 1980s and developed in the men's magazines in the mid to late 1980s. It is within these representations that I want to explore the distinctiveness of the "new man" representations (including the forms of spectatorship associated with them). Before I can do that, though, I need to account for the shifts within magazine culture itself which set the institutional conditions for the formation of these representations.

# PART IV

# Magazine culture and the "new man"

# Introduction

I have laid stress so far in this account on two nexus of institutional practices which formed key determinants of the regime of "new man" imagery. I suggested in Part II that developments in the design and selling of menswear set important terms for the formation of the "new man" imagery (through the developments in menswear design) and that menswear shops were themselves an important site at which the "new man" was represented (through the coding of shop space and the signification of the garment ranges). In Part III I set out a specific formation of advertising knowledges and practices – essentially, those associated with creative advertising – and argued that these knowledges and practices were also a key determinant on the regime of "new man" imagery. It was through the television and press adverts produced within this formation of advertising that the developments in menswear design were again resignified and a specific set of visual codings of masculinity deployed in targeting new male consumers. In Part IV, I turn to a third set of institutional practices which impacted on the formation of the regime of "new man" imagery: the publishing knowledges and practices associated with two sectors within UK magazine publishing, the "style press" and "general interest men's magazines". It was through these magazine sectors that publishers and advertisers attempted to address new male readerships through a magazine form in the mid to late 1980s and where commercial interest in the "new man" was forged within magazine publishing. In Chapter 9, I set out the publishing trade debates that surrounded the formation of a sector of "general interest men's magazines" in the UK. The formation of this sector was important not only because it revealed particularly clearly the advertising/ publishing nexus focused upon new male readers, but also because the launch of these magazines extended the volume of photography based coverage of menswear in the UK. In Chapter 10, I consider in more detail the journalistic characteristics of the three magazines that were pivotal to the shifts within magazine culture in relation to new male readerships. In particular, I comment on the forms of cultural knowledge these magazines offered their male readers. In Chapter 11, I put together an account of the fashion photography produced within these magazines. My account of this fashion photography carries special significance for the book as a whole. My reading of these representations is shaped by a concern to look critically at the codings of masculinity produced within this imagery. These representations not only formed part of the regime of "new man" imagery. More than that they represented the privileged site in this regime of representation. It is within the magazine fashion photography associated with the new magazine culture that the "new man" first emerged and where these visual codings were consolidated and elaborated. It is in relation to these representations, then, that I advance an argument about the specificity of the regime of "new man" imagery as a whole, including the forms of spectatorship coded in relation to these representations.

## CHAPTER 9

# Looking for the Holy Grail: male readerships and the general interest men's magazine

Ann Cooper, reporting in *Campaign*'s "Close-up" section on developments in publishing in June 1984, noted the boom in what she called "men's lifestyle titles" in the USA. *Esquire* and *GQ*, the more established among these titles, were the main beneficiaries of this boom and both magazines had achieved their highest recorded circulation figures and largest number of pages of advertising in 1983. (*Campaign*, 29/6/84: 12).[1] Cooper quoted John Veronis, of the media analysts Veronis Suhler and Associates, in offering an explanation of this boom. He suggested,

> Men's lifestyle magazines have touched the interest of the marketplace – an interest not around five or ten years ago. Readers today are very much more self-focused and these magazines have found an editorial format that's having a dramatic effect on the marketplace (*Campaign*, 29/6/84: 12).

Two years later, *Media Week* also focused on the success of *Esquire* and *GQ* in the USA, and again attempted to characterize what lay behind the transformation of the magazines' fortunes. For Art Cooper, editor-in-chief of *GQ*, quoted in the *Media Week* article, the new success of the magazines stemmed from the way

> men have become far more conscious of style and fashion . . . the magazines have benefitted from that. I think more and more men are discovering that it feels good to look good, so part of it is a result of the fitness mania in this country (*Media Week*, 2/5/86: 14–17).

Lee Eisenberg, editor of *Esquire*, added that "in the wake of the women's movement, a different kind of male came about. Their interests have changed and become more mature" (ibid.).

Both the *Campaign* and *Media Week* articles used the reporting of the developments in the USA men's magazine market and the diagnoses of their success, to pose the question of whether the time was right for the launch of a UK equivalent of these magazines. Had a comparable shift occurred in the attitudes and lifestyles of British men (or at least a significant enough minority of them) to make possible a UK version of a men's lifestyle magazine? The posing of this question fed into (in both 1984 and 1986) a vociferous debate among magazine publishers and media analysts within advertising agencies about the possibility of opening up this sector of magazines in the UK. In a concerted way from 1983, publishers and advertising practitioners had been preoccupied with what *Media Week* called the "next rich publishing seam" – what was known in the UK trade as the "general interest men's magazine".

In this chapter I set out the advertising and publishing knowledges that intersected in these debates and which were important determinants upon the formation of a sector of general interest men's magazines in the UK. I advance an argument, in particular, about the way these knowledges and their associated practices were stitched together around a shared concern among media practitioners (within advertising and publishing) to address a new consumer readership through the form of glossy magazines: what were recurrently referred to as style-conscious young men.

## A new magazine market

Publishers look at women's magazines, their circulation figures and bottom line and they think, "If we could put together a road test of a new Porsche with an in-depth interview with Giorgio Armani and some stuff about personal finance, then we've hit some sort of composite male who has all those interests." (Zed Zawada, *Campaign*, 29/8/86: 41).

Conventional wisdom says that men buy fashion and sports magazines in the US and Europe; that men's interests are well catered for in the Sunday supplements and dailies; that advertisers prefer to reach them by TV; that men don't buy magazines, period; and that there must be a market out there (Steve Taylor, *Campaign*, 29/8/86: 41).

The publishing formula of "general interest men's magazines" which provided the focus of much of the advertising and publishing debates between 1983 and 1989 was a simple one. It was also the product of a straightforward logic. Women's magazines dominated the consumer magazine sector in terms of circulation figures and income from display advertising. Publishers believed, as Zed Zawada's comments testify, that an equivalent male title would deliver to them an aggregate of the diverse male readerships traditionally dispersed across specialist magazines – car and photographic magazines, the hobbies press and soft porn magazines – and, hence, the kind of circulation figures and advertising income enjoyed by women's magazines.

This formula was, however, the site of competing arguments voiced by different formations of media practitioners. At the heart of these arguments were a number of contradictory assertions about men's culture on the ground; in particular, arguments about men's propensity to buy a general interest magazine. What was often invoked – as Steve Taylor's comments make clear – were a series of truisms or common-sense wisdoms about what was recurrently referred to as the "typical British male" and his media consumption habits. These truisms were most clearly articulated by practitioners sceptical of the possibility of launching a UK general interest men's magazine. At their least sophisticated and most doctrinal, these commentators saw men as difficult and elusive media consumers, as highly discerning, and as unwilling to pay out for a glossy magazine (*Campaign*, 29/8/86: 41). A more conceptual rendering of these arguments was also advanced. For Simon Marquis, commenting in a "state of play" article in *Campaign* at the height of the trade debates in 1985, a general interest men's magazine was unlikely to succeed because,

> While women become "friends" with their magazines there is an inbuilt male resistance to the idea of a magazine that makes public and shares ideas about being a man. To men it is an unacceptable contradiction. Self-consciousness is permissible, even attractive, in a women; it is perceived as weak and unmanly in a man (*Campaign*, 26/7/85: 37).

Men, in addition, he went on to argue, did not need the kind of club provided for women by their magazines. For men, "contact with other men has been their historical perogative" (ibid.).

This interpretation of men's culture and the norms of masculinity associated with it, was echoed by Zed Zawada. Zawada, like Marquis, took issue with the notion that a general interest men's magazine could be successfully launched in the UK. He said,

> Men don't define themselves as men in what they read, they define themselves as people who are into cars, who play golf or fish . . . Successfully launching a general interest men's magazine would be like finding the Holy Grail (*Campaign*, 29/8/86: 41).

Other practitioners took a less pessimistic view of the possibility of finding the Holy Grail of glossy magazine publishing. At the heart of these practitioners' optimism was evidence from consumer research about shifts in groups of men's "values and lifestyles". For these practitioners, this research pointed to a new constituency of men who would buy a generalist men's magazine.

Paul Keers, a journalist who began his career with *Cosmopolitan* and then went on to edit *Expression*, the magazine for American Express cardholders and to be commissioning editor for the *Sunday Telegraph Magazine*, was a key evangelist amongst the publishing advocates of men's magazines. National Magazines' production of a banded supplement, *Cosmo Man*, for its women's monthly, *Cosmopolitan*, in November 1984, gave him the opportunity to develop his arguments in a practical context and an institutional space from which to carry forward his conception of a general interest men's magazine. Keers's argument drew strongly on an account of the success of the USA men's magazine market, and, in addition, on evidence of shifts in the culture of groups of men in the UK. In a letter to *Campaign* in 1985, he argued that

> The reason why US men's magazines have been successful is not to do with the size of the audience, nor with any differences in social and sexual attitudes, but simply because they have worked on isolating the male yuppie audience. And that audience has reading and lifestyle habits distinct from those of earlier generations of men. So the men's magazine I and others would like to see would be aimed at this yuppie male audience . . . By isolating

the interests of this specific, large, wealthy and image-conscious demographic bulge in the male market, a UK men's magazine could succeed (*Campaign*, 2/5/85: 20).

Choosing more cautious language, Simon Marquis reported similar positive shifts in groups of men's consumption, values and tastes. Marquis suggested that the "seedlings of new attitudes and behaviour in 1985 . . . may give publishers hope" (*Campaign*, 26/7/85: 38). The men most implicated in these attitudinal and behavioural shifts were not, for Marquis, yuppies but men who corresponded to the male consumers identified as "avant guardians" in the advertising agency McCann-Erickson's "Man study". These were men who, for Marquis (quoting from McCann's report) "have an optimistic outlook on life and a strongly contemporary view of masculinity" (ibid.). These attributes, for Marquis, were most clearly evidenced through "avant guardians" ' interest in clothes; an interest defined by Marquis as being shaped by the entry of style into the vocabulary of British men and pursued without the approbation of women.

Other practitioners were also optimistic about the shifts in the "values and attitudes" of groups of men. They derived this confidence not only from consumer research (like the "Man Study"), but also from developments within magazine culture itself. What loomed large in this respect was the success of a new sector of youth magazines in the 1980s: the "style press".

## The style press

The "style press" was a term applied to three magazines which launched almost simultaneously in 1980. These were *The Face, I-D,* and *Blitz.* The term was deployed as a form of trade and journalistic shorthand for the kind of journalism and editorial mix which characterized the magazines. The magazines themselves were all produced by independent publishers – Wagadon (*The Face*), Jigsaw (*Blitz*) and Levelprint Ltd (*I-D*) – and who, among the company of publishing giants like IPC, National Magazines, Condé Nast, and even a smaller publisher like EMAP, were marginal enterprises.

*The Face* was the most successful of the three magazines, reaching a circulation peak of around 92,000 between 1985 and 1987, as well as picking up a number of trade awards (*Benn's Media Directory,*

1983–8). It is the most important of the three for my account and I consider its distinctiveness as a magazine more fully in the next chapter. Publisher and editor Nick Logan had developed the initial idea of the magazine in the late 1970s while editing IPC's flagship music paper *New Musical Express*. Logan had joined IPC from the *West Essex Gazette*, the local paper on which he had worked after leaving school at 16. Logan, a self-proclaimed "East London mod" and Labour Party supporter, edited *NME* for ten years before moving to EMAP. It was while at EMAP guiding the early days of *Smash Hits*, however, that Logan eventually launched *The Face*. Logan's original concept for the magazine was built around the notion of a well written magazine that, he said, he would have liked to read when he was 18 years old. That is, a magazine that would cast its net quite wide to comment on a diverse range of subjects. The independence of Wagadon was important to this project. Putting it somewhat prosaically, Logan said,

> The only reason I'm an entrepreneur, if I am, is because that's the only way you can have the freedom to follow your own instincts. My period working for publishing corporations [was] depressing and frustrating (*Direction*, 9/1988: 32).

The space to develop the format of the magazine outside the restrictions of a big publishing company – cushioned a little in the first year by Logan's job at *Smash Hits* – allowed *The Face*'s distinctive style and format to grow. Logan said,

> When I started it, I believed people like IPC who told me that there was no market for a *general* title. Therefore I made it music based and gradually brought in other stuff to make it, after a couple of years, what I had wanted it to be in the first place (*Campaign*, 29/6/86: 42; my emphasis).

*The Face*'s circulation expanded strongly in 1983 and 1984. In the second half of 1984 sales rose by 20 per cent from 66,500 to 80,000 (*Media Week*, 3/5/85: 22). As the magazine grew, Logan's strong sense of the "look" of the magazine led to a somewhat idiosyncratic approach to competing for advertising revenue. Initially, he had planned that *The Face* would be able to survive on cover sales alone, and although Logan had been forced from early on to take advertising, *The Face* did not have an advertising manager until 1984. Logan's antagonism to advertising derived from his sense that advertising spoiled the "look" of the magazine. In particular, half-page or smaller adverts were anathema to Logan in his concern to develop the design of the magazine (*Direction*, 9/1988: 32).

Rod Sopp's arrival as advertising manager in 1984 marked a more engaged – if still disingenuous – view of advertising in relation to the magazine. Sopp skilfully crafted Logan's dislike of the way advertising broke up the aimed for layouts of the magazine, into a piece of media folklore about *The Face*'s preparedness to refuse adverts on aesthetic grounds. More significantly, Sopp produced for the first time a worked-up picture of the type of persons who read *The Face*. Sopp presented *The Face* to advertisers as the perfect media form through which to target the consumer groups we have already encountered in Part III: namely, "innovators" or "opinion formers". These were groups of consumers who, for Sopp, were at the forefront of social trends; taste-shapers who – and he gave this example – were behind the classic mid 1980s style for young men of a plain white T-shirt, Levi's 501s, white socks and bass weejun loafers.

Sopp's representation of *The Face*'s readership of "innovators" through the figure of the stylish young man was significant. Attention to menswear and male style was an important element of the magazine's editorial between 1983 and 1987. As Logan acknowledged, in what is a telling comment for my argument in this chapter,

> One area where we are particularly strong is in men's fashions, which is pretty badly represented generally. I keep reading about the need for a men's magazine, but I think we're closer to that than anyone. Two thirds of our readers are men. At the moment I'm caught between trying to attract more women readers, or expanding the trend towards men (*Media Week*, 16/3/84: 56).

Other commentators, like Jane Reed of IPC, saw *The Face* as shaping up a new market of young male readers. She argued that the magazine had established "new territory for young men", particularly in terms of promoting style and consumption (*Campaign*, 26/7/85: 37). Even critics recognized the address *The Face* made to young men. Thus, publisher Peter Jackson, castigated the magazine for being "narrow, mannered and obsessed with males" (*Campaign*, 27/3/87: 20).

It was *The Face*'s association with this consumer subject, however – the stylish young male "innovator" – that attracted advertising media buyers to the magazine. *Media Week* succinctly enunciated the thinking behind media buyer's interest in the magazine when it suggested that "*The Face*'s 63% NRS male readership is used by hapless media planners [or buyers] stuck with the perennial problem of reaching the young male through the colour press" (*Media Week*, 12/2/88: 4).

The placing of *The Face* high up the media buying lists of advertising media buyers and planners was itself dependent upon the shifts in media buying practice detailed in Part III. Thus, despite its relatively small circulation, *The Face* was identified by media buyers as an effective place in which to advertise both because the magazine was read by key groups of consumers ("innovators", "the style-conscious male") and because it provided a sympathetic context in which to place adverts for, in particular, a range of lifestyle orientated goods and services: clothing, financial services, records, alcohol and consumer electronics. Two high profile advertising campaigns which ran in the magazine between 1985 and 1987 illustrated the way *The Face* was classified by advertising practitioners within this form of "qualitative" media buying. These were the adverts produced for Way In and Levi's 501s. It is appropriate briefly to consider these campaigns.

## Way In

Way In had been established as a boutique within the Harrods' department store in the 1960s. In 1985, a decision was taken by the Harrod's management to redesign Way In in order to give it a stronger identity and to reposition it in relation to developments in fashion retailing. The acclaimed retail designer, Eva Jiricna, was chosen to carry out the revamping of the boutique. Fenella Walsh of Harrods described the type of consumers that the redesign was targeted at.

> People who buy at Next go there because they want to be helped to co-ordinate their clothes. That is the last thing we're trying to do. We believe that our customers have their own style and know how to put it together. Our market is not commercial. It's a boutique market. Coming to Way In is like shopping in the whole of South Molton Street (*Media Week*, 8/11/85: 23).

Lynne Franks PR, who undertook the advertising that accompanied the redesign of Way In, spent a significant proportion of the £60,000 budget on two press advertisements. *Media Week* (8/11/85: 23) described them as "deliberately pretentious and arty black and white ads". Both adverts used high-contrast black and white images (in one of the adverts, the image consisted of a fingerprint and an eye) with sans serif typeface and print of different sizes. The copy selected comprised arch quotes – one from Barthes on photography, the other from a song by Stephen Duffy on provincial shopping and Parisian arcades. Both adverts invoked a knowing metropolitan sophistication, underlined by the play on the 1960s page layouts and typeface.[2] The media chosen as the most appropriate place or context for these adverts was the "style press" – including *The Face*, where one of the adverts ran on the back cover of the magazine.

## Levi's 501s

BBH's press campaign for Levi's 501 jeans, which followed the broadcasting and screening of the "Bath" and "Launderette" television and cinema commercials in January 1986, was even more explicit than Lynne Franks PR's work for Way In in the way it selected *The Face* in terms of "qualitative" media buying criteria. As we saw in Part III, the television and cinema adverts produced by BBH were aimed at a mass market of consumers ("early adopters", in BBH's terms) and motivated by the ambition to make the Levi's 501s a compulsory purchase for anyone within this segment interested in fashion. A major concern, however, surfaced for the agency with this strategy.

> The early indications of the potential success of the 501 programme, gave us one major concern. We feared that, as 501s went "public", the opinion leaders who had discovered the product without the aid of advertising would abandon the brand. We had to reassure this small (but very important) group that 501s really were the great classic they had always believed them to be (Broadbent 1990: 188).

The press campaign put together by BBH was designed to do precisely this. John Hegarty art directed five adverts which displayed the 501s laid out on a flat surface as part of a coordinated "look". Each advert was immaculately styled and accessorized by contemporary British fashion designers – Scott Crolla, Wendy Dagworthy, Jasper Conran, Joseph Ettedgui and Paul Smith. The adverts ran in *The Face* – directly targeted by BBH at "innovators" (*Campaign*, 24/1/86: 12, *Media Week*, 29/4/88: 28).

The interlinking of these forms of advertising media buying practice and creative strategy on the pages of *The Face* – exemplified in both the Way In and Levi's 501 adverts – drew the magazine, then, very directly into the advertising arguments about targeting new male consumers through the colour press; arguments which – as I have suggested – were an important determinant of the formation of men's magazines. In classifying *The Face*, however, the media buyers at BBH or Lynne Franks PR did not hold all the cards. What was distinctive about the relationship between *The Face* and advertising practitioners at this time (1984–7), was the ability of the magazine to lay claim to this group of young male consumers. In other words, the magazine – and especially Rod Sopp – was extremely successful in persuading advertising media buyers that *The Face* was not only the perfect media vehicle through which to target new male consumers, but also that the magazine's staff had a developed sense of this group of consumers' tastes, values and sensibilities. This last point was particularly critical. In a period where – as we saw in Part III – advertising practitioners had evidence of shifts in the "values and lifestyles" of groups of men and yet were uncertain about how to represent the new male consumer, *The Face* offered the precepts of the necessary cultural knowledge to target these "new men". Pivotal to this, as I hinted in my comments on the Levi's 501 and Brylcreem adverts in Part III (and which I come to in the next section), was the styling of menswear in the magazine and the codings of masculinities that this threw up. These exerted considerable influence over a wider range of representations targeted at new male consumers.

As well as being central to the way advertisers targeted this segment of male consumers through the colour press, *The Face* was also subject to close scrutiny from other consumer magazine publishers. For a number of publishing practitioners, the success of *The Face* between 1984 and 1986 really testified to a shift in the magazine reading habits of important groups of young men. In particular, it was seen to have educated a generation of young men into reading a general interest magazine for men. In doing so, as we will see in the next chapter, *The Face* also shifted the terms of what the format of a general interest magazine could be; namely, one based upon a style-led journalism and editorial approach rather than on the format offered by women's magazines. These findings gave considerable impetus to the formulation of a general interest men's magazine aimed at the segment of men in the age group above *The Face*'s target readership. That is, men aged between 20 and 45. It is to these developments that I now turn.[3]

## The general interest men's magazine: *Arena* and *GQ*

In September 1986, Condé Nast, publishers of *Vogue*, began dummy preparations for a free-standing "Vogue for Men". Their concern to produce a general interest men's magazine in the UK formed part of a long standing ambition to produce such a magazine in all the markets in which they operated. As we saw earlier, in the USA Condé Nast's *GQ* was a successful magazine, while in Italy, *L'Huommo Vogue* and in France, *Vogue Hommes* were equally profitable products (interview with Keers, 1989). The decision to launch in the UK at this time, however, was strongly driven by the arguments I have introduced already. On the one hand, Condé Nast were confident that the success of magazines like *The Face* had established a new market for men's magazine. As readers aged and moved away from *The Face*, Condé Nast aimed to attract them to a magazine geared to more mature interests. On the other hand, an identification of shifts in men's attitudes to fashion at Condé Nast loomed large in their calculations. Richard Hill, Condé Nast's deputy managing director, was very explicit about the importance of this finding, if still cautious about the depth of the change:

> people are always saying that men are becoming peacocks and while that is certainly true in Europe, I'm not sure whether we've got the full plumage here yet. But we are almost there and what we want to find out is whether its enough to make a separate Vogue for Men viable (*Campaign*, 26/9/86: 7).

Two formats were produced and tested by a market research company for Condé Nast. One version was based on the USA *GQ* format, the other was "a quirkier, harder version" (*Campaign*, 5/6/87: 19). The results of these testings, however, were not encouraging.

The market research company summarized its findings as follows:

> [You] would have great difficulty in achieving 50,000 and shouldn't go ahead unless [you] felt the magazine could be made viable at circulations between 25,000–30,000 (*Campaign*, ibid.).

Mark Boxer, editorial director of Condé Nast, commenting in the spring of 1987, remained troubled by the whole concept of a generalist male title – even following the success of *The Face*. He said,

> I think there's a problem with men's magazines. Men are already well served for sport, the City and politics by newspapers . . . They're now getting freebies sent to Diners Club and American Express card holders. There is too much to read already. The one area there might be a gap is for a style magazine – but in that area Englishmen are uneasy, they don't admit to taking fashion seriously (*The Observer*, 26/4/87: 29).

Condé Nast's cautious manoeuvrings were overshadowed in November 1986, however, by Nick Logan's launch of a general interest men's magazine, *Arena*. Given the importance of *The Face* in the advertising and publishing debates between 1984 and 1986, as we have seen, it was quite fitting that the formation of this new sector should have come from Wagadon. Commenting prior to the launch, Logan described *Arena* as "a 132 page perfect bound bi-monthly glossy, pitched at the 25–35 year old male, with a circulation of 45,000–50,000" (*Campaign*, 8/8/86: 6). For *Campaign*, in a telling characterization, this was to be the magazine "really liberated males will leave lying around their hi-tech studios" (*Campaign*, 15/8/86: 18).

Logan, in fact, saw *Arena* occupying a more precise cultural niche. As he said,

> I only decided a couple of months ago that I will do a magazine with fashion and good articles and that will look great. I am still inventing it. I don't have any big philosophy of the new man . . . Take people like myself who became interested in fashion as mods in the sixties, or the soul boys and Bowie fans of the 70s and 80s. If you become involved in fashion with that intensity I think it stays with you (*Campaign*, 15/8/86: 18).

The immediate reaction to *Arena* in terms of sales was good. "It's going like a train", announced advertising manager, Rod Sopp, two weeks after the launch. Importantly the magazine also found favour with media professionals. *Media Week* awarded it a commendation in the "Launch of the Year" category of its consumer magazines awards. In the words of the judge,

> *Arena* has increased the advertisers ability to target an extremely elusive consumer. Before its launch, young male fashion magazines were taboo. Its success is a credit to the judgement and nerve of a small publishing team which really knows its readers (*Media Week*, 1/7/87: 10).

Steve Buckley, editor of *Media Week*, underlined this assessment of the magazine by emphasizing *Arena*'s importance in establishing the new magazine market for men. He said, "*Arena* is tiny but significant. It has dispelled the taboo on publishing magazines for men whose interest and income stretch beyond sensible cars" (*Independent*, 26/10/88: 15).

The evaluation of *Arena* among advertising media buyers generally mirrored the comments made by Buckley and *Media Week*. Practitioners identified it as a good media vehicle for targeting "innovators" or opinion forming young men. Two campaigns, which ran in *Arena* in 1987–8, evidence this categorizing of the magazine by advertising media buyers. These were the adverts for Levi's Chinos and Clark's Desert Boots.

The Clark's Desert Boots campaign ran from the summer of 1987. BMP, the advertising agency handling the account, put together a strategy which was concerned to reposition the brand in the UK as a "classic" and fashionable item. Working with a small budget, BMP's first move was to define as tightly as possible the target consumers. The agency focused on what they called, "young style-conscious men" as the core group of consumers to be targeted (Broadbent 1990: 236). The central problem then became how best to target these consumers. BMP explained,

> Given a media budget of £30,000 and a sparse but nationally distributed target audience, the media department was given the task of finding a medium that would allow us to reach as many of this target audience as possible whilst providing an environment

that gave our style claim credibility. They came up with a selection of "style magazines"; publications . . . that captured precisely the young style leaders we were aiming for. The title list included *The Face, I-D* [and] *Arena*" (Broadbent 1990: 236).

BBH's framing of the consumer target and the media planning for the press adverts they produced for Levi's Chinos deployed a similar attitudinal classification of *Arena*. As they put it, "Our audience was difficult to define – broadly speaking we were looking for ABC1 15–25 year old men. But the "style leaders" definition transcended traditional demographic categories . . . They have a major desire to lead rather than be led, they are opinion formers" (*Media Week*, 29/4/88: 28). With this conception in place, BBH's concern was to execute the advert and then place it in the appropriate media. The agency described the thinking behind the choice of media for the advert:

> In order to fulfil the advertising strategy for the brand, media choice for Chinos set out to reflect elements of youth culture itself, and attempted to influence the target group through a number of identifiable components . . . We set out to identify the titles which were held to be most credible by the youth elite" (ibid.).

*Arena* was chosen by BBH as a title that fulfilled these criteria. The selection of the magazine by BBH (and BMP) also registered the success of the practitioners at Wagadon – and especially, Rod Sopp – in presenting *Arena* to advertisers. In fact, Rod Sopp was as canny as he had been with *The Face* in representing the readership of *Arena* to advertisers. With *Arena* he even raised the stakes. *Arena* declined to be audited by the National Readership Survey (NRS). For Sopp, placing the magazine on the NRS – which produced a break down of magazine readership in terms of the JICNARS definition of social class – "puts the magazine on the media shopping lists at the less clued up agencies . . . Clearly, there are ABC1s and ABC1s, and a planner who fails to look beyond this data is doing considerable disservice to the title" (*Media Week*, 12/2/88: 2). Instead, Sopp emphasized the way *Arena* was read by "innovators" and opinion forming males with greater purchasing power than their younger equivalents who read *The Face*.

The circulation figures of 65,000 which *Arena* achieved for its first audited circulation, together with the interest shown by advertising media buyers, gave the trade debates on men's magazines – still dominated in 1986–7, it is important to underline, by extreme caution from most interested publishers – a new urgency. These developments, together with changes of personnel, prompted Condé Nast to act. A key figure in Condé Nast's more confident approach to the general interest men's magazine was Stephen Quinn.

Quinn had been a strong advocate of the general interest men's magazine since the early 1980s. His own background provides some clues to the shape of the sort of magazine he envisaged. Quinn worked for *Nova* in the late 1960s, before moving to National Magazines to publish *Harper's & Queen*. As he said, "I began my love affair (then) with rather clever, intelligentsia type magazines, and it has never ended." While at *Harper's & Queen*, he began to identify a market of male consumers he wanted to reach and attempted to integrate some editorial elements into the magazine to attract these readers. This process was partly fuelled by advertising interest. As Quinn acknowledged "Advertisers such as Harrods, Harvey Nichols, Jaeger, Yves Saint Laurent and Estée Lauder have often told me that they long for a clever, sharp and witty magazine aimed at men" (*The Times*, 24/6/87: 28).

In 1983 he proposed such a title (what elsewhere he has called a "classy men's magazine") to the board of National Magazines (*Media Week*, 4/11/88: 47). They turned the idea down. A second proposal in 1987, producing the same reaction, precipitated Quinn's move to Condé Nast.

Quinn's move to Condé Nast coincided with Paul Keers's arrival fresh from editing the *Sunday Telegraph* magazine and *Cosmo Man*. This combination of two such strong advocates of a general male title formed the guiding hands behind Condé Nast's entry into this market (and their first independent British launch for 30 years) (*Campaign*, 13/5/88: 33).

Further market research was undertaken. Working with a narrower base of upmarket male consumers, the magazine's name was tested and the mixture of editorial worked on. The name GQ was favoured over Vogue for Men because of the feminine connotations of the latter, and the sense that it implied a derivative magazine (*Daily Telegraph*, 27/7/88: 10; interview with Keers, 1989). More importantly, the research suggested that

cautious conservative professionals, including lawyers, accountants and estate agents, were very unsympathetic to the idea of
a men's fashion magazine per se. The more contemporary professional men – architects, designers and advertising agency
executives – on the other hand, found the idea no problem at all
(*Campaign*, 1/4/88: 19).

Advertising demand, as Quinn's comments earlier hinted at, was also
significant in setting some parameters for the magazine. *GQ* in fact
tailored itself quite precisely to the sort of advertising it courted
(fashion and luxury brands like Tuscany, BMW, Champion, Rolex
and Porsche) (*Campaign*, 7/7/89: 27). Deliberately – in the words of
Quinn – leaving the "trendy young Londoner to Logan", *GQ* pitched
itself at rising "success driven men" (*Campaign*, 13/5/88: 33) Drawing on figures from the boom in High Street spending and, more
importantly, the sales of premier suits (like Armani, Hugo Boss and
YSL), *GQ* was positioned to become "the essential reading for a particular kind of man – a lifestyle manual for the professional who has
achieved success with style" (*Daily Telegraph*, 27/7/88: 10). Nigel
Lawson's tax cutting budget of 1988 also provided *GQ* with a further
point of identification for its putative reader: "Our readers will be
forty per centers aged between 25–45", purred Mark Connolly, *GQ*
assistant fashion editor (*The Observer*, 30/10/88: 15).

The response to *GQ* from advertising media buyers was generally
to greet the magazine enthusiastically. As *Campaign* put it, here
at last was someone from the publishing establishment who had
understood the new importance of style. Anxieties did surface however. Jonathon Durden, of the advertising agency WCRS Mathews
Marcantio, in a comment that took to task not only *GQ*, but also
*Arena, The Face* and their advocates in advertising, suggested

> The so-called style magazines appeal only to certain types of
> men. *GQ* is a specialist interest. Its a lovely market but its just
> not important yet. As yet the whole thing is still embryonic
> (*Campaign*, 7/7/89: 27).

Burden's comments went right to the heart of the whole debate on
the "general interest men's magazine" between 1983 and 1989. His
comments underscored the clear fractures of opinion within the trade
about general interest men's magazines. In raising the issue of the

small circulation figures achieved by *Arena* and *GQ*, in their elision of the difference between the magazines (*The Face, Arena* and *GQ*), and in their problematizing of the post-style definition of what a general interest magazine was, Burden's comments touched on some deep anxieties about male readerships and general interest magazines prevalent within consumer magazine publishing and advertising media buying; anxieties which persisted despite the formation of the sector by *Arena* in 1986 and its consolidation by *GQ* in 1988.

## Conclusion

What, then, can we draw out from this account of the advertising and publishing knowledges and practices that drove the formation of general interest men's magazines in the UK? What has my attention to the advertising/publishing nexus associated with the "style press" and men's magazines delivered? First, it is important to emphasize that the account I have put together reveals the extent of the interest from groups of media practitioners (within magazine publishing and advertising) in a new type of magazine for men in the period between 1983 and 1989. Secondly, the concern specifically to target men through new magazines was dependent, as we saw, on a sense amongst these practitioners of shifts in young men's "values and life-styles". This was largely drawn from evidence from consumer research, but also from assessments of developments within magazine culture itself. Thirdly, the concern to target men through new magazines was also dependent upon the production of new products and services by advertisers and the refocusing of the marketing of existing products in relation to the new male market. Fourthly, the identification and servicing of new male readerships was led by independent publishers. Thus, the development of a sector of UK general interest men's magazines was marked in its formation by the success of the "style press" and the publishing practices of the independent publishers, Wagadon. It was the style-based format that set the precepts for general interest men's magazines in their formation. Fifthly, the shifts within advertising media buying practice detailed in Part III were critical to the advertising arguments and practice that shaped the formation of the new sector and provided its economic underpinning.

Putting together an account of these advertising and publishing knowledges and practices also has other pay-offs. It sheds light, in particular, on the way a central institutional determinant of the magazines functioned; that is, the economic relations between advertisers and publishers. It is to repeat a well worn conceptualization to suggest that these economic relations regulated the production of the magazines. For publishers, securing and maintaining healthy levels of advertising revenue and achieving sufficiently large circulation figures formed the *sine qua non* of their operations as commercial enterprises. However, rather than take on trust the assumption from economic theory that these economic relations and their associated commercial imperatives constituted a primary level of determination on the production of the magazines, the account I have offered in this chapter prompts us to consider their operation in different terms. First, it points us to the key relationships that constituted these economic relations. From the account it is clear that we are talking about relations produced between some specific practitioners. Namely, those figures who loomed large in this chapter: advertising media buyers and magazine advertising managers. It was this key relationship that effectively constituted the economic relation between advertisers and publishers. Secondly, foregrounding these knowledges and practices revealed the way in which representations of the imagined target readerships were central to the operationalizing of these economic relations. In other words, it was through these shared representations of the consumer that the relationship between media buyers and advertising managers functioned. This suggests, then, that the economic relations between advertisers and publishers themselves had cultural conditions of existence; cultural conditions of existence made up of the way the market of consumers was represented through specific cultural practices. It is not to overplay the argument to suggest that this work of representation was as much a condition of existence of these economic relations as the exchange of money between advertising agencies and publishers.

## CHAPTER 10

# From "The world's best dressed magazine" to "The men's magazine with an IQ": magazine journalism and new male readerships

In the previous chapter, I offered an account of specific advertising and publishing knowledges and practices which intersected in the targeting of new male readers through the colour press between 1983 and 1989. What loomed large in this account was the sense that the advertising/publishing nexus was an important site for the public formulation and development of general interest men's magazines. As we saw, much of the debate animating the commercial relations between publishing and advertising practitioners was devoted to defining in concrete terms the mix of contents and style of journalism of general interest men's magazines. I suggested that the editorial mix and journalistic approach developed by the "style press" – and especially by *The Face* – was pivotal to this debate. The ability of *The Face* to attract young "opinion forming" men through an innovative style-based format meant that its format set some of the precepts for the contents and journalism of UK general interest men's magazine. What remained underdeveloped in this account, however, was a substantive sense of the contents and journalistic style of the three magazines. It is necessary to explore these more fully now. What was the distinctiveness, then, of the format and journalism of *The Face* and how precisely did it impact on the journalism of *Arena* and *GQ*? How did these magazines address their male readerships? What form of knowledge and visual pleasure did they offer? I want to begin answering these questions by turning to *The Face*.

## *The Face*: "The world's best dressed magazine"

> One thing about *The Face* from the very beginning was having
> the best. It was on paper when everything else was on newsprint.
> It had good colour standards, and all those things have improved
> over the eight years – from stitched to perfect-bound: from
> 100 pages to 132. It was saying: "Why should Vogue have a
> monopoly on the best paper?" (Nick Logan, *Media Week*, 22/7/
> 88: 29).

*The Face* was launched by Nick Logan and his company Wagadon on
1 May 1980, while (as I noted in Ch. 9) Logan was still in charge of
EMAP's teenage pop magazine *Smash Hits*. This launch date was
later memorialized by the magazine with typical *élan*. As its third
birthday editorial put it, this was the date "Historians will tell you,
the Dark Ages officially ended and the Age of Enlightenment began".
From its launch, as Nick Logan's comments above make clear, the
team producing *The Face* was committed to bringing the surface
qualities and "look" of the traditional upmarket glossies (like
*Vogue* or *Paris Match* and *Life*)[1] to the domain of youth publishing.
Launched as a music magazine – its first subtitle was "Rock's final
frontier" – *The Face* was conceived by Logan to stand out from the
newspaper-type magazines that dominated this sector. In addition to
emphasizing the design and the glossy "look" of the magazine, Logan
introduced from early on elements that extended the conventional
content and subject matter of the music press. Through the early to
mid 1980s, *The Face* addressed in an increasingly seamless way popular music and those elements that constituted the wider pop process:
the dress codes of pop consumers, together with the design of record
sleeves, glamour, the stars and pop video. This interest in the packaging and visual presentation of pop stemmed in part from the influence on the magazine of arguments associated with the promotion of
punk, "New Pop" and Two Tone. All these musical movements had
been marked by an explicit concern amongst their key players and
promoters to exert control over the packaging, design and marketing
of their products. Thus, in the case of Two Tone, Jerry Dammers had
placed great emphasis on wresting control from the record companies over the whole "look" of the way records and the bands were
packaged.[2]

The journalistic interest in these practices had a number of con-

146

sequences. First, it meant that figures traditionally marginal to pop journalism were drawn into the magazine as the subject of features. Designers were a significant inclusion in this sense, and they provided an important link between the magazine's guiding interest in popular music with the wider fields of the visual arts and media industries. In issue 19, for example, the work of the designer Barney Bubbles was the subject of a long feature. Centre-stage in the article was an exploration of Bubbles's work on album covers. The article, however, also ranged further to include a consideration of his work with the Conran Design Group and his furniture designs (*The Face*, November 1981: 32–5).

A consideration of design and, from that, a reflection on its place in the processes of marketing and promotion, had a second consequence for the journalism of *The Face*. It drew into the magazine the conceptual arguments that informed these processes. Most important in this respect were theories of art and commercial cultural production associated with these (often art school educated) practitioners. Situationism, theories of montage and appropriated critiques of mass culture were some of the theories that were alluded to or explicitly referenced.[3] This produced a distinctive amalgam of tones within features. Interviews with pop stars or media practitioners or reviews of pop videos were scattered with questions about the nature of pop stardom, and the subversive possibilities of pop or cinema or painting, together with a more familiar form of pop questioning which interrogated performers on what aftershave they were wearing, or what their idea of luxury was (*The Face*, November 1982, for example).

The interest shown by *The Face*'s journalists in the wider pop process produced a third important dimension to the magazine's journalism. The interest, specifically, in the dress codes and styles of both stars and pop consumers allowed the magazine to locate itself quite self-consciously within a subcultural history. Shaped in part by the influence of Dick Hebdige's book, *Subculture*, journalists writing for *The Face* put together accounts of defining stylistic moments – both for themselves and for the wider public they addressed.[4] Robert Elms's article on David Bowie, from issue 61, was a particularly developed example of this style of journalism.

Elms's article was based around an invocation of David Bowie's 1976 appearance on the American television show, *Soul train*. Bowie's appearance on the show followed the release of his album,

*Young Americans*, and the unveiling of his new "look". The songs on the album marked, for Elms, a break with the glam rock styles of Bowie's preceding albums, drawing instead on black American soul music. Bowie's "look", meanwhile, marked, for Elms, a new stylistic sophistication. This was signified most clearly by Bowie's haircut: a wedge cut ("heavy on top and falling over one eye, but karate chop short at the neck") dyed chestnut brown with bleached strands at the front. For Elms, this "look" and the appropriation by a white performer of the "stylised, fake and expensive" sound of black American soul (specifically, "Philly [Philadelphia] Soul") were the seminal elements of the impact of Bowie's performance on *Soul train*. As such, they formed part of Elms's reflection on the mid 1970s London soul scene; a scene in which – for the white boys especially – Bowie was a central figure.

What is significant in Elms's account was the way that it built into the magazine a memory of this subcultural moment. Elms's comments on the importance of Contempo Records were particularly evocative:

> The clientele had a look and a music all of their own . . . Somehow it all seemed to come from the States via special "in" place in central London. To paraphrase Colin McInnes they were "young England, half English". The other half was, well, young American (*The Face*, May 1985: 51).

Elms's article was entitled "All you have to do is win", and it celebrated the enterprising aspirations of the working-class boys of the soul scene. This was not accidental. A celebration of success was a further significant element of the magazine's journalism which partly flowed from its interest in the mechanics of the music industry, design and marketing. By 1985, in its fifth anniversary issue – and at the high point of the magazine's success – its editorial asserted that "Nothing succeeds like success. Its the credo of the decade." Success was defined through the example of selected figures. A 17-page feature set them out. They were – as the magazine put it – "the nascent style-shapers of the late-eighties . . . a new breed of serious achievers – from modelling to music to architecture" (ibid.: 28). The gallery of figures or "faces" included individuals like Neil Jordan, Miranda Richardson, Nigel Coates, Sean Penn and Nigel Finch.

I want to underline two things about this selection. First, it was strongly avant-garde in its orientation. In other words, the feature introduced individuals who were on the verge of more mainstream success. Secondly, the selection of "style shapers" testified to the coming into formation of a generation of artists, film-makers, actors, fashion designers, models, stylists, musicians and writers. The emergence of these individuals and the success of many of them well beyond the stage presented by *The Face*, was central to the influence of the specific late 1970s post-punk London culture which *The Face* both came out of and helped to organize into a distinctive "public".

The magazine's celebration of the success of these "new glitterati" took for granted the importance of entrepreneurialism: the ethos, that is, of going it alone, of vigour, boldness and the ability to take risks. However, the connotations of entrepreneurialism were accented in a distinctive way by the magazine. There was a sense that being enterprising for *The Face* connoted being either a freelance photographer or stylists or having a stall in Kensington Market, and allowed individuals to engage in activities that blurred the conventional distinctions between work and leisure. It offered, in other words, a different vision of work and a model of the good life that was set against the notions of incremental advancement rooted in the cultural languages of social democracy.

The magazine also, however, registered the risks of operating outside established job and career structures and the greater uncertainties experienced by all young people through the 1980s. Insecurity lay close to the surface. The government's Youth Training Scheme was as much a part of the world *The Face* addressed as "success culture". In the fifth anniversary editorial, from which I have already quoted, the invitation to "front" or "hype" your way out of "hard times" pointedly rested upon – as it put it – "a self-conviction that is the only faith left".

Charting the new successes of the decade within the cultural and media industries sat alongside a form of critical social commentary by a number of the young journalists associated with the magazine. Through the cryptic space of the "Disinformation" section of the magazine, Marek Kohn offered biting and witty observations on a broad range of contemporary events. Thus, from August 1986:

One area of the NHS overdue for deregulation is the scale of the fees charged for private operations. Some major operations can cost up to £2,500 more to perform than the maximum permissable charge. £2,500 is over four months salary for the average NHS nurse.

. . . If the chief constable of Hampshire could mistake an air rifle allegedly found in a Peace Convoy vehicle for a "high-velocity rifle", what would he make of the devices in his own training centre's firing range which are said to resemble rocket launchers?

. . . By the end of the year the Greyhound bus may be no more. Buy your ticket, pack an 8mm Handicam and pre-empt the *Arena* retrospective.

. . . Britain's top five supermarkets – Tesco, Sainsbury, Asda, the Co-op and Finefare – are all reducing stocks of South African produce. The Co-op is phasing out apartheid imports altogether, and individual Tesco stores are authorised to bow to local pressure, as in the St. Paul's district of Bristol. But Safeways, the International/Gateways chain, Scotland's John Low, Waitrose and Marks and Spencer are still backing Botha. Liberals will have to take a trip down market (*The Face*, August 1986: 98).

These critical commentaries ran with features on subject matter of an entirely different order. This produced some peculiar juxtapositions of material. Consider the following feature on Paris from July 1986 which was emblematic of the kinds of juxtapositions staged in the magazine as a whole. In the introduction we were invited to explore the prime movers of Paris life. These were represented in the following terms: "Who shapes Paris life? Eurostyle teens, post-marxist thinkers, starlets and street-gangs? All these. And the twenty four pictured over . . . " (*The Face*, July 1986: 56).

This combination of subject material (fashion, contemporary theory, street gangs), and the confident way the magazine moved across these elements, giving equal weight to each, was characteristic of the form of cultural knowledge *The Face* coded in this period. Dick Hebdige, in his influential reading of the magazine, dramatized well these innovative juxtapositions which *The Face* held together. He suggested: "anything imaginable can happen, anything at all. The permutations are unlimited: high/low/folk/popular culture; pop music/opera; street fashion/advertising/haute couture; journalism/ science fiction/critical theory; advertising/critical theory/haute couture . . . " (Hebdige 1988: 161).

From its commentaries on dress codes or style, to the way it reviewed galleries, clubs, bars, films, books, drinks and so on, *The Face* brought to bear an aesthetizising gaze on its subject matter. This produced a number of effects. The first was that the magazine's journalism drew more strongly than it would have liked to acknowledge on the genre of the consumer guide or directory. The apparently perverse juxtapositions of material that is sanctioned ultimately rested on their shared stylishness or aesthetic value. As the earlier quote on Paris suggested, "post-marxist thinkers" could be brought within the same frame as "starlets" because they were each "chic". Both represented the allure of Parisian life. A place where, as one of the shapers of Paris life put in the feature, "culture is so beautifully done" (*The Face*, July 1986: 56).

This mode of commentary, however, was rooted in distinctive criteria of judgment. Part of this stemmed from an attention to detail, to the line and form of objects – in a word, to specific design characteristics – which were key to the selection and review of the consumer objects the magazine commented on. This applied equally to a range of objects, whether they were furniture, a Sony Walkman, club interiors, or clothing. A preference for minimalism in design loomed large in this selection process. Paul Rambali's 1985 feature entitled "Towards the matt black dream home" was pivotal in this respect. The story was built around a double page spread featuring a range of matt black objects. The objects were placed against a flat white background, individually lit, and photographed in ways that confounded their true relative sizes. The spread represented these objects as beautiful, precious objects; qualities guaranteed by their (minimalist) design content. The valorizing of these objects was underlined by their unexceptional nature: a toothbrush, scissors, a calculator, nutcrackers, a goblet.

The large amounts of space devoted in *The Face* to photographs and the overall design of the magazine meant that many of its juxtapositions of material were rendered in very visual terms. Neville Brody's design – especially his use of typeface, his disruption of the conventions of page layout (including the use of large amounts of white space), and the way he cropped photographs – was central in this respect and highlighted the surface qualities of the magazine.

151

The visual organization of the magazine's "Intro" section (where reviews, information and new products were piled together) for example, mixed different sizes and types of typeface, small tightly cropped photographs and objects simply presented against the white page background. The effect was to disrupt conventions of layout and the established practices of consumer magazine art directors. The layout was at once economical, disciplined and jarring.

The look of the magazine – particularly the references to modernist design in Brody's typeface – together with its editorial focus, were defiantly metropolitan. A version of metropolitanism, in fact, was key to the repertoire of knowledge and taste the magazine coded. In other words, the magazine established a specific set of ways of experiencing the city – be that London, Paris, New York or Berlin. The city was mapped through urban dress codes, certain galleries, bars and clubs, and through the movements of music, styles and people between these cities. Club culture was an important underlying element of this mapping of the city. The regular dancefloor columns and features on nightlife not only contributed to a mythologizising of clubs and their minor glitterati, but were also one point of entry for urban black culture – especially music and style – into the magazine. House and hip-hop – from the Bronx to Brixton – in particular, were a further part of *The Face*'s version of metropolitanism.

The style of journalism put together by *The Face* and its editorial format represented, as I have suggested a number of times, a new type of general magazine for young male readers. There are a number of directions in which it would be possible to track the influence of *The Face*.[5] What concerns me here, however, is the way the type of journalism developed by *The Face* was influential on the formats of men's general interest magazines. This influence is strongest on the magazine that opened up this market in 1986: *Arena*.

## *Arena*: "A new magazine for men"

> Since the 1960s men have been interested in fashion and style. You can see that in everything from rockers to the New Romantics. When they reach 25 and perhaps get married, they don't suddenly stop buying clothes and music (Nick Logan, *The Times*, 6/9/89: 15).

*Arena* was implicated in a special way in the type of style-based journalism initiated by *The Face*. Produced by more or less the same group of staff at the independent publishers, Wagadon, *Arena* developed in a very immediate sense upon the journalistic traditions of *The Face*.

Nick Logan, the publisher and founding editor of both magazines, had been considering producing another magazine for some time and had originally planned to produce a sports magazine. This decision had been motivated in part by the desire to keep hold of certain key individuals – Neville Brody and Ray Petri in particular – who had been important to the success of *The Face*. Logan felt they were becoming restless. His strategy to retain their services was to invite their co-operation in this new project.

*Arena* was lauched as a quarterly magazine and arranged around a distinctive mix of editorial, with a strong focus on men's fashion. Four regular sections formed the basic format of the magazine: "Spectator", "Vanity", "People" and "Avanti".

The "Spectator" section, which came towards the front of the magazine, carried critical reviews of forthcoming events: the new show at Saatchi's Boundary Road Gallery; a review of Greil Marcus's edited collection of Lester Bang's writings; a review of a Picasso show and a recommendation to go and see Wim Wender's "Wings of Desire", for example (*Arena*, Summer 1988).

"Avanti" was a series of directory-style spreads and featured various commodities laid out in impeccable style across a double page, in a format that Brody had first deployed for the "Matt black dream home" piece for *The Face*. Furniture, "postmodern picnic sets", and witty accessories were set alongside each other in the "Avanti" pages. Amongst the products selected was the work of up and coming designers along with the repeated appearance of "label names" – Mont Blanc, Chevignon, Issy Miyake, Ted Baker, Chipie, Ray Ban and Timberland. This coded, in similar terms to *The Face*, a distinctive repertoire of taste in which minimalism in design loomed large. A preference for certain materials was important in this regime of taste. Notably, aluminium, chrome and matt black finishes. Also strongly present were products, objects and materials from Italy, France and Japan – key cultural reference points for *Arena*.

The "Avanti" spreads also displayed the latest extraordinary innovations in products and accessories. Miniature black plastic razors from Japan, coffee in an aerosol can, designer cloth band-aids, or a

153

metal accessory in the shape of Rodin's sculpture of "The Thinker, were some of the objects selected for ironic enjoyment as outrageous trifles.

*Arena* also evoked the notion of classic design in aligning the commodities it selected. What loomed large, then, were objects like a "Le Courbusier" chair, or – when it came to clothes – American Oxford cloth button-down shirts, wing-tipped brogues, Bass-Wegan loafers or Willis and Geiger US Army Air Corps A2 leather flying jackets (*Arena*, Autumn 1987). This ascription of the term "classic" to clothing was particularly important. It shaped a way of talking about menswear in the magazine which was characterized by a reverence for good quality materials, attention to the details of the way the garment was finished (such as linings), and a scrutinizing attention to the cut of trousers or the yoking on shirts. In one sense this language drew on conservative – and highly gendered – notions of menswear; notions of menswear in which its timeless characteristics set it apart from the trivial excess of change, colour and disposability of women's clothing and fashion. *Arena*'s deployment of the term, however, did not straightforwardly reproduce these conservative connotations. The emphasis on "style" in *Arena*'s ascription of the term shifted the meaning of "classics". Thus, Dylan Jones, in a brief feature celebrating "Katherine Hamnett pegs", defined their "classic" status through a highly contemporary sense of style:

> Baggy at the waist, tapered at the ankles, with four front pleats, turn-ups, deep-side pockets, brace-buttons, button-fly and with a deep crotch, these creaseless pants are the perfect counterpart to everything from a Paul Smith polo top to a Botany wool turtleneck. Whether underneath a double-barrelled suit or a leather MA–1, Katherine Hamnett's Classic Brace Pants are the consummate match . . . and fashion hyperbole notwithstanding, they are, it has to be said, probably the best pair of trousers in the world (*Arena*, Spring/Summer: 146).[6]

"Vanity", the third regular section of the magazine, consisted of short written commentaries on various aspects of everyday life. These were usually consumption orientated. Each commentary was no more than a column and a half long and was replete with what Brody called "antiquated" illustrations. "Vanity" cast its net quite widely, drawing in features on skin care, shopping for clothes, whisky, shaving and even tackling pieces on circumcision ("First cut"), masturbation ("One from the wrist"), the male figure ("True gut"), and masculine rituals ("Stag club"). What emerged in these pieces were witty, often ironic, commentaries which also brought together a certain critical mass of information on the subject being discussed. "Vanity" also extended the directory-style journalism of the "Avanti" sections of *Arena*. A guide to selected retail outlets – usually menswear shops – figured prominently in this. The shops selected were invariably independent outlets where much sought after label names could be bought or where imported shoes or jackets were available. The reviews of shops also made much of the "look" of the shop interiors. Thus, in his review of the Quincy menswear store in Floral Street, Covent Garden, London, Dylan Jones not only expounded on the range of menswear stocked in the store, but detailed its retail design: "With its acres of Lake District slate, moulded wood, hospital walls and geometric shelving . . . this third Quincy shop is really the epitome of the shop as sculpture" (*Arena*, Winter 1988–9: 82).

Other consumer services were also detailed in the "Vanity" section. Cafés and restaurants where the "best bagel or biryani" could be bought were listed, while clubs and cinemas were also critically reviewed and recommended. These consumer reviews not only provided a service to readers, in addition they mapped London (and it was almost always London) in distinctive ways. Like *The Face*, *Arena* constructed for its readers through these features a particular way of experiencing the city which was built around the familiarity with certain shops, bars, clubs, sought-after menswear outlets and significant street names. This represented – as with *The Face* – an "avant-garde metropolitanism".

"Vanity" also circumspectly explored specifically masculine anxieties and reflected on the shared experience of maleness amongst its particular readership. One dimension to these commentaries was the question of men's relationships with women. In line with the tone of this section, these commentaries were often marked by considerable irony. Nonetheless, there was a recognition by the male journalists writing on these subjects of the limits set by feminist injunctions to men. The felt sense of this was often registered in the pieces through the invocation of female friends and partners. The following example conveys the tone through which some real tensions were played out:

> The stag night presents a perplexing dilemma for the modern man. Whilst male friends expect him to attend and indulge heartily in the phallic frivolity, female friends regard his presence at this macho ritual as a severe contravention of feminist etiquette.

It continued, concluding:

> The rite as it is stands as an anachronism in this age of male (and female) liberation, but as one "new man" said to me recently, "We must preserve the stag – after all, opportunities to get your chopper out are getting rare these days" (*Arena*, Summer/Autumn 1988: 162–3).

The piece is pulled in different directions by the disjunctures between the competing masculine scripts it signals. It draws on the "cred" of the pro-feminist man (conceived very narrowly in the piece as following what is disparagingly called "feminist etiquette"), while at the same time taking pleasure in a more traditional masculinity. The humour of the denouement, however, certainly invites the reader to identify with the fantasy of "lower body" exhibition ("getting your chopper out") in favour of a cerebral politeness (sticking to "feminist etiquette").

Similar disjunctures between competing masculine scripts were even more self-consciously played out in another site in the magazine where women were the exclusive focus of attention. This was the occasional feature, "Distinguishing features". "Distinguishing features" focused upon one "distinguishing" physical feature of a woman celebrity from television, music or cinema. Consisting of a short column of text and a photograph, the feature indulged in a celebration of her "looks". Thus, actress Brigitte Fonda's chin was the subject of one "Distinguishing features", while in issue 18 actress Melanie Myron's eyes were selected as objects of desire:

> Her eyes, those large, drowsy pools of forgiveness, eyes older than her face. Though her luxurious mouth (with its lop sided smile) is hard to miss – as is her hair, her voice and almost everything else – it's her eyes which send out the signals . . . bright, forgiving, rueful eyes with weary lids and expectant pupils. She is thirtysomething's sleepy-eyed Princess (*Arena*, Autumn/Winter 1989: 100).

These features were, on the one hand, committed to a problematic form of visual scrutiny of women, while on the other hand there was a recognition – registered through the irony of the written text (the excess of celebration) and the title of the feature ("Distinguishing features", the descriptive supplement of passport photographs) – of the shortcomings of judging women solely in terms of their physical appearance.

"People", the fourth of the regular sections within *Arena*, was a more straightforward section. Four or five individuals – from actors, through television producers, bespoke tailors and footballers to politicians – were profiled in an interview-based format. The individuals selected corresponded to the range of individuals who appeared in *Arena*'s longer feature articles. In these articles, extended interviews with film and (established) pop stars, architects, designers, fashion designers and media folk, sat alongside a form of cultural journalism on subjects like art sponsorship or the changing nature of the movie hero in the western. This form of cultural journalism also informed the travel features that appeared in the magazine. These features were shaped by a mediated sense of the places they detailed. In other words, they drew into the commentaries those media representations and public fantasies that impacted upon the allure – and certainly the meaning – of the places being detailed. These travel features, then, more often than not, included old photographs of the places featured in the articles. The rationale behind the selection of these images was important. These images represented the historical moment or period with which the place was most closely associated in the popular imagination. Thus, for example, an article on Coney Island from issue 13, "Coney Island days", was based around a contemporary drive around the resort. The ghosts of the island's "glory days" were both summoned in the written text of the article and literally represented in the photograph that accompanied the story. The photograph chosen was a 1940s shot of the resort at its peak in the era of mass working-class leisure. The photograph did not simply inform readers of the resort's more prosperous days. It implied that the contemporary appeal of Coney Island for *Arena* readers was framed through a fascination with the "look" of the earlier historical moment of 1940s America.

A similar style of journalism was often employed in *Arena*'s coverage of sport. In issue 18, Neil Lyndon reflected on the 1960 European Cup Final. The article was dominated by sepia-toned photographs of the football match and it celebrated the cultural significance of the game; in particular, its place within a specific generational experience. As Lyndon put it,

> Nothing in a post-war childhood in England had prepared us for an apparition of such other-worldy grace and ferocity . . . The 1960 European Cup Final held in Glasgow introduced Britain to a new era of skill, grace and glamour. Real Madrid's 7–3 rout of Eintracht was not only the greatest display ever seen by a club team, but a proclamation of a new age, the sixties (*Arena*, Autumn/Winter 1989: 181).

The identification in Lyndon's article with Spanish football was an identification with a different version of masculinity, one separate from – as Lyndon put it – the "stifling disciplines" of the class codes of English masculinities. Central to this identification with the Spanish version of masculinity represented by Real Madrid, however, was the "look" of the team ("the Angels in white"). In this sense, Lyndon's article registered a second element of *Arena*'s coverage of sport. Namely, sport was read in terms of style and fashion. There was a reverence in this attention to label names and the stylish qualities of sportswear. In addition, the sportsmen the magazine featured were both heavily styled in the photographs accompanying the written commentaries and an interrogation or interest in their "look" was invariably present in the article.[7]

The design and art direction of *Arena* was important in adding a further set of meanings to the editorial and features of the magazine. In similar terms to his design for *The Face*, Brody's page layouts (especially his use of two columns of type and lots of white space), his selection and cropping of photographs and his choice of typeface, emphasized the surface qualities of the magazine by making type and various invented typographical signs, for example, themselves an object of visual attention. He also signified through these typographical elements a reference to modernist experimentations with typeface and design and a strongly urban modernity.[8] The "look" of the magazine underlined its "avant-garde" self-positioning.

## GQ: "The men's magazine with an IQ"

The "new man" is just as keen as the so-called Cosmo girl on learning how to "make it" and how to dress for success (Condé Nast Media Information, June 1989).

I'm really quite in love with Britain in a way. My present heroes are David Owen and Michael Heseltine. Both believe passionately in the market economy as well as a just and egalitarian society (Stephen Quinn, *Media Week*, 4/11/88: 47).

Launched by Condé Nast two years after *Arena*, GQ reproduced many of the editorial elements present within *Arena* – most notably, the organizing of the magazine around menswear and style. Specific correspondences also occurred in a number of sections. For example, GQ had four regular sections dealing with grooming, information and product displays ("Body and soul", "Objects of desire", "Material world" and "Backstab") which corresponded to *Arena*'s "Vanity", "Avanti" and "Last detail" sections. In addition, between 1986 and 1989, a number of stories occurred in both magazines: The French Foreign Legion; Kenneth Branagh; "Life without women"; Motorbikes; The Polo Shirt; and Jonathon Ross.

GQ, however, was a very different kind of magazine to *Arena*. Its mode of attention on subjects amounted to a very different coding of cultural knowledge. GQ pitched itself at a more serious minded, conservative older reader than *Arena*. Coverage of popular music was absent and the kind of figures interviewed or profiled in GQ tended to be traditional professionals rather than the media–fashion–art based individuals *Arena* was interested in. GQ signalled this distinction very clearly with its first cover star: Michael Heseltine. Heseltine represented for GQ both a conservative version of "style" and – importantly – the centrality of success and the making of money. The editorial prefacing the extended feature on Heseltine underlined this combination. It stated,

> Success with style – that's the ethos around which GQ has been created for British men . . . GQ will be featuring men such as Michael Heseltine and Terence Stamp who embody both taste and achievement; running features by the very best

159

contemporary writers and journalists, which combine the intelli-
gent with the irreverent . . . and covering menswear, from the
influence of top designers, to suits and accessories appropriate
for the modern professional. From aspirations to relaxations,
from work to weekends, *GQ* is a manual for those who want to
enjoy success with style (*GQ*, December/January 1988–9:
120–21).

Looming large in this celebration of "success with style", was the
figure of the enterprising young executive. In a pivotal article from
issue 2, titled "Farewell to the company man", *GQ* compared the
attitudes of executives under 45 years old to those of an older generation. What emerged was a picture of clear differences of approach
between the two groups. Gone for the young executive were notions
of company loyalty (let alone public service) and steady advancement
through a company. In their place, was an emphasis on individual
success and a representation of themselves as enterprising men. "The
modern young executive", the article concluded, "is fleet of foot and
hard of heart. One has to conclude that the corporate man is a dying
breed" (*GQ*, February/March 1989: 154).

These were precisely the men targeted by *GQ*. In another feature,
it set out more clearly who these new "Hotshots" were. Tempering
the more aggressive entrepreneurial rhetoric expounded in "Farewell
to the company man", "Hotshots for the 1990s" brought together
ten men under 35 years old in order to define the nature of "success
and masculine achievement". The fields of work from which the men
were chosen was significant. Alongside a writer (Kazuo Ishiguro), a
record industry executive (Nick Gatfield) and an athlete (Steve
Backley), the men chosen were a mixture of professionals within
the high profile sectors of the late 1980s: advertising, retailing, the
City, insurance and computing. (*GQ*, December/January 1989–90:
123–30).

The modern executive or professional also figured prominently in
the magazine's "Style and substance" section. This was a feature
which detailed the "wardrobe" of a public figure, commenting on
favourite shoes, jackets and accessories as well as passing comment
on the individual's career and leisure interests. The men that *GQ*
chose for this section were not the "style leaders" that *Arena* centre-
staged in its section "Essential wardrobe". Rather, they were usually
more mainstream successful men. Thus, while *Arena* detailed the

"essential wardrobe" of figures like Don Letts, former pop video director and member of the group "Big Audio Dynamite", and Tony Wilson, television presenter and co-owner of Factory Records, "Style and substance" featured men like Robin Wight, advertising executive and former Conservative prospective parliamentary candidate, barrister John Hilton, and Vinda Saax, a period roof restorer.

GQ's leisure and news based features, while they often shared subjects in common with *Arena*, deployed a different style of journalism. For example, both magazines ran features on motorbikes. In *Arena*'s feature, "Transports of desire", bikes were located within the mediated forms of post-war popular culture. It painted a picture that thrilled in the iconographic aura of the "commodity" and its place within specific social relations (from Rockers to the 1980s reworking of 1950s imagery). As the introduction put it,

> Bike culture encompasses every male stereotype, be it bohemian rebel, his designer pastiche, or purveyors of a cartoon machismo – owners of Triumphs, Nortons or Harleys, sub-sonic chrome angels, transports of desire, this is the story of the strung-out Californian GI, the Hell's Angel, the British Rocker and their modern day counterparts, a story born to run and run . . . (*Arena*, Spring 1988: 76–89).

In the accompanying photograph, the bike was photographed in a highly aestheticized way. Credited to the fashion photographer Nick Knight, the Harley became a gleaming mass of chrome and muscular parts.

Meanwhile, in a piece called "Racing back", *GQ* interrogated the British built Norton motorbike. The piece was written and photographed in the style of the motoring trade press – with evenly lit photographs of the bikes shot in the forecourts of garages with the proud owners posed stiffly next to the machines. A central thrust of the piece was a concern with the technical qualities of the bikes and with the business strategy that the company's new owner was developing in order to turn around the company's fortunes.

Another story run by both magazines – this time on the French Foreign Legion – repeated these distinctions. In addressing this exclusively male domain, *Arena* again cast a captivated, style-preoccupied eye on the legion. Strikingly cropped photographs of boots and shaven heads were mixed with captioned photos. Thus: "Corporal de

161

Arofo wears a navy/wool cashmere 3/4 length reefer jacket, £1506",
or "Corporal Saint Remy wears sunglasses, £54 by Cutter and Gross,
and black cotton shirt" (*Arena*, Spring/Summer 1989: 45). *GQ*'s
piece, on the other hand, was built around a Legion desertion tale –
charting the brutality, hardness, deprivation, adventure and excite-
ments of the Legion in a form of exposé journalism.

This latter feature was representative of the way *GQ*'s journalistic
style drew much more strongly on the conventions of established
news journalism than did *Arena*'s journalism. Underlying this was a
deliberate concern to position the magazine somewhere between the
"style press" and magazines like *Newsweek* and *The Spectator*. Paul
Keers, the first editor of the UK *GQ*, emphasized this positioning
through the inclusion within the magazine of what he called heavy-
weight pieces. Thus, *GQ* ran feature articles, for example, on a death
row lawyer, divorced fathers, and dangerous dogs.

*GQ* also tackled the issue of men's relationships with women in its
feature articles. These articles were driven in large part by a sexualized scrutiny of women and a sense of the incommensurability of
the cultures of men and women. William Leith's profoundly paranoid invocation of heterosexual domestic relations in his article "Life
without women", brought together both of these concerns. The
article drew strongly on masculine codes of romance, in which pos-
sessing a woman was cast as the ultimate goal of men's lives. Thus he
suggested,

> Just take a look around you, at your options, your life choices. All
> routes lead back to women. Why work? For money and status, of
> course. Why do you want status? For the sake of women. The
> more status you have the better woman you get (*GQ*, February/
> March 1989: 110).

The imperatives of this romantic concern with women posed dangers
for men however, Leith claimed. They threatened masculine independence. He illustrated this by detailing the signs of dependency
that overtook men when they tried to "give up" women. The signifiers of dependency he chose were the reverse of the familiar signs
of the addict's dereliction. Thus, freedom from "the habit" was conceived of as a "phase of defiant self-neglect", only to be followed by
the inevitable falling back into old ways: "Four weeks later, he
remembers pulling out the bottom drawer of his bedroom chest and

finding a couple of pairs of knickers in there. Clean. Folded. He was back to square one" (ibid.: 111).

If finding oneself driven back into the routine of self-care in order to engage in (what Leith called) "pair bonding" wasn't bad enough, then worse could befall a man: he might reach the point of not wanting women. Focusing on two such individuals, Leith read the signs of pathology, "You never quite know what they're up to. What are they doing all the time that the rest of us are going out with our girlfriends? What do they do with all that extra money?" (ibid.: 113).[9]

GQ was on surer (and less hysterical) ground with its regular style sections. Rather than code what I've called an "avant-garde metropolitanism" in relation to The Face and Arena, what I want to call a "modern conservative metropolitanism" was strongly coded through these features in GQ. A central element of this version of metropolitanism was a play on the notion of the gentleman. For Keers, reclaiming the notion of the gentleman was a spin off from the centrality of success that the magazine promoted. He suggested that the image of the gentleman represented an image of "lifestyle success, an image of quality" (interview with Paul Keers, 1989). "Body and soul" and "Agenda" were central to the coding of these gentlemanly competencies. They framed the representation of commodities around a traditional notion of the "gentlemen's toilette" and refined, but unfussy consumption. The coding of the objects invited a leisurely, connoisseur's appreciation. An article on port, for example, made much of the drink in terms of financial investment. It suggested that "with Port rapidly becoming an investor's market, this is the ideal opportunity to buy in at your own level" (GQ, December/January 1989–90: 25). A short feature on wristwatches, "Time is money", emphasized the importance of investing in quality watches because "(although) luxury watches depreciate in value as soon as you walk out the shop, . . . fine craftmanship ensures they stay looking good" (ibid.: 116). GQ, in this sense, drew on older notions of de luxe consumption for men.

This conservative version of metropolitan consumption was underlined by the design and layouts of GQ. Compared to Brody's design for Arena, the use of familiar serif and sans-serif typefaces, together with conventional page layouts and photograph cropping, gave GQ a more sober feel.

## Conclusion

What conclusions can we draw from this consideration of the editorial mix and style of journalism of *The Face*, *Arena* and *GQ*? A central part of my argument has been to draw attention to the centrality of the vocabulary of "style" to all the magazines. The vocabulary functioned as an important element of continuity across the magazines and guided the way each of them framed and presented the objects of consumption and leisure around which they were focused. The vocabulary of style was clearest, of course, in the written commentaries on menswear and grooming. In relation to these objects, it shaped an emphasis on the selection and combination of garments and accessories in the construction of an overall "look" and put a premium on attention to detail within this process. Style, most importantly, signified across the magazines the expression of a distinct sense of masculine individuality through dress and appearance. Being stylish meant having the necessary knowledge to put together a "look" and to carry it off with enviable ease.

As a mode of attention and assessment applied to other objects, the style-based journalism developed in the magazines centre-staged the packaging and presentation of objects, the quality of their finishes, their line and form. It was the criteria of judgement built into this mode of attention, however, which – I suggested – differed across the magazines and which produced different masculinities in relation to the coding of cultural knowledge. While *The Face* and *Arena* coded an "avant-garde metropolitanism" based around the modernity of urban consumption, *GQ* represented a "modern conservative metropolitanism" which drew much more strongly on older notions of quality and luxury consumption. The individuals who populated the pages of the magazines underlined these different formations of taste, lifestyle and consumption. Whereas *The Face* and *Arena* selected individuals from the cultural and media industries associated with the new style of consumption, *GQ* identified itself with more conservative men associated with a subtly updated version of de luxe masculine consumption.

Differences of age and income played their part in reinforcing these distinctions across the magazines. Although, clearly, the forms of taste and individual consumption framed by the magazines were not reducible to age, there was a generational dimension which the magazines themselves signified within these distinctions. Stephen

Quinn's comment (which we encountered in the previous chapter) that *GQ* would leave the "trendy young Londoner" to Nick Logan was a case in point.

The representation of relationships with women was the significant joker in the pack for *Arena* and *GQ*. In both magazines sexualized visual representations of women were marginal (if not entirely absent), while, as we saw, clear tensions were played out within the written commentaries addressing relationships with women. Both magazines' self-conscious sense of addressing an exclusively masculine public prompted a heavy-handed reflection on the shared norms of maleness. Regarding relationships with women, this meant that a well established post-permissive sexual script loomed large, with women functioning as objects of sexual scrutiny and as absolutely different from men. *Arena*'s deployment of irony in such matters did, certainly, open up a space of critical distance within these sexual scripts although it never managed to move beyond their terms. The possibility of friendships with women, for example, were entirely absent from the discussions of relationships with women.

The alignment in the magazines of representations of highly elaborated masculine competences in relation to style, grooming and individual consumption and the masculine scripts associated with relationships with women were themselves accented by another set of representations within the magazine that has been missing from my account so far. These were the visual representations of masculinity within the magazines fashion pages. It is to a consideration of these forms of representation that Chapter 11 is devoted.

## CHAPTER 11

# Distinguishing looks: magazine fashion photography and the "new man"

A striking feature of *Arena* between 1986 and 1989 and *GQ* between 1988 and 1989 was the sheer volume of visual representations of men. From adverts for clothing and toiletries to celebrity portraits, the magazines were a bulging visual parade of masculinities. What figured most prominently in this visual parade, however, were pages devoted to fashion coverage. With a third of the editorial space of both magazines given over to fashion spreads (and with *Arena* regularly having 40 pages of fashion in an issue), the dominant visual representation of masculinities in the magazines was produced in relation to the editorial display of menswear. This emphasis on extended fashion coverage in the form of photographed fashion spreads was a central part of the format of general interest men's magazines. In itself, this coverage massively extended the volume of photography-based coverage of menswear available in the UK. For style-conscious men prior to the launch of *Arena* and *GQ*, access to such imagery was largely limited to imported men's magazines or to the rather dull coverage offered in the menswear trade press (magazines like *Menswear*). The only other significant source of such visual imagery came from the "style press". *The Face* was a particularly key publication in this respect in the early to mid 1980s. Through its regular "Style" features or through its "Fashion expo" pages, it offered young men innovative stylings of menswear in a glossy magazine format. This coverage, as I noted earlier in Chapter 9, was a key element in the magazine's relationship to new male readerships and in turn guaranteed the strong fashion element in the post-style format of general interest men's magazines in the UK.

In this chapter I want to consider the fashion images produced in *The Face*, *Arena* and *GQ*. The account I put together centre-stages three recurrent "looks" which were coded within this fashion coverage. These were the stylings of menswear as "street style" associated with Ray Petri's "Buffalo" look for *The Face* and the plays on what I call "Italianicity" and "Edwardian Englishness" in the styling of menswear. These latter "looks" were a strong feature of the fashion imagery in *Arena* and *GQ*. In delimiting these three "looks", what I have to say is guided by a concern to unpack the visual languages of masculinity produced within this imagery and to put together an account of the forms of spectatorship associated with these representations. These concerns go right to the heart of the account I advance of the "new man" imagery in the book. Let me be clear, then, about what is at stake in this reading.

I suggested in the Introduction to the book and have reiterated on several occasions since, that the new magazine culture associated with the "style press" and men's general interest magazines represented a privileged site in the regime of "new man" imagery. This rested upon two principal factors. First, these magazines were the site where the most significant developments in the consumer institutions underpinning the formation of the "new man" imagery intersected. Thus, the developments in menswear design and in the knowledges and practices of marketing and selling associated with these markets (consumer research, media buying practice, publishing knowledge and so on) interlocked in the fabric of the magazines. Secondly, and more importantly, the magazines' fashion pages were the site where the new visual languages of masculinity associated with the "new man" first emerged and where they were consolidated and elaborated. The magazines' fashion spreads, then, offer us a privileged way into the formation and development of the "new man" imagery and its associated forms of spectatorship. In this sense, they allow us to develop a proper response to the question I posed in the Introduction. Namely, what was the distinctiveness of the "new man" imagery?

In putting together an account of the distinctiveness of the visual codings of masculinity produced in the fashion pages of *The Face*, *Arena* and *GQ*, I want to consider this imagery in relation to an earlier moment of representation; specifically, in relation to the fashion images produced in *Town* magazine between 1962 and 1968. The reason for making this comparison is straightforward. The imagery from *Town* allows me to establish a norm against which I chart the new representational elements that characterized the "new man" imagery. The pay-off from making this comparison is double-edged, however. While it allows me to narrate a clear set of distinctions, it also produces a less ambitious picture of the "new man" imagery in relation to wider fields of masculine representation.

The imagery from *Town* which I consider, however, is far from an arbitrary norm. The magazine began life in 1953 as a "gentleman's tailoring magazine", *Man About Town*. In 1960 it was bought by Michael Heseltine and Clive Labovitch and extensively redesigned to become – as the *Press and Media Directory* (1968: 62) put it – a magazine of "social comment and features on events in Britain and the world in general". In a highly visual format which owed much to the photojournalism developed in magazines like *Picture Post* and *Life, Town* devoted itself to "politics, fashions, theatre, films, opera, ballet, music, jazz, books, and profiles on interesting people" (ibid.). It was, in its own terms, the general interest men's magazine of its day. The space the magazine gave to photographed fashion coverage, though minimal compared to *Arena* and *GQ*, was significant. The magazine used its fashion pages to report on the developments in menswear which grew apace through the 1960s. Three elements were pivotal to these shifts in menswear. First, a whole range of new designs in menswear was produced – from skin-tight pants to brightly coloured suits. Hepworth's decision to hire Hardy Amies as a design consultant in 1961 – at the time the best-known women's couturier in England – was emblematic of this new dynamism in menswear design, and the changing parameters of menswear even in the world of ready-to-wear men's tailoring. As Nik Cohn noted, not only did Hepworth's decision bring the vocabulary of design to menswear for the first time, it also was part of a process whereby the sense of fashion as an exclusively feminine domain was broken down (Cohn 1971: 72). Secondly, the availability of new synthetic and lightweight materials impacted on the design of menswear, laying the basis for the use of new colours and cuts. Thirdly, menswear retailing was transformed by the emergence of new techniques of selling. These were most clearly articulated – as noted in Part II – in the development of boutique-style retailing in menswear shops like John Stephen's "His Clothes" in Carnaby Street, London.

*Town*'s coverage of menswear was interlinked with this expansive and transformative period for menswear through the 1960s. In displaying the new menswear, *Town* deployed a set of visual conventions within its fashion photography which formed part of an established set of norms for the coding of masculinity in relation to menswear. It is these codings that are important for my argument in this chapter. It is precisely against these conventions of fashion photography that the "new man" imagery can be most usefully charted.

## *Town*, menswear and fashion photography

I want to consider four fashion spreads from *Town*, together with an advert featured in the magazine which drew on the format of the fashion spread. These are "High fahrenheit fashion and fun" (July 1967); "What about the people in the middle?" (September 1967); "Dress rehearsal for the seventies" (August 1964); "You need not be a father-figure to wear this autumn's shirts" (September 1964); and "Jantzen breeds a new kind of man" (November 1966). The use of locations and props together with the forms of *mise en page* deployed in these spreads give an indication of the range of fashion coverage produced in *Town* between 1962 and 1968.

I want to begin by considering the choice of models used in these spreads. The choice of models – in terms of their physical "look" – alerts us to an important visual code in fashion photography: namely, the code of casting. The first point to make regarding this code is that the models used in *Town* were exclusively white, with clean-cut, thin-lipped features. There was little fleshiness or sensuality in their features. The "look" was also predominantly mature. In other words, young or boyish looking men were marginal to these spreads. This casting was particularly clear in "Dress rehearsal for the seventies" and "High fahrenheit fashion and fun".

The codes associated with dress and grooming formed a second key element in the signification of masculinity in *Town*'s fashion images. The range of menswear presented in these spreads produced some distinctive masculine profiles. The design and cut of the clothes worked to produce an assertively narrow and straight-lined body shape. We can see this in the formal lines of the suits and in the casual and leisure wear displayed in the spreads. From single-breasted suits with sloping shoulders and a waisted cut, through narrow hipsters and polo shirts, to roll-neck jumpers and V-neck sweaters, the masculine body was signified within a long, lean silhouette. In "Dress rehearsal for the seventies", it is the smooth lines of the lightweight suit and the tight cut of the Reefer jacket that stand out. As one picture in this spread also makes clear, this was a silhouette in which the sharp cuts and the hyper-neatness of the subcultural "look" developed by mods were a strong point of reference.

The importance of casualwear and of less formal cuts in jackets was also a significant feature of the fashion coverage in *Town*. The advert for Jantzen made much of the importance of a smart casual wardrobe through its figure of the "four sweater man". Apart from the chunky-knit "morning sweater", the coding of the body in these images was again narrow and straight-lined.

In addition to the cut and finishing of menswear, a sense of extravagance and modernity was often displayed in the choice of colours and fabrics used. A clinically cut, high-collared space suit and a Jacobean print jacket in purple and red on black from the spread "What about the people in the middle?" represented different versions of this. The selection of new colours loomed large in the suits. Although – as in all the *Town* fashion pages – this colour was not signified through the choice of film stock in the image, an accompanying written text revealed a chromatic exuberance: white jackets, mulberry pink suits (also available in faded pink and grey-blue, we are told), with neon-coloured wide silk ties. The use of these colours for the garments marked a clear break with established notions of sobriety in the selection of menswear colour schemes. It signified menswear, importantly, as fun, fashion and leisure. These selections of colour underlined the newness and – importantly – the youthfulness signified by the slim-lined profile of the masculine body through the clothes.

A third set of codes that were important in the signification of masculinity in the spreads concerned expression. I want to consider these together with a fourth set of codes, those of posture. "High fahrenheit fashion and fun" begins with a close-up of the model's head and shoulders (Fig. 11.1). His facial expression and the angle of his head in this image are reminiscent of the modern day gangsters of Godard's and Truffaut's early films. Specifically, the expression and pose – with a fat cigarette held at an arrogant angle in the mouth – are Belmondoesque! More significantly in other pages of the same spread, the model's posture is stiff and angular, while his gaze is assertively directed at the viewer. The coding of posture and expression are rather different in "Dress rehearsal for the seventies". Here the models are more formally posed, standing upright and square on

**Figure 11.1** High fahrenheit fashion and fun, *Town*, July 1967. Courtesy of Haymarket Publishing Services Limited and by permission of the British Library PP5242bbc.

in three-quarter length shots in ways which draw on the conventions of portraiture. In the case of Figure 11.2, the pose – with one hand in his trouser pocket and the other supporting himself – is confidently manly. The expressions of the models in both these images are significant. Both look away and out of the frame, as if contemplating an imagined distant horizon. A further version of this form of expression was coded in the spread – "What about the people in the middle?" Here, amidst the subterranean shadows and seediness of the boutique, the model looks upwards – in a look and pose accentuated by the camera angle. The look of the model in the Jantzen adverts is also turned away from engaging directly with the viewer (Fig. 11.3). However, rather than looking up and out of frame, he looks down, narcissistically self-contained. The expression and posture coded in this image represent a departure from the dominant forms of posture and expression more usually found in *Town*; postures and expressions which connoted an assertive masculine independence.[1] Here the passivity of the model's pose and his melancholic expression connote a different version of masculinity. I shall return to the significance of this image later in the chapter.

The lighting of these fashion shots and the settings used represent two further important codes at work in these images that require attention. Most of the spreads deployed lighting in order to construct a uniformly lit image. Thus, what was generally signified was the transparency of the image. In "Dress rehearsal for the seventies", however, the decision to deploy an almost chiaroscuro form of lighting marked out this spread from the others. The effect of the form of lighting chosen was to dramatize the images, in particular reconnoting the codes of posture. In Figure 11.4, the model's masculinity is strongly signified through his sophisticated, slightly dangerous ("cool") pose and expression; a form of posture and expression which the codes of lighting (suggesting danger and enigma) work to underline.

The settings used across the spreads in *Town* were varied. They ranged from the minimally coded studio of "Dress rehearsal for the seventies" to the foreign location setting for "High Fahrenheit fashion and fun". In the latter spread the "sunshine trip" to Torremolinos was important in situating the menswear worn by the model in relation to forms of consumption: in this case, information about currency restrictions, places to visit and comments on the quality of local food together with an inventory-style listing of recommended basic grooming items. "What about the people in the middle?", on the other hand, invoked consumption in a different sense by placing the clothes in relation to the leading contemporary London boutiques. In the Jantzen advert elements of an exclusive and privileged consumption were signified by the inclusion of a private plane in one of the photographs. An important element in the selection of settings across the spreads in *Town*, then, was the signification of menswear in relation to the signs of individual consumption.

**Figure 11.2** Dress rehearsal for the seventies, *About Town*, August 1964.
Courtesy of Haymarket Publishing Services Limited and by permission of the
British Library PP5242bbc.

**Figure 11.3** Jantzen breeds a new kind of man, *Town*, November 1966. Courtesy of Haymarket Publishing Services Limited and by permission of the British Library PP5242bbc.

House of Swedish Fashion's gunmetal grey parka (above) in shower-proofed cotton gabardine. Press-stud fastened front also has a fully zipped flap inside. Fleece lining in the body and hood, quilted sleeves, belt detachable. Also in dark brown. About 16 gns at Lillywhites, Piccadilly. Protector of Austria's self-lined lightweight nylon anorak (above, right) with hidden hood, zipped pockets, knitted collar and cuffs, approximately 49/- available September at Simpson, Piccadilly. Melka's long-sleeved jersey shirt in cotton/wool mixture with concealed front placket; 59/6d from Sweden at Smart Weston, Coventry Street, W.I. Wide, blue canvas belt with heavy leather trims and brass buckle, by Canterbury of America, about 50/-. Alpaca and wool six-button cardigan (right) with buttoned side tabs and wide sleeves, by Catalina of California, about 9 gns. Sabre's zipper shirt in tridebal Bri-Nylon with button cuffs and cadet neckline, in red and black, 63/-. Bulova Accutron feeless watch with electronic movement, £55 at Garrard, Regent Street. Braemar's golden wheat-coloured cardigan (far right) with four buttons, in looped mohair; also in black, stone, blue, and green; 9 gns, available mid-September at Aquascutum. Arrow's University Club sports shirt with soft tip collar in blue and grey variated stripe drip-dry poplin, has breast pocket, single cuffs and tapered body, 42/-. Stroem's light brown and grey Donegal tweed trousers, with belt loops, plain fronts, side pockets, plain bottoms; available mid-September at Selfridges, 5 gns.

I have so far emphasized six visual codes in this reading of *Town*'s fashion photography: the codes of casting, dress, posture, expression, lighting and setting. Taken together these codes worked to produce a distinctive version of masculinity across the imagery. This was an exclusively white masculinity in which the attributes of an assertive independence and a youthful modernity figured prominently. Considered in another way, however, these codes also constructed a look for an imagined spectator in the organization of representational space. In other words, they organized a particular way of looking at the model in the image. How are we to conceptualize this spectatorial look? One way to proceed would be to turn to the account of looking developed within film theory. I suggested in Part I that this body of work (in particular that influenced by Laura Mulvey's account of cinema spectatorship) is good at centre-staging questions of gender and the organization of looking. It is not without its problems, however. Looming largest in this respect is the universal psychoanalytic account of subjectivity that underpins this work. As I argued in Part I, it has been impossible to square this account of subjectivity with the insistence on historical specificity derived from Foucault. However, rather than write off this psychoanalytically informed work on the look, I have appropriated elements of its conceptual vocabulary but now understood in more contingent, historical terms. Three concepts have been important in this respect. The attention to the gendering of the look and the distinction between distinct registers of the look: on the one hand identification and on the other a pleasure in looking at an external object or person. Let me be clear on how I am understanding these terms and what they deliver to my analysis of spectatorship in *Town*.

The gendering of the look is an important part of the analysis of spectatorship. It orientates the visual pleasures coded in the representation to wider formations of gender and, often, sexual identity. In other words, who looks at whom and in what way. However, whereas in the psychoanalytically informed work the gendered positions of looking are related to the ambiguous structuring of unconscious drives into active/masculine and passive/feminine and the fundamental positions of sexual difference, I want to insist that the way spectatorship is gendered is centrally an historical question. My argument in Chapter 5 concerning looking and shopping spectacle carries its full weight in this regard. Certain kinds of masculinity

appear to have been pivotal to the emergence of modern technologies of perception – notably through the figure of the expert and
the professional. It was men's dominance over these visual technologies that formed the dominant split in relations of looking
between the coding of femininity as visual spectacle and the positioning of masculinity as the bearer of the look that a range of writers
have identified across different visual media (Mulvey 1989, Coward
1984).[2] Attending to the historical formation of modes of spectatorship also reminds us that looking can be not only gendered but
marked in terms of (notably) class and "race" (Tagg 1988, Mort
1987).[3]

In relation to the representations from *Town*, the spectatorial look
was formally staged between the male readers addressed by *Town*
and the male models in the text. What was coded, then, was a
masculine–masculine look. The marking of this look was important.
It framed the way the visual pleasures coded in the fashion images
were organized. What figured prominently in this respect was the
organization of identification in the look. Or, to put it another way,
the narcissistic register of the look. It is clear that the images I
described from *Town* were constructed so that the male reader was
literally invited to buy into the "look" of the model; that is, to identify with his "look".

Identification with the "look" of the male model within the spectatorial look, however, was not the only register of the look coded in
the images. Visual pleasures associated with the display of the menswear were also in play in the representations. The cut of jackets, the
shine of shoes and the overall construction of "looks" invited pleasure in the images themselves – including the male models. These
visual pleasures, together with the coded elements of masculine passivity, were explicitly re-connoted as normatively heterosexual. The
Jantzen advert (Fig 11.3) offers a particularly good example of the
importance of this heterosexualization of masculine display. It is a
good example precisely because another sexualization of the display
is almost sanctioned. In the image, the model reclines on a rug, his
body relaxed, almost languid. More than that his expression establishes a sexual ambiguity. His gaze is narcissistically self-absorbed and
slightly melancholic. He is, in a certain sense, a "sad, young man". As
Richard Dyer has suggested, in the 1950s and 1960s, the figure of the
sad young man often worked to signify male homosexuality (Dyer
1993). The masculine–masculine look coded between the model and

the reader, then, is accented in ways which potentially register homo-sexuality. This sexuality, however, is disarticulated by the presence of the female model. Her positioning in the image is important. The male model has his arm protectively positioned around her. She leans into him. The positioning of their bodies in this relation-ship, then, connotes a normative heterosexuality and makes possible the displacement of homosexuality which might have been signified by the coding of passivity and connotations of a melancholic mas-culinity. The softness of his profile and the passivity of his pose are rather directed towards the women as sexual accoutrement.

There is a further point to make about conceptualizing spectator-ship emerging from *Town*'s representations. It concerns the bifur-cation between identification and the pleasure in looking at the image posited within the psychoanalytic conception of spectatorship. *Town*'s fashion representations walk a fine line between inciting identification on the part of the reader with the "look" displayed and the marking of visual pleasures around the model through which he himself potentially becomes the "object" of a desiring look. This interplay of both identification with and pleasure in the represen-tational other in the coding of spectatorship is a tension within all the images I consider in this chapter. It suggests a more mobile and ambivalent relationship between identification and pleasure in the image than the too rigid distinction advanced within film theory in particular.[4]

I cannot leave this discussion of spectatorship without underlining again the nature of my appropriation of the psychoanalytically informed work on the look. While I fly the flag of the concepts of identification, the pleasure in looking at an external other and the gendering of looking, they operate without their precise psycho-analytic connotations. This is critical in terms of how I understand the effects of these forms of spectatorship. As I argued in Part I, the coding of forms of looking involves processes of identification on the part of the spectator and more importantly the operationalizing of this look through techniques of looking and associated practices of the self. It is in this latter sense that the forms of spectatorship coded in the fashion imagery have to be located as part of a wider technol-ogy of looking. They cannot be read back to positions of looking structured by the primary structures of sexual difference and set by a universal oedipal order.

## From buffalo boys to Edwardian gents: fashion photography and the "new man"

The distinctiveness of the forms of spectatorship coded in representations of masculinity is a central element of my argument about the fashion imagery produced in the magazines for men in the 1980s. I want to begin putting together an account of these images by turning to the fashion stylings produced by Ray Petri for *The Face*. These images, as we will see, marked the biggest break from those produced in *Town*.

### Buffalo boys

Ray Petri is an important figure in my account. He was the most successful of a group of fashion stylists who rose to prominence with the success of the "style press" through the mid to late 1980s. At the root of Petri's impact – and the ascendency of stylists – was the greater emphasis that was placed in magazine's like *The Face* and *I-D* in the early to mid 1980s on a style-based approach to fashion. Style, in fact, was explicitly counterposed to fashion, and the role of the stylist was to produce an innovative "look" rather than to present a

Figure 11.5    Buffalo, *Arena*, 1987. Courtesy of Marc Lebon; styling Ray Petri.

designer's new range or the latest seasonal "looks". Petri was an accomplished stylist. In *The Face* between 1983 and 1987 he produced regular stylings under his trademark "Buffalo" label. These stylings were built around a close group of models and associates including the photographer Jamie Morgan and the models Zane and Nick and Barry Kamen. "Buffalo", in fact, was very much a "family affair" (as a headline to one of Petri's stylings once put it) characterized by the regular casting of "Buffalo's" familiar faces. This was no accident, as Petri identified casting as the essential element in defining the "Buffalo" look.

Away from the established catwalks, Petri's stylings drew on and helped shape a distinctive repertoire of urban style. Most famously his styling of the MA–1 flight jacket turned the item into an essential element in "tough", street style. Testifying to Petri's influence, *The Face*, in its review of 1989, suggested "Who could argue that the combination of MA–1 flight jacket, Levi's 501s and Dr. Martens is the urban uniform of the decade?" (*The Face*, October 1988: 50).

The fashion styled by Petri asserted a tough, muscular masculinity that drew tangentially on the representational genres of 1950s' bodybuilding and boxing portraiture. This was a significant break from the slim-profiled bodies through which masculinity was signified in *Town*. In line with the often ambiguous and ironic tone of *The Face*'s journalism, Petri's "Buffalo" look knowingly played on this "simpler" and fixed sense of masculinity. References to this prepermissive manliness were spliced with the contemporary paraphernalia of style to carve out a striking and distinctive repertoire of codings of masculinity.

In the image from the January 1985 issue of *The Face* (Fig 11.6), the model chosen is young and physically well built, with strong, hard features. Together these elements produce a mixture of boyish softness – connoted through the clear skin and re-connoted by the hat pushed back on the head – and an assertive maleness – connoted by his physical solidity. This combination of "boyishness" and the solid body form represent one of a number of contradictory elements of masculinity held together in this image, and was typical of the Buffalo stylings.

This ambivalence of "soft" and "hard" is reinforced by the casting of a light black model. This casting is important beyond its function as a signature element of "Buffalo" and the metropolitanism of *The Face*. In terms of the signification of masculinity, two connotative

**Figure 11.6** Portrait of a buffalo boy looking hard in the yard, *The Face*, January 1985. Courtesy of Marc Lebon; styling Ray Petri.

"moments" come into play: an equivalence of "light black" with sensuality; and of "black masculinity" with hyper-masculinity. The equivalence of "black masculinity" with a hyper-masculinity is easiest to read. As a popular representational regime it has a long history, shaped by a pathologizing of blackness and is the site of pronounced fantasies about black men's sexuality and physical prowess. These connotations of black masculinity operate as an important trace within the signification of the light black male; they impart the connotations of an assertive masculinity. However, "light black" has a partially separate set of connotations. The light black model makes possible the sanctioning of masculine sensuality. It does this through the indices of skin tone and features. The casting of the light black model makes possible the playing off of "soft" and "hard".

In the styling of the clothes in the Buffalo spreads a recurrent allusion is to workwear. In this example it is the labourer's hat, the rolled up sleeves, and the heavy-duty cotton top. There is also a clear reference to the "collage dressing" of punk style, in which various inappropriate objects and materials are assembled together; to wit, the safety pin worn as accessory in punk style. The effect in this image, as with punk styles, is to disrupt established ways of dressing and to present the body as a surface on which objects and images can be plastered and hung. This styling draws attention to the construction of a "look", to the process of "bricolage".[5] In another Buffalo plate ("Hard is the graft", *The Face*, March 1985), an oversized jacket was worn with a hat plastered with a newspaper headline style banner. Both were set off by a patterned silk tie and large encrusted earring. A range of accessories, in fact, loomed large in the stylings: US military tie-pins and more "dressy" jewels, which reworked male jewellery in a bricolage spirit. This was, on occasions, pushed to outrageous limits: the combination of jewelled bracelets and long black gloves worn with sportswear vest top and tracksuit bottoms, signalling both "masculinity" and "femininity", "physique" and "elegance" in the same "look".

This assemblage of elements threw up a range of further combinations across the fashion Petri styled. Motorcycle boots were worn with trunks or lacy boxer shorts by muscly models, topped off with tank top and jacket. Dr Marten boots were mixed with a jumper and trunks accessorized with knuckle duster. Less emphatically suits, ties and waistcoats were combined with both the accessorizing jewellery and also clumpy boots and sunglasses. Elements in this fashion were drawn from US military style – the tie pins, the leather jacket, the aviator Ray Bans and even, perhaps, the greased quiff. They testified to an "American cool", and the pursuit of what is explicitly called in one of the images a "more serious pose".

Petri's Buffalo fashion was resolutely, stylishly masculine. The accessories – and occasionally the revealed body – extended the conventional repertoire of menswear. This process represented a loosening of some fixed significations around masculinity: the styles were about a "knowing", self-conscious sense of maleness that was pushed to the edges of camp. All of which was worked with the distinctive choice of models and recurrent kinds of grooming: cropped hair, sideburns, quiffs and hair boyishly brushed forward, glowing and shiny skins.

The posing and the models' expressions stood out in this fashion. Eyes, mouth, chin, nose and sometimes muscular arms and thighs were foregrounded. The conventions of modelling were knowingly drawn upon, in order to attain the perfect pout and that moody stare. The use of conventions was often particularly marked, playing on the posture of an aggressive masculinity or parodying assertively masculine ways of standing. Across these images the postures and forms of expression gave a distinctive gloss to what we might call the romantic individuality of male youth. These were streetwise, pretty hard boys of popular mythology, from James Dean on. These romantic masculine identities offered resources for a "tough", stylish masculinity – men who carried their maleness with a self-contained poise. A certain pre-permissive feel was important in accenting this masculine romanticism. This was brought into sharper focus in some of the Buffalo images by the Kobal-esque finish to the black and white photographs. Glamour, evoked through the seamless surface of the photo, had a nostalgic edge here; the polished gloss of 1940s and 1950s film star portraiture applied to the art of "lookin' good" in 1980s street style ("Hard is the graft", *The Face*, March 1985).

The Buffalo stylings were marked by the strongly narcissistic absorption or self-containment of the models. Posed usually alone, their gaze is often focused downwards or sideways out of frame, registering self-reflection and (in certain spreads) a hint of melancholy. Part of this relates to Buffalo's accenting of the codes of male romanticism and individualism in terms that register the restrictions on young men in 1980s' "Hard times" culture (reduced life-chances, lack of money, the authoritarian shifts in social life).[6] More significantly, however, the conventions of posing and expression established in the spreads invite the viewer into complicity or identification with the models' narcissistic absorption in his "look" or self-presentation; complicity in the ways he carries his "looks" and appearance. What is important for my argument is the way this invited complicity in the model's narcissism is focused upon men's bodies that are at once highly masculine and openly sensual. Two aspects are crucial here. First, the attention staged upon the model's appearance and the pleasures this establishes (in the quality and styling of the clothes, in his grooming, his "looks", in the lighting and quality of the paper) are not directed towards an imagined feminine spectator who would triangulate the look between the male model and the imagined male viewer as we saw in *Town*. That is, there is no woman in the representation or implicitly addressed by the staging of the image to encode this masculine–masculine look as normatively heterosexual. Secondly, the choice of the models and some of the elements of clothing in the stylings have a strong intertextuality with certain traditions of representation of masculinity aimed at and taken up by gay men. (Namely, the valorizing of a "tough" masculinity.) The Palmano Man calendar for 1987 produced a particularly explicit example of this intertextuality. Advertised in lesbian and gay magazines like *Square Peg*, and featuring "thirteen classic male images . . . the perfect present for someone special", the calendar was styled by Petri and featured black and white men shot in three-quarter length shots displaying muscular arms, chests and shoulders in vest tops and chunky accessories.

I am not suggesting, however, that the Buffalo codings were gay male codings; or rather that they were straightforwardly that. There was a limited displaying of the surface of the body in the fashion spreads and the choice of models broke with the tighter generic figures of some more explicitly sexualized gay representations (such as the denim clad boy or the cop). Buffalo was strongly rooted in the stylistic community that it both invoked and simultaneously represented, and this was not strictly defined in terms of sexuality. What was pivotal, however, was the way the styling organized a masculine–masculine look that drew upon a gay accent without either pathologizing that accent or re-inscribing a binary coding of gay or straight.

## Classics go Latin: Italianicity

As I pointed out in Chapter 9, above, one of the reasons behind Nick Logan's decision to launch *Arena* was to maintain the services of those individuals who had been important to the success of *The Face* but whom he feared were wanting to move on to new projects. Ray Petri was prominent amongst these individuals and one of the first names pencilled in by Logan in the early stages of *Arena*'s genesis. Petri's preliminary test stylings in the pre-launch preparation of *Arena* were important in defining the "look" of *Arena*'s fashion coverage. It was no accident – in addition – that these test stylings should later form the basis of the publicity materials used in *Arena*'s launch.

The work Petri produced for *Arena* bore a strong continuity with the look he had established under the Buffalo label. In particular the casting of models remained distinctive. In important ways, however, Petri's work for *Arena* did represent a break with the Buffalo stylings. Apart from the disappearance of the trademark name, two new elements in particular were present. First, the stylings in *Arena* moved towards a highly styled presentation of classic menswear and away from "street style". Secondly, a more extensive narrativization of the fashion images was deployed. Location shoots appeared and the spreads ran over ten or more pages. This broke with the much shorter Buffalo spreads and the exclusive studio setting of these images. One look figured prominently in these shifts. This was a look which I have called "Italianicity". Although not exclusive to Petri, his stylings figured strongly across the range of this look.

In describing these images, I use the term Italianicity to refer to the "condensed essence" of a mythical Italian masculinity.[7] The casting of the models was important in establishing these connotations of Italianicity, connotations which were often further anchored by titles for the spreads (such as "Roma", *Arena*, Summer 1989; "Latin Groves", *Arena*, Winter 1988). The particular index of skin tone, strong features and a marked sensuality (the lips, in particular, were pronounced) were prominent among the models chosen. As with the Buffalo stylings, these physical features signified both sensuality and hardness. Or a mixture of both "soft" and "hard". Thus, the sensuality connoted by the dark skin, eyes and full lips intersected with both strong chins and noses and the connotations of the bravado and swagger of an Italian "macho", an appeal to Roman pride and passion. The casting of Italian-looking models, then, worked to produce a set of connotations of masculinity similar to those signified by the casting of light black models.

The location settings chosen for the spreads were also key in the signification of Italianicity. Two versions of Italy are notably present. The northern city at night provides the backdrop in "After dark", while in "Chianti fields of green" the lush fields and clear light of the Tuscany countryside form the context for the display of menswear.

Italianicity was evoked in a third sense in the images; through the clothing itself. A central element of this was the bravado of the styles: generously cut suits were worn with trashy, bad taste ties and silver shirts, topped of with flashy dark glasses. Wide-profiled overcoats and jackets figured prominently. These were big and bold clothes which emphasized and accentuated a broad masculine frame.

The assertive masculinity of the menswear and its styling were carried through in much of the posing of the models. In "After dark", a strong element of the spread is the theme of the gang and the staging of rituals of aggression and display. This produces a stylized bravado of stares, pouts and tensed bodies; a regime of posture and expression which evokes the frisson of controlled confrontation in the city at night. "Dateline Milan" worked with a similar coding of posture and expression. Moody stares and upright poses produced a rock solid bodily regime. The physicality of the masculine body was also foregrounded in these images. In addition, well established codes of expression – similar to those coded in *Town* – were drawn upon: upward focused stares; a gaze sideways and away from the imagined viewer. Narcissistically absorbed looks – like those in the Buffalo images – were also coded. One spread gave a particular twist to this narcissistic look. The model is – as the title puts it – "Lost to his sweet (day) dreams of youth". His pose is relaxed, and this is a relaxation underlined by his casual clothes – in particular by the boxer shorts loosely framing his thighs. A spectatorial look is established here which draws the eye to the cusp of where the clothing (the shorts) meets the leg. As if to register this look and disperse its possible homosexual connotations for the imagined male reader, a wall-hung photograph of a woman mediates between the reader and the model. Perhaps she is the subject of his "sweet dreams"? She certainly triangulates the relation between the reader and the model within the terms of heterosexuality. That is, the picture stitches the look invited at the bared thighs into a display that is primarily directed at a woman. The smallness of the photograph, its marginality in the frame, and the way that the model's attention in the narrative of the image is not upon the photograph, however, leave his relationship to her open and ambiguous. They suggest that another kind of sexualization of the look is also possible.

The cropping of the images across the spreads, together with the use of lighting and colour film stock, staged other pleasures in looking. A striking feature was the intensity coded in many of the images through the cropping of the photographs. Mouths, noses, chins and glowing skins were foregrounded by this cropping in ways which markedly broke with the conventions of cropping used in *Town* and in the Buffalo stylings. The lighting used further emphasized the gloss of skin, eyes and hair, together with the texture of the clothing. Colour film stock, tinting and glossy black and white also played up the surface qualities of the images inviting a much more developed set of visual pleasure in the texture of the image itself than those coded in the images in *Town*. These techniques shaped a masculine spectatorial look across these images which sanctioned the display of sensuality in relation to assertively and stylishly masculine models. This invited, then, both identification with and pleasure in the pleasures coded around these masculinities.

## "How very English": Edwardian Englishness

An invocation of what I have called "Edwardian Englishness" shaped the third "look" which loomed large across the fashion spreads. It was a "look" which was especially strongly represented within the pages of *GQ*. The casting of the models was key to producing this "look". The models all had pale white skin, with lighter hair and softer features than the Italian-looking models who featured in the Italianicity look and Buffalo stylings. The styling of the hair, however, was particularly important to the coding of the Edwardian Englishness look. It was cropped at the sides and back, but left long enough on top to be pushed back. Slightly dressed with hair grease, the weight of the hair on top was also cut to flop forward. This combined the Romantic associations of long hair, with the connotations of the masculine discipline and civilized neatness of the "short back and sides".

The repertoire of clothing worn was also key to signifying "Edwardian Englishness". Plundering a casually formal wardrobe, the emphasis was on linens and cottons in white, soft hues and "country" colours. In Figure 11.7, for example, a white linen jacket was worn with a paisley cravat, and taupe, cream and beige jackets and trousers set off with coloured silk ties, cravats and waistcoats. Courduroy and brogues compliment the soft edges of a cream rain-coat and a straw hat. The choice of fabrics is important here. The emphasis on the texture of "traditional" materials like cotton, linen and wool and their association with quality and craftmanship are very different from the synthetic modernity of *Town*'s terylene and polyester. The choice and cut of materials used across the menswear in this look, then, evoked a colonial, aristocratic Englishness.

Empire and aristocracy figured prominently in the selection of materials for the sets and props. In one spread, the clothing and styles are glossed as an "Englishman abroad" by the set and props. Embroidered oriental rugs, cane chairs and a wickerwork elephant are some of the key signfiers. These are men – as the title to the spread puts it –

Figure 11.7   Colony club, *GQ*, April/May 1989. Knut Bry © *GQ*, The Condé Nast Publications Limited.

189

down at the "Colony Club". Alternatively, in another spread, the wind blown spring skies and flat, sandy coastlines of a "temperate isle" England formed an evocative backdrop to the menswear.

Ways of standing and looking animate the coding of masculinity in relation to these styles and settings. The "Colony Club's" aura as an exclusively masculine domain is connoted in the posing of the models. The formality and stiffness of their poses signifies the appropriate indices of class and power. The models pose square on and upright, staring back assertively to camera. Meanwhile, the social context of the club is confirmed by the grouped posing. A more languid set of posture is coded in other images.

The choices associated with lighting, cropping and film stock bring to bear further meanings across these spreads. Lighting is especially important. In a number of the images, the connotations of "Edwardian Englishness" are signified by the selection of lighting. This happens in two ways within the spreads I have selected. First, early evening light is suggested. The light is soft, connoting spring showers and the peculiarities of the English climate. Secondly, the lighting has a grainy, amber glow. This infuses the image with a warm, rich light which re-connotes the colonial context of the menswear.

The version of "Edwardian Englishness" produced through the codes of casting, clothing, posture, expression, lighting and setting, in these images drew on an important set of contemporary intertexts: specifically, the cinematic and televisual representation of inter-war Britain and Empire. Looming large in this were the "Raj genre" of films, including David Lean's *A passage to India* (1985) and Central Television's *Jewel in the crown* (1982). Also important were Merchant and Ivory's *A room with a view* (1986) and *Maurice* (1987), and Granada Television's *Brideshead revisited* (1981). The success of these films and serializations was rooted in their emphatic reproduction of colonial, Edwardian England through costumes and sets. In *Brideshead revisited*, for example, Jeremy Irons looking dashing in period costume against the backdrop of the splendour of Castle Howard was as important as the prestigious literary adaptation. One element prominent in some of these representations of Edwardian Englishness was the connotation of the "sexual aberrations" associated with this aristocratic English masculinity. The fashion spreads do not go so far as to signify this masculinity as homosexual, but it does deliver to them a stylized, almost aesthetisized sense of identity. They are prissy young gentlemen.

This repertoire of "Edwardian Englishness", however, also had other strands operating within it. If, as writers like Forster testify, the turn-of-the-century and the inter-war years were important in consolidating a new version of Englishness within which a representation of the English countryside and a conservative modernity figured prominently, Conservatism in the 1980s drew strongly on these formations in its attempts to articulate a new version of "little Englandism". Thatcherism, as Stuart Hall and others have argued, made much of appeals to a version of late Imperial Englishness. This stood as a moment of greatness and Imperial confidence in which the values of a "true" Englishness were built (Schwarz 1984, Schwarz 1986, Hall 1988, Mercer 1988). The reproduction of a narrowly based version of Englishness – and English masculinity – is at stake, then, in these fashion images in as much as the connotations of "Edwardian Englishness" were closely articulated with this new Conservative project.

The version of masculinity coded within these spreads, then, was strongly marked by the interplay between on the one hand the assertive masculinity associated with a dominant version of Englishness and on the other the Romantic connotations of narcissistic young manhood. If the nature of this tension was less marked than the highly ambivalent sexual identity coded in Petri's Buffalo stylings or even the Italianicity stylings, it nonetheless coded a spectatorial look in which identification with the models (especially in terms of the power of their imagined Englishness) sat alongside the sanctioning of visual pleasures in the cut of clothes, lighting and the look of the models themselves.

## Conclusion

It is appropriate to take stock at this point and consider what my reading of the three looks has revealed about the distinctiveness of the representations produced within *The Face*, *Arena* and *GQ*. Clear differences have certainly emerged between the moment of representation associated with *Town* and the 1980s images. First, the breaks in terms of casting were strong. Not only were the 1980s models resolutely younger looking, but they were more markedly groomed (their skins in particular were very glossy) and had stronger and more sensuous features. The casting also, importantly, included not only white models but black, light black and southern-European looking men. Secondly, the selection of menswear and its shaping of the masculine frame were very different from those coded in *Town*. Clothes were assertively masculine, with big wide profiles or cuts which emphasized – and on occasions revealed – the new importance of a solid, muscular body. Thirdly, there were disjunctures in terms of the codes of posture and expression. In the 1980s images, expressions were often more extravagant and exaggerated, while the conventions of assertive masculine posing were played upon. Fourthly, the codes of lighting and film stock used were very different in the 1980s images. There was more emphasis on dramatizing the stylings through the use of lighting. Lighting and film stock were also more extensively used to emphasize the surface qualities of skin, hair and the texture of clothing. Fifthly, the cropping of the images was also important. A greater intensity was coded in the 1980s images through this cropping. The spectatorial eye was brought up much closer to the surface of the masculine body.

Across key visual codes, then, the representations from *The Face*, *Arena* and *GQ* broke with the representational conventions deployed within *Town*. Continuities did persist, however, between the two moments of representation. Particularly important in this respect were the continuities in the codes of posture and expression. The signification of masculine independence and assertiveness through these codes was present within both moments of representation. Important differences within the 1980s images also complicated the nature of the break between the images from *Town* and those from *The Face*, *Arena* and *GQ*. Petri's Buffalo stylings represented the most ruptural set of representations. They went furthest down the road of displaying sensuality in the coding of masculinity – including displaying the surface of the body. The deliberate jumbling of the conventions of menswear in the Buffalo stylings – especially the mixture of tough outerwear with camp accessories – produced some sexually ambivalent codings. The Italianicity stylings re-coded some of the elements found in the Buffalo stylings – in particular the mix of assertive masculinity and sensuality. The choice and styling of the clothes, however, was less disruptive of the conventions of menswear than those styled by Petri under the Buffalo label. The Edwardian Englishness stylings on the other hand drew very deliberately on a nostalgic (and conservative) version of menswear and sanctioned less display of the surface of the body and a more limited coding of masculine sensuality.

These differences between the three looks which I centre-staged had implications for the forms of spectatorship coded in relation to each of them. While all the representations staged forms of masculine–masculine looking in which identification between the imagined reader and models loomed large, disjunctures between the three looks were manifest in terms of the interplay between these looks and sexual identity. The coding of a sexually ambivalent masculine–masculine look again marked the Buffalo stylings out as the most ruptural. It was the way these images set up pleasures in looking drawing on forms of looking that were historically the prerogative of gay men – without pathologizing that look – which made them so distinctive. This sanctioning of an ambivalent mas-culine–masculine look was also present in the Italianicity stylings, though less assertively so and often combined with a clear hetero-sexualization of masculine display. The ambivalence around sexual identity in the look was even less clearly marked in the Edwardian Englishness looks and the coding of masculine display at times drew upon the presence of a female model to orientate this display towards the norms of heterosexuality.

Drawing the distinctions between the Buffalo, Italianicity and Edwardian Englishness looks has broader implications for my argu-ment in Part IV as a whole. First, the different versions of masculinity coded in these three looks return us to the distinctions between the three magazines that were set out in the previous chapter. Although there is no neat fit between the three looks and the editorial contents of the three magazines, there are correspondences between the address to an "avant-garde metropolitan" masculinity in *The Face* and *Arena* and the Buffalo and Italianicity looks produced in their respective fashion imagery and the address to a "modern conserva-tive metropolitan" masculinity in *GQ* and the Edwardian Englishness look which was best represented in its fashion pages. A large part of the knowledge coded within the magazines' editorials complemented their fashion spreads in as much as it was concerned with menswear and related forms of individual consumption. Secondly, the Buffalo, Italianicity and Edwardian Englishness stylings demonstrated that more than one version of masculinity was produced through the styling of the developments in menswear within the magazine fash-ion photography. To put it more pointedly, more than one version of the "new man" was coded within this site of representation. Thirdly, emphasizing the differences between these three looks also enables us to periodize two phases of representation in relation to the new masculinities coded within magazine fashion photography. It is clear that the production of the Buffalo stylings between 1984 and 1986 represented the formative moment for the new representations of masculinity within magazine culture. It was these stylings that established the importance of a solid and muscular body shape, the highly groomed appearance of skin and hair and the possibility of displaying masculine sensuality (including the surface of the body) in the casting of the models and in the styling of the clothes in this imagery. Buffalo, in this sense, was the formative influence on the peculiarities of the 1980s "new man" imagery. It was within Petri's Buffalo stylings that this look first emerged. Elements of this Buffalo look were thus appropriated in the two key adverts focused on in Part III, namely, the Levi's 501 jeans and Brylcreem adverts. In the case of the Levi's advert the appropriation was extremely specific. Nick Kamen, the model in the "Launderette" advert, was one of Petri's most regularly used "Buffalo" boys.

The second phase of representation between 1986 and 1989 saw the consolidation of the new representational elements as well as the pluralization of these new codings of masculinity. The fashion imagery produced in *Arena* and *GQ* – specifically, the Italianicity and Edwardian Englishness looks were the case in point.

Periodizing these representations leads me to a fourth important point. This concerns the ability of Petri's stylings to command such an influence over fashion-based representations addressed to new male markets in the mid to late 1980s. How do we account for Petri's influence? The account of the advertising and publishing knowledges and practices set out in Part IV directs us towards the conditions under which Petri's stylings were able to pass from their base in the elite avant-garde culture of *The Face* into a wider set of representations of masculinity. These conditions were the commercial manoeuvrings of advertisers and publishers in relation to new male markets. It was, as I have argued on a number of occasions, the ability of practitioners at *The Face* successfully to address new male consumers at a time when other publishers and advertisers were uncertain about how to address or represent these consumers which gave *The Face* considerable cultural authority over this market. This meant that the magazine's format and address to "style-conscious young men" or "innovators" formed the necessary starting point for other media practitioners in addressing this market and in representing the "new man". At the heart of this process were Petri's stylings. It was within these stylings that a new and distinctive version of masculinity was available.

# Conclusion

Where has this account taken us? I have ranged from the innovations in menswear garment design and the associated merchandising and retail design decisions of retailers, across questions of advertising organization and the knowledges and practices of advertising production to an account of developments in magazine publishing and a reading of the visual codes deployed within magazine fashion photography. The importance of taking in these multiple sites has been a central contention of the book. I have argued that the "new man" imagery had to be understood as a regime of representation. The imagery precisely signified across more than one form; we found the "new man" in more than one place. Taking into consideration this range of commercial sites, however, has had an additional significance. I suggested in the Introduction that a central ambition of the book was to put together an account of what drove the formation of the regime of "new man" imagery. Institutional practices have figured prominently in my response to that question. I have argued that by breaking open these commercial institutions – the menswear design and retail trade, advertising and magazine publishing – it has been possible to locate the production of the "new man" imagery within a specific set of nexus each made up of a range of practices and forms of expertise.

Setting out the specificity of each of these institutional nexus has been a central aim of the book. Across the accounts I have pieced together, however, a consistent theme has emerged. Namely, that the institutional practices I have detailed were governed by calculations about shifts in forms of masculine culture outside the consumer institutions. These were quintessentially commercial calculations made by the cultural practitioners who have loomed large in my account. It was their concern to target what they identified as new male consumers that gave the commercial impetus to the mobilization of new visual codes across these sites. The formation of the regime of "new man" imagery was precisely shaped by the intersection of these commercial and cultural calculations. What also emerged across Parts III and IV, in particular, was the way in which forms of cultural authority were woven into these cultural calculations concerning the deployment of the new visual codes of masculinity. The uncertainty amongst advertising practitioners and the large magazine publishers (notably, Condé Nast) about how to appropriately address new male consumers, set the terms for the formative influence of a set of innovative, avant-garde codings of masculinity (Petri's "Buffalo look" for *The Face*) upon the regime of representation. The coding of masculinity constructed in Petri's stylings was able to hegemonize the representations addressed to the new male consumer; it was these codings that provided the necessary elements to mark out the distinctiveness of the visual address to new male consumers.

There was a further dimension to these forms of selling, marketing and commercial display which made its presence felt at various points throughout the account. This was the way that the "new man" imagery was tied in with the operationalizing of marketing and selling techniques geared towards a more segmented view of mass consumer markets. The forms of marketing and selling with which the imagery was interconnected, therefore, told us something about the formation of a culture of flexible specialization within these consumer institutions – most particularly in middle and mass market menswear retailing.

In foregrounding in the book these institutional practices and the commercial imperatives with which they were associated, however, my ambition has not been to push for a form of economic reductionism in the analysis of the "new man" imagery. Rather, my account has been driven – as I made clear on a number of occasions – by the concern to rethink the usual relations of determination that are assumed between economic and cultural practices within the tradition of post-Althusserian cultural analysis; a tradition that continues to broadly frame, in an often unacknowledged way, a good deal of cultural analysis. At the heart of my disagreement has been the ambition to delimit the imbricated and interdependent nature of some of the economic and cultural practices within the sphere of cultural production I have centred on. This has meant, in particular, opening up for critical scrutiny the role played by cultural practices in the formation and operation of the "new man" markets. What followed from this was of paramount importance: specific cultural practices emerged as important determinants on the formation and operation of the "new man" markets as markets. As we saw in Part III, for example, the establishment and playing out of a set of relations of exchange between producers (like Levi-Strauss), cultural intermediaries (like BBH) and groups of consumers was conducted through representations of (what was variously specified as) "innovators", "style-conscious young men" and so on. It was the mobilization of these representations of a new market of male consumers that was a necessary part of the articulation of these economic or commercial relations. It shaped the organization and channelling of technical and financial resources. These representations, then, were a key determinant on the formation and operation of this market.

These findings have clear implications for the cultural analysis of commercially produced cultural forms. It is no longer enough to put together sophisticated accounts of these cultural forms in which economic practices only ghost across the analytic scene as shadowy but ominous constraints or blocks to the play of language, representation or other symbolic practices. Economic processes do quite clearly act as determinants of the process of commercial cultural production in so far as they set certain limits and exert certain pressures on cultural production.[1] As we have seen in relation to the "new man" imagery, however, the relations between "the economic" and "the cultural" are not best conceptualized as the effect of an autonomous, primary domain of practices and processes (the economic) on another "relatively autonomous" domain of practices and processes (the cultural). Rather, as I have suggested, it is more useful to emphasize conceptually the interdependence of economic and cultural practices and their relations of reciprocal effect in the sphere of cultural production. Such an approach is also, quite clearly, distinct from advocating a return to political economy. It is the attempt to analyze the economic discursively that is at stake and not the return – as in political economy – to the economic understood as a fundamental level of determination. In this sense, fully exploring the imbricated relationships between "the economic" and "the cultural" is the real challenge for cultural analysis. One of the hopes of the book is that future work will produce more empirical work on the discursive operation of economic relations and practices in the sphere of commercial cultural production and take up the challenge of charting what we might call (following both Foucault and Laclau) the correlations and mutual relations of effect between the incompletely formed entities of culture and economics.

The ability to attend to these relationships between economic and cultural practices is one of the more important pay-offs from rethinking the usual priorities of textual analysis developed in the book. Extending the net of the cultural analysis of the "new man" imagery to include the institutional practices and forms of expertise governing and regulating their production, has profoundly marked the empirical substance of the book. If the visual texts themselves have remained key to my argument, the magisterial centrality they might have commanded within a more narrowly text-based form of analysis has been significantly diminished. What have loomed large in my account, then, have been those places which most cultural critics of popular representation have often been reluctant to enter. Namely, the commercial institutions that dominate these fields of representation. Not only, as I have just suggested, has this emphasis forced a rethinking of the model of determination deployed within cultural analysis, but it has also delivered a challenge to the narrow semiotic emphasis on a set of exemplary texts. The story the book has told has demonstrated the necessity of grasping the way the "new man" imagery signified across a number of sites of representation and within different cultural forms as a regime of representation. This included, as we saw, sites of representation (retail interiors) which conventionally fall outside the lens of those forms of semiotic textual analysis shaped by a preference for the more tightly delimited visual or literary text.

This book, however, has not only been about an account of the institutional practices and forms of commercial expertise that shaped the production and circulation of the "new man" imagery. I have also explored the cultural significance of this imagery. This was based upon an analysis of the visual codes associated with the "new man". In the conclusion to Part IV, I detailed at some length my arguments about their specificity. The following points are worth underlining again. A central characteristic of the codings was the signification of an assertive masculinity with the sanctioning of the display of sensuality. Casting was important in this coding of masculine sensuality. The use of light black and Italian-looking models was key to delivering these attributes and characteristics. The resignification of the developments in menswear design were also key. They reinforced the coding of an assertive masculinity – both through the reworking of classic menswear and in the appropriation of elements of "street style" that emphasized and revealed the importance of a solid, muscular body. The intensity of the framing of masculinity was also a significant element in the distinctiveness of these visual codings. Techniques of cropping and framing were important in this respect. They guided the eye of the spectator across the faces and (occasionally) the revealed surface of the body of the models and onto the displayed clothes.

The intensity of the looks staged in relation to the coding of masculinity was one part of the distinctiveness of the forms of spectatorship coded in relation to the "new man" imagery. I argued that more than one form of spectatorship was coded across this regime of representation; different forms of spectatorship related to the different versions of the "new man" produced across the field of imagery. The three "looks" detailed in Part IV were emblematic in this respect. The fashion photographs associated with Ray Petri's "Buffalo" stylings were important in staging a form of masculine–masculine looking in which a sexual ambivalence was coded. This represented the most ruptural organization of spectatorship across these images in that it drew on, as I suggested, forms of looking historically associated with gay men without re-inscribing the binary split between "gay" and "straight". An explicit heterosexualization of masculine display sat alongside these ambivalent masculine–masculine looks in other forms of spectatorship coded across the representations. In addition, forms of identification figured prominently across the forms of looking staged by all the representations. In this respect, the narcissistic register of the look loomed large in the formal organization of spectatorship. The effect was to produce a range of masculine–masculine looks within the magazines.

The coding of these forms of spectatorship had implications not only for the forms of looking staged in relation to magazine fashion photography but also in relation to advertising representations and, perhaps most crucially, in relation to the spectatorship spatialized within menswear shops. This was an important characteristic of the regime of "new man" imagery I have highlighted. It brought together a series of intertextual looks staged by magazine fashion spreads, advertising imagery and the frontages of shops and their interiors to constitute a distinctive regime of looking. This regime of looking was central to the distinctiveness of the "new man" imagery as a whole.

The cultural significance of these forms of spectatorship and the visual codes through which they were formally staged rested upon their relationship to established formations of masculinity and masculine culture. Frank Mort, in his "Boy's own" essay, advanced a particular reading of the significance of the "new man" imagery in relation to the lived culture of young men. His central contention was that this imagery addressed men self-consciously as men and therefore set the terms for a more provisional, gendered sense of maleness. This in turn made possible a reconfiguration of relations between young men and women. I have not attempted in the book to test out this claim. The account I have developed, though, does offer up a challenge to his contention that this gendered address to men was in any sense new or – in his terms – potentially progressive. Although the imagery I have considered does certainly stage highly stylized forms of masculinity, the way in which it addressed men as gendered (rather than unmarked) subjects was consistent with a whole range of other forms of fashion marketing and selling to men. In fact, in relation to consumer markets like menswear and grooming and toiletries, addressing men as gendered subjects is a *sine qua non* of their operation. As we saw in relation to the imagery from *Town*, there is nothing disruptive to the norms of masculinity in this kind of gendered address.

What was distinctive about the "new man" imagery, as I have argued, was the space it represented for the display of masculine sensuality, the sanctioning of a highly staged narcissism through the codes of dress and grooming and (at its most ruptural in Petri's styling) for the coding of sexual ambivalence – especially in the organization of spectatorship. In this sense, then, I do want to concur with the spirit of Mort's general argument in his "Boy's own" essay about the importance of this moment of representation. Something significant was at stake for the formations of gender and sexual culture in the representations I have detailed. The images represented a particular loosening of the binary opposition between gay and straight-identified men and extended the space available within the representational regimes of popular consumption for an ambivalent masculine sexual identity. An identity, furthermore, which had precedents within the metropolitan contours of post-war popular culture – most spectacularly, within mod subculture in the 1960s, amongst soul boys and Bowie fans in the 1970s and within the experimentations of "Blitz" culture and "New Pop" in the early 1980s.

Developments since the end of 1990 in the men's markets centre-staged in the book have underlined this reading of the cultural significance of the "new man" imagery. At the heart of these developments has been the explicit ambition – most clearly articulated within magazine culture – to establish a break with the figure of the "new man" and an attempt to close down the space of sexual ambivalence associated with it.[2] The publisher Condé Nast's decision to introduce a new editorial mix into GQ in January 1991 (backed up by a high profile advertising campaign) offered the hardest version of this explicit backlash against the "new man" within magazine publishing. With undisguised relish, Condé Nast's publicity proclaimed, "GQ is proud to announce that the New Man has officially been laid to rest (if indeed he ever drew breath). The 90s man knows who he is, what he wants and where he's going, and he's not afraid to say so. And yes, he still wants to get laid" (Condé Nast press release, January 1991). Figuring strongly in this new editorial approach was the introduction of what was rather euphamistically called "glamour" in the trade. By this publishers meant the inclusion of sexualized visual representations of women as a main feature in the magazine and an accompanying sexual scrutiny of women in editorial pieces.[3] The introduction of these features marked the more assertive articulation of the post-permissive masculine heterosexual script which, as I argued in Part IV, was evident in a less strident form within GQ from its launch.

Editorial changes, however, were not unique to GQ. Arena also reworked its editorial mix at this time. Its new approach was strongly signalled in its Winter 1990–91 issue which featured a woman on the cover of the magazine for the first time. The cover star was the model Tatjana Patitz, one of the women featured in the issue's main story "Girls! Girls! Girls! Arena's 100 favourite women (and 20 belles from hell!)". The piece drew upon a regular feature called "Women we love" from the American magazine Esquire, and offered a "celebration" of women within cinema, comedy, fashion, music, the literary world and sport. Unsurprisingly, the feature largely revolved around a scrutiny of the women's physical looks, though the tone of the written copy was informed by Arena's trademark irony and witty irreverence. Thus, in the category "Word up, literary spectacles", Jeanette Winterson's entry was accompanied by the line "What's it with her and fruit?", whilst Marge Simpson, the fictional cartoon character from The Simpsons, featured in the "Women etc., lest we forget" category together with the line "Homer, are you blind?"

Accompanying these developments in its editorial, *Arena*, self-reflexive as ever, offered a cultural analysis of the new masculine identity which it saw its new editorial mix as being addressed to. This was the figure of the "new lad". For Sean O'Hagan, author of the piece, the "new lad" was "a rather schiziod fellow. He aspires to New Man status when he's with women, but reverts to old man type when he's out with the boys" (*Arena*, 27, Spring/Summer 1991: 23). For O'Hagan, the "new lad" was a culturally and generationally specific identity:

> he tends to be part of the thirtysomething generation – educated, stylish, more often than not well groomed and totally in tune with the shifting codes of contemporary culture . . . [H]e is well versed in the language, and protocol, of post-feminist discourse and he will never ever, even after a few post-prandial brandies, slip into Sid the Sexist mode like a regular (Jack the) lad might" (*Arena*, 27, Spring/Summer 1991: 22).

As with *GQ*'s editorial rethink, *Arena*'s address to the "new lad" marked the more confident articulation of the sexual scripts already established in the magazine and instituted a deepening of its celebration – shot through, in this instance, with *Arena*'s particular avant-garde metropolitanism – of the shared culture of young(ish) heterosexual masculinity and its updated post-permissive scripts of "cars, girls, sport and booze".[4]

These editorial rethinks were also accompanied by shifts in the visual codes of masculinity that appeared in the magazines – particularly within the magazine fashion photography. Three shifts were particularly noteworthy. The first, and perhaps most important, was the less intense framing of masculinity within the images. The second was the decline in the display of masculine sensuality which came largely through changes in casting. The third shift was the display of a harder musculature amongst the models. It is important to state that none of these shifts amounted to a dramatic change in the visual codes of masculinity produced within the magazines. Nonetheless, in the context of the changes in the magazines' editorial material, they did mark the pulling away from the more ambivalent display of masculine sensuality sanctioned in the period 1984–90.

The refocusing of the format of the general interest men's magazines from the end of 1990 around a new target consumer suggested their repositioning in relation to wider formations of masculinity and masculine culture. This was a repositioning driven, like those commercial initiatives around the "new man" the book has charted, by calculations about shifts in the lived culture of groups of men. I have suggested that these recent development shed illuminating retrospective light on the cultural significance of the visual codes associated with the "new man". They underline the novelty of the break the book details and the importance, as I have argued on a number of occasions, of the space of masculine sexual ambivalence opened up in this moment of representation. There are other lessons, however, that we can derive from the emergence of the "new lad" within magazine culture. The first is that the "new lad" is a post-"new man" phenomenon. By this I mean that many of the elements of the "new lad" were already in place within the representation of the "new man" (most clearly within magazine culture). This included not only the sexual scripts I have referred to in the conclusion already, but also the persistence of the more elaborated codes of style and individual consumption for men associated with the "new man". Secondly, though the language of "glamour" developed within the magazines certainly marked the confident articulation of an updated post-permissive masculine heterosexual script, it needs to be set in the context of the contemporaneous appropriation of highly feminine and sexualized femininities by young women within magazine culture and beyond. Thus, the use of the terms "babe" to signify a certain kind of femininity was deployed within the men's magazines as well as appearing in young women's culture as a term positively laid claim to by groups of women. This suggests that to fully understand the significance of these new languages of masculinity and sexual identity we need to situate them within the wider field of gender relations. Such an exercise would also reveal that the "new lad" has not been the only new masculine identity to emerge in relation to these consumer markets since 1990. Northern Shell Plc's attempt to explicitly address a mixed male readership of both gay and straight-identified men in its magazine, *Attitude*, built upon the space of sexual ambivalence opened up by the "new man". In particular, *Attitude*'s attempt to mobilize the identity of "strays" – "straight men who act and think gay or at least hang out with gay men" (as the *Guardian* rather clumsily put it) was unthinkable without the impact of the "new man" on magazine culture.[5] Likewise the emergence of queer as a term of self-identification adopted by groups

205

of gay men can be partly attributed to a more entrenched articulation of difference and positioning in relation to the blurring of gay and straight signified by the more ruptural versions of the "new man". As such, then, the "new lad" is one of a number of outcomes within popular representations of masculinity that have followed the emergence of the "new man".

Perhaps, however, the most important lesson of the emergence of representations of the "new lad" in relation to the images discussed in this book concerns the way it points up the difficulty of re-inventing masculine heterosexual scripts. This relates to a clear limit position within the shifts in masculinity associated with the "new man". Thus, while the moral language of antisexism associated with the sexual politics of the new social movements clearly impacted on the debates about the "new man" (putting a limited block on the more trenchant sexualized scrutiny of women within magazine publishing, for example) no alternative sexual scripts were fully elaborated. The most interesting development within magazine culture, as I suggested earlier, was *Arena*'s deployment of irony to establish a critical distance from these sexual scripts. However, because no new heterosexual scripts were articulated – scripts that were both sexy and antisexist – the opportunity for established scripts to re-emerge was always left open. The "new lad" represents the return of that particular repressed.

In assessing the cultural significance of the "new man" imagery it is quite clear, however, that there are limits to what a purely formal reading can deliver. I have insisted throughout the book that the effects of the "new man" imagery on the masculinity of real historical men could not be read-off from the representations. Their actual cultural impact upon specific lived masculinities and forms of masculine culture depended upon the way the attributes and characteristics coded in the imagery (including the modes of looking) were operationalized or performed through everyday practices and upon the articulation of these attributes and characteristics with the competing masculine investments of the men successfully interpellated by the imagery. Making further judgements about the significance of the imagery in this respect requires the production of a different kind of knowledge to that set out in this book. In this sense, it means holding out against the temptation to slip between a formal reading of representation and assessments about shifts in lived culture. This is where I strongly depart from studies that move too quickly from a formal reading of representation to inferring shifts in lived culture. There are, though, perhaps two particular sets of lessons to be taken from the story the book has told in relation to charting the dynamic between regimes of representation and lived cultures. Both relate to the politics of masculinity. The first concerns the model of sexual/cultural politics that has shaped my account. The second concerns the cultural practitioners and intermediaries who have loomed large in this story.

I suggested in the Introduction that the impetus for the account the book develops came out of a particular model of engaged cultural criticism; a model of cultural criticism informed by a version of sexual/cultural politics. Frank Mort's argument in his "Boy's own" essay was influential on my thinking in this respect and reflected a broader Gramscian-informed interest in popular culture as a domain of "containment and resistance" to a range of social hegemonies (including those of gender and sexuality). The pay-offs from such an approach are significant. The first of these concerns the way it breaks with those conceptualizations of popular culture that read it as a wholly manipulated domain and as the site (from the perspective of sexual politics) of the most regressive versions of masculinity. Rather, the neo-Gramscian version of sexual/cultural politics points to the way progressive shifts in gender and sexual cultures might register quite rapidly within popular culture, whilst retaining a sense of the tensions between dominant and subordinate gender and sexual cultures built right into the domain of popular culture. Secondly, this version of sexual/cultural politics forces any project of transforming masculinity to engage with popular experience; that is, to root the transformative ambitions of sexual politics in genuinely popular forms rather than imposing itself on them from the outside. The notion of cultural politics as a politics of articulation and counter-hegemony pitched at the level of representation is enormously generative in this respect.

There are, however, some marked limitations to this mode of cultural intervention. Both Frank Mort and Tony Bennett, in auto-critiques of their own work, have argued that a high degree of instrumentalism informs this kind of analysis of the popular (Mort 1992, Bennett 1992). Such readings of popular culture tend to run a calculus through popular forms: "Is it progressive?", for the projects of gender, sexual and social equality. This has a number of implications. First, it can tend to produce a highly skewed account of cultural relations and the field of popular representation and experiences. What are centre-staged are those cultural forms and practices that can be most clearly fitted into a model of hegemony. The positive emphasis on taking the popular seriously and of being attentive to the moments when a range of social hegemonies are challenged within popular culture, can exclude the more mundane and unspectacular range of cultural practices. An emphasis on the subversion of dominant cultural formations, additionally sidelines attention to "non-progressive" cultural forms and practices. Because these cannot be tied into an imagined project of counter-hegemony, their position and persistence within the field of cultural relations is underplayed.

The model of intervention that guides this kind of cultural politics also draws on precepts from a longer tradition of cultural regulation. Mort and Bennett both emphasize the continuities that exist between cultural politics and a history of the administration and regulation of the "habits and life" of subordinate groups. These projects of social reform – such as the interventions of the Rational Recreations and public museum movements – were driven by the concerns of middle-class reformers to remake popular experience. Of course, the project of cultural/sexual politics has more radical ambitions than its precursors; a concern to produce a genuinely democratic culture for a start. Nevertheless, the relations of cultural authority between reformers and subordinate cultures remain very similar. This is not to suggest that this mode of engaged reading of the popular – such as that conducted in this book – be ruled out of court. Rather, it is to suggest that a clearer sense of the politics of reading the popular be spelt out. As Bennett has argued, what is characteristic of this method of engaged reading of the popular is its largely rhetorical sense of intervention. A critical reading often remains the limit of intervention. Again, this is not to argue against this kind of method of engagement with popular representations, but to insist on explicitly acknowledging the limits of what this can deliver in itself. This method of reading has specific institutional conditions of existence within higher education and makes most sense to those who have been through this experience of learning. A lesson of this book is that effective intervention, if this is being proposed, needs to be grounded in the translation of these forms of knowledge into other contexts and their imbrication with other forms of knowledge and practice. As we have seen in relation to the various practitioners who populate this account, such an exercise will require negotiating some obstinate forms of professional expertise.

There is an additional stumbling block, however, with the politics of masculinity shaped by sexual/cultural politics from which this book emerged. This concerns the language of emancipation which still haunts its transformative ambitions. The central problem with this notion of emancipation is the underdeveloped sense of what a post-emancipation settlement might look like in relation to gender and sexual relations. What is generally invoked is a utopian picture of social relations that allow the expression of fully human potentials. In effect, such a politics posits a gender and sexual future without antagonism or conflict; a future in which the distinctions of gender and sexuality carry no, or less, significance and a future set at an unbridgeable distance from the realties of the existing conflictual configuration of gender and sexual relations. As both Jeffrey Weeks and Chantal Mouffe have argued in relation to more general arguments about social change, however, recognizing the diversity of ways of life and definitions of the good needs to be the starting point for any grounded project of progressive social change (Weeks 1991, Mouffe 1991). In this sense, the story the book has set out about the "new man" has been instructive. The different versions of the "new man" produced within the particular field of representation I have focused on remind us of the need to ground any project of transformation in a plurality of masculinities. This suggests a future of ongoing negotiations between differently constituted and shifting groups of masculinities and femininities in which the provisional nature of the particular claim of any group has to be recognized.

The second principal point concerning the politics of masculinity is of a rather different order. I have centre-staged in the book the producers and cultural intermediaries within the consumer institutions linked to the production and circulation of the regime of "new man" imagery. One provisional finding from this was a sense of the different formations of practitioners operating within these institutions. Within magazine publishing, for example, there were clear differences between the practitioners associated with the independent publishers Wagadon and those associated with Condé Nast. Significantly, there are grounds for suggesting that this was partly rooted within the way each formation of practitioners was itself linked with the new forms of masculine consumption and leisure articulated within the magazines and beyond. Charting the relationship between the "new man" imagery and lived masculinities might fruitfully be put together through an analysis of these practitioner cultures and – in particular – the forms of work-based masculine identities written into them. This would also allow an exploration the relationship between these new masculinities and coterminous formations of femininity; specifically, the femininity of the groups of women also working in these institutions. Such an approach would provide a way of assessing the impact of shifting gender and sexual scripts upon masculinities at a popular level as an alternative to focusing on an analysis of the consumers of the imagery: via the intellectual and cultural formation of the practitioners behind its production and circulation. To explore the gendering of the workplace culture of these industries, however, is to begin a new line of enquiry and to embark on another account.

# Notes

## Introduction

1. See, for example, G. Melly, "Why the tables have turned on macho males", *Campaign*, 18/7/86: 40–41; B. Kennedy & J. Lyttle, "Wolf in chic clothing", *City Limits*, 4–11 December 1986: 10–12; S. Moore, "Target man", *New Socialist*, January 1987: 4–5; "Where are the new men?", *Media Week*, 15/7/88: 47; M. Jones, "We'll make a min of you", *Campaign*, 19/2/88: 43; Moore (1988); Rutherford (1988); Chapman (1988).

## Part I

## Chapter 1

1. For an influential account that takes up the insights from semiotics and also attempts to hold onto an account of the processes of production and consumption associated with media representations, see Hall (1980). Hall's model is one point of departure for David Morley's work on media consumption and his opening out of the processes of "decoding". The development of Morley's arguments can be traced in his *Television, audiences and cultural studies* (1992). Morley's work belongs to the most proliferating body of work within media studies over recent years: work devoted to conceptualizing and empirically evidencing the process of consumption of media texts. This has offered a sustained critique of the semiotic-informed emphasis on media "texts" from the perspective of consumption. See, in addition to Morley, Radway (1984); Ang (1985); Walkerdine (1985). Other highly suggestive work on the processes of consumption and its relationship to the distribution of cultural capital can be found in Bourdieu (1984)

(especially his distinction between the "pure gaze" and the "popular aesthetic", pp. 9–97) and C. Mercer (1991).

2. Foucault's conception of discourse is most explicitly developed in Foucault (1972). His attention to the verbal or written components of discourse is complimented by a focus on the setting into practices of a wider range of phenomena in Foucault (1977a, 1978).

3. John Tagg gives a detailed example of these power relations of looking in relation to nineteenth century prison photography, in *The burden of representation*, ch. 3 (Tagg 1988).

4. On the importance of these arguments in the appropriation of Foucault's work see Weeks (1982). On the economic as part of the domain of extra-discursive practices see Foucault (1991). Ernesto Laclau's arguments in Laclau (1990) are also significant in terms of rethinking a model of determination.

5. On the formation of a more or less coherent sense of self, see Dawson (1991: 118).

6. Colin Mercer's essay "After Gramsci" in *Screen Education* 36, Autumn, 1980 alludes to the importance of this element of Foucault's argument in *The history of sexuality, an introduction.* Mercer attempts to advance a larger argument about bringing together theoretically the works of Gramsci and Foucault.

7. Foucault most explicitly details this process in Foucault (1977a; 1980: 186; 1982).

8. I have in mind here the body of work stretching from *The order of discourse* (Foucault 1981 [1970]) to *The history of sexuality, an introduction* (Foucault 1978).

9. Freud most directly elaborates on what he means by identification in "Group psychology and the analysis of the ego" (Freud 1977 [1921]).

10. For a developed argument about the value of Kleinian – as opposed to Lacanian – psychoanalysis for cultural theory see Dawson (1994: ch. 2).

11. Mulvey has reworked the arguments developed in the "Visual pleasure" essay in a number of forms. The fundamental elements of her argument, however, have remained consistent (see Mulvey 1989). The importance of addressing differences within the category of masculinity and an emphasis on a more ambivalent relationship between a visual text and its audiences is illustrated by Kobena Mercer in his reading of Robert Mapplethorpe's photographs (see Mercer 1992).

12. Lacan's work on the gaze also probematizes accounts that emphasize the successful positioning of individuals within particular systems of representation. This notion of the gaze represents – as both Joan Copjec and Slavoj Zizek have argued – a shift away from the earlier attention in Lacan's work on the subject's successful insertion into the imaginary in relation to the world of objects (Copjec 1989, Zizek 1989). The gaze

induces a paranoid relation to the visual. Individuals are in a constant (and impossible) attempt to place themselves at the punctual point of the gaze; a position that always eludes them. They are left, as Zizek has put it, like the spectators of Hitchcock's *Psycho* in the scene where Lilah approaches Mrs Bates's house: "the subject sees the house, but what provokes anxiety is the uneasy feeling that the house is somehow already gazing at her, from a point that escapes her view and so renders her utterly helpless" (Zizek 1989: 8). This anxiety or paranoia distinguishes the gaze from a subjective point of view and, for Lacan, prevents individuals from being totally bound in an imaginary relation to the world; they are anxious to see more than is apparently visible, disturbed by what seems to be beyond representation.

13. Juliet Mitchell describes the way Freud and Lacan are concerned with processes that (in her words) "forge the human in culture" (Mitchell 1984: 237).

14. See Foucault's comments on practices of the self in Rabinow (1984: 369). The four major types of "technologies" that Foucault specifies are: technologies of production; technologies of sign systems; technologies of power; technologies of the self. (In Foucault 1988, esp. p. 18.)

15. My comments on performance here owe something to Judith Butler's rendering of the notions of performance and performativity. In particular, Butler's description of performance as a "stylized repetition of acts" that constitute identity in time (and, I would add, space) is equivalent to the way I use the term here. Butler has subsequently attempted to move away from the voluntaristic gloss she gives her notion of performance in *Gender trouble,* towards an emphasis on the performativity of discourse. That is, the way performance as a bounded set of acts depends on the citation and reiteration of norms and the simultaneous exclusion of the "unperformable". (See, in particular, Butler 1993: ch. 8.)

## Chapter 2

1. Alain Lipietz's work is the most accessible of the French Regulation School's approach to Fordism and post-Fordism. (See, in particular, Lipietz 1982; 1984; 1987.) For general accounts of regulation theory and its multiple variants, see M. de Vroey (1984); Jessop (1988, 1990). Robin Murray's arguments on post-Fordism can be found in Murray (1987, 1989). The work of Bob Jessop and his co-authors can be found in Jessop et al. (1987, 1988, 1990). Useful summaries of Piore & Sabel's conceptualization of flexible specialization developed in *The second industrial divide* are offered by Cutler et al. (1987) and F. Murray (1987). Hirst & Zeitlin's arguments about flexible specialization are set out in Hirst & Zeitlin (1989, 1991). For accounts of mass production

techniques, see Cutler et al. (1987); Meegan (1988); and Murray (1989).

2. See, in particular, Hirst & Zeitlin (1989, 1991).
3. Hirst & Zeitlin (1989, 1991) and Jessop et al. (1990).
4. On these characteristics of the UK economy, see Massey (1984: ch. 4).
5. Hirst & Zeitlin advance this argument in Hirst & Zeitlin (1989).
6. In firms where flexible manufacturing systems were embraced the pay-offs were often limited. As the CMG Management Consultancy report in 1989 confirmed, the piecemeal take up of FMS or computer integrated manufacture had led to under-use of the novel features of the machinery and a failure to evaluate the organizational implications of new production methods properly. The report concluded: "manufacturing companies have to set competitive lead times and the first factor that must be recognized is that marketing should lead manufacturing" (*Financial Times*, 22/3/89: 42). For a discussion of the practical difficulties of introducing just-in-time, see "Easier said than done", *Financial Times*, 4/1/89: 42.
7. For a discussion of the fortunes of S. R. Gent, see "Back from the brink", *Independent on Sunday*, 25/2/90: 25. On the implementation of CAD, CCC and Epos, see "Cutting lead times", *Fashion Weekly*, 11/5/89: 12 and "Packing in the power", *Fashion Weekly*, 31/8/89: 58–9; "The store of tomorrow" and "Electronic point-of-sale (Epos) systems" in "Financial Times survey, retailing technology 2", *Financial Times*, 28/3/88.
8. Further information on the sourcing of men's suits in the UK can be found in C. Hird, "The clothes we wear", *New Statesman*, 3/10/80: 12–14; B & MR Reports (1989); Key Note Report (1987); Key Note Report (1989); "A structure suited to quality", *Financial Times*, 8/9/89: 16; "German quality is taking over on the clothes rails", *Financial Times*, 25/5/89: 12. For evidence of local sourcing of menswear for the designer menswear market, see Crewe & Forster (1993).
9. The UK clothing industry has a number of distinctive characteristics. First, through most of the twentieth century clothing retailers have dominated producers. Specifically, it was the concentration of retailing in the inter-war and early post-war years that established the power of multiple retailers over dependent manufacturers. It was these retailers, as Zeitlin argues, that provided the major impetus towards the introduction of more standardized, long run clothing manufacturer (Zeitlin 1988:214).

The power of retailers in this sector also contributed to the highly segmented nature of the industry in the post-war years. Two types of firms dominated the sector: large multi-plant companies usually linked to large retailers or textiles groups like Burtons, Tootal or Courtaulds;

and small, usually family owned firms often employing less than one hundred workers, and concentrated in London and the urban peripheries (Massey 1984; Zeitlin 1988).

In the extensive small firms sector, the production process, as Massey suggests, was (and remains) organized around the individually operated sewing machine based in small workshops. Mechanization – like conveyor belts – and long runs were rare. Production was geared around the top and bottom of the market, or towards subcontracted work for larger manufacturers or retailers. In this latter regard, small firms were drawn into the processes of standardization central to mass production. This usually took the form of producing part of a standardized product – such as jacket buttonholes (*Financial Times*, 19/11/88: 25).

The large multi-plant firms were the sites where adapted forms of mass production technology were brought to bear on clothing production. These technological developments were most marked in the postwar years in the mass markets in menswear and workwear – especially in men's suits and shirts (Zeitlin 1988). In the core parts of these markets, as Zeitlin suggests, competition between retailers and their manufacturers was mainly geared around price and the physical quality of the garment manufactured (Zeitlin 1988: 214).

From the mid 1960s, as Massey argues, the clothing sector witnessed a marked decline in levels of employment. In the 1970s this was mainly occasioned by heavy import penetration. In this sense the industry, as Massey suggests, was an early victim of the emergence of a new international division of labour on the back of the growth of mass production in newly industrializing countries.

The decline in employment in the industry continued through the 1980s. However, through the decade import penetration slowed down and output rose by 20 per cent from its low point in 1980 (Zeitlin 1988: 211). For Zeitlin, it was the implementation of flexible manufacturing that laid the basis for the improvements in its fortunes.

10. Some of the essays in Hall & Jacques (1989) and Lash & Urry (1987) come close to this.

# Part II

## Introduction

1. I do not deal with the developments in the men's toiletries and grooming products markets, except when I discuss the marketing of Beechams's "Brylcreem" in Part III. They are, though, the other key product area in relation to which the "new man" imagery was mobilized. For a sense of

the developments in this area see, "Shulton's cautious climb to the top", *Campaign*, 13/8/82: 25–7; "Make way for the scented male, *Marketing Review*, June 1986: 8–9; "The message in a bottle", *Campaign*, 6/3/87: 37–41; "Spray it again, Sam", *Observer*, 26/5/88: 81; "Sensitive spenders", *Media Week*, 26/8/88: 26–33; "New man is alive and raring to buy", *Marketing Week*, 28/10/88: 25; "Scent packaging", *Marketing*, 5/1/89: 27–8; "A high degree for Fahrenheit", *Financial Times*, 4/1/1990: 8; "Is he fragrant? Yes, the new man is", *Independent*, 17/12/90: 12. The men's fragrance market is conventionally split into "Fine fragrances" and "Mass market" fragrances. Between 1980 and 1990, the significant products were: "Rapport" and "Insignia" (Shulton); "Sybaris" (Puig); "Jazz" and "Kouros" (Yves St Laurent); "Tuscany" and "Aramis" (Estée Lauder); "Obsession for Men" (Calvin Klein); "Fahrenheit" (Christian Dior); and "Polo" (Ralph Lauren). Sales of men's fragrances increased by value from £74 million in 1981 to £211 million in 1989. In 1981 approximately one third of men's fragrances were bought by men. This had risen to two thirds by 1990. ("Is he fragrant? Yes, the new man is", *Independent*, 17/12/90: 12).

## Chapter 3

1. Dack and King envisaged the EMDC as a network for promoting the development of menswear, particularly in relation to export markets. It also aimed, as Dack put it, to "act as a kind of research and development arm of the manufacturing industry, and we've been working as closely as possible with them, so they've gradually come round to understand that the market we've aimed at is their market as well – and if it isn't, it should be, can be" ( *I-D*, September 1986: 21). EMDC's most important intervention, however, was in organizing the "Designer Menswear Show" in 1986. This was something of a caesura in the industry. Dack and King set out their motivations in launching the show as follows: "We got sick of the buyers having to wade through mountains of jeans stalls before they got to ours – that's if they were in the country of course. Basically we want a trade fair and fashion show that reflects the quality of the clothes and the time and effort that went into making them. And that doesn't mean girls in bikinis giving out free cigarettes" (ibid.). Their prime targets in these comments were both IMBEX and the trade organization, MAB. MAB – the Menswear Association of Britain – was the dominant professional association in British menswear, representing (along with the Drapers' Chamber of Trade) 4,000 businesses and more than 10,000 men's and womenswear outlets (*Fashion Weekly*, 12/11/87: 1).

2. For an example of the mutual admiration between Gaultier and *The Face*, in particular, see Gaultier's illustration for the magazine's one hundreth issue. *The Face*, no.100, 1988: 113.
3. The Burnsteins also either introduced to Britain or showcased the work of Calvin Klein, Armani and John Galliano. Richard Creme's L'Homme in Manchester was also significant as an outlet stocking new designer menswear outside the capital.
4. *Arena* devoted one of its regular "Avanti" sections to Armani's new range of menswear in 1988. See *Arena*, Spring 1989: 128–31.
5. See Sudjic (1990: 10–11).
6. For a fuller discussion of Comme des Garcons' womenswear – from which I have drawn – see Evans & Thornton (1989: 156–65).
7. Kawabuko's relationship to fabric producers was important in relation to this emphasis in her work for Comme des Garcons. See Sudjic (1990).
8. In Hepworth's company report in the year to February 1985, pre-tax profits were up to £9,656,000. Next for Men was "making an increasing contribution to [this] profitability" (*Fashion Weekly*, 25/4/85: 14). By November 1986, with the group profits at nearly £28 million, a further report noted that the "menswear shops were performing particularly well" (*Fashion Weekly*, 6/11/86: 5).
9. The Next for Men in-store catalogue, Autumn/Winter 1987, underlined this concern well. It stated, "To ensure exclusivity of our designs some items are only available in selected stores" (Back cover, Next for Men, in-store catalogue, Autumn/Winter 1987).
10. See C. Hird, "The clothes we wear", *New Statesman*, 3/10/80: 12–14.
11. A discussion of these retailing techniques follows in Chapter 4.
12. Profits in the period 1981–5 rose from £16.4 million to £80.2 million, before tax (*Independent on Sunday*, 22/7/90: 10).

## Chapter 4

1. For commentaries on the developments within the design industry see Gardner & Sheppard, (1989b); "International design industry", Financial Times survey, *Financial Times*, 22/2/89: I-VI; "A cottage industry gaining maturity", *Financial Times*, 30/3/89: 32. The UK design industry – especially those companies with large investments in retail design – suffered rapid losses with the downturn in consumer spending and the increase in interest rates from 1989. For a discussion on the impact of these developments, see "Going public, going bust", *Design*, January 1991: 13–20.
2. On Conran's mission to extend popular interest in design, see Jane Lott's review of B. Philips, Conran and the Habitat story, (*Design*, May 1984: 6).

3. For an interesting account which touches on shifts in retail design in the 1960s, see J. Woudhuysen, "How design got high street cred", *Campaign*, 16/9/88: 38–40.
4. The most significant other ex-Conran employee for my account is David Davies of DDA.
5. See DR (*Drapers Record*), 22/10/88: 32–3; C. McDermott (1987: 103).

## Chapter 5

1. Benjamin sets out this relationship very explicitly in Benjamin (1973: 55).
2. Benjamin quotes Baudelaire from his "Salon de 1845". Although he is speaking of the painter, the forms of self-consciousness Baudelaire describes could apply equally well to the *flâneur*. Thus, "More than anyone else, the painter, the true painter, will be the man who extracts from present-day life its epic aspects and teaches us in lines and colours to understand how great and poetic we are in our patent-leather shoes and our neckties. May the real pioneers next year give us the exquisite pleasure of being allowed to celebrate the truly new" (Benjamin 1973: 76–7).
3. See N. Green (1990: 40).
4. On the expansion of art dealing in Paris from the 1820s, see N. Green (1990: 23–7).

# Part III

## Introduction

1. Advertising expenditure in the UK rose from 1.1% of GDP in 1980 to 1.6% in 1988. Expenditure increased by 11.4% in 1986, by 9.9% in 1987, by 15% in 1988 and by 13% in 1989 (Jordans 1988: 13; *Financial Times*, 17/10/89: 32; *Campaign*, 19/2/88: 5; *Independent on Sunday*, 12/8/90: 6).

## Chapter 6

1. For a discussion of the fortunes of these agencies, see "Going public: trailblazers that paved the way for today's city hopefuls", *Campaign*, 20/6/86: 40–41.
2. For a critical exposition of Coca Cola's marketing in relation to the UK, see "Can Coke put a bit of fizz back into the real thing?", *Campaign*, 9/8/85: 28–9.

3. The theory of three distinctive waves of post-war advertising in Britain represented a widely subscribed-to piece of popular history within the profession. It worked in at least three registers: as a sales pitch to clients; as a form of professional self-organization and formation; and as a useful chronology of trends. A familiar version went like this: in the 1950s and 1960s British advertising was dominated by large USA owned agencies and their British subsiduaries. These agencies – like J. Walter Thompson, Young and Rubican, Ted Bates and Ogilvy and Mather – were a response to the expansion of the consumer sectors of the UK economy and represented the exporting of forms of commercial knowledge and expertise from the USA. These agencies formed the First Wave. This First Wave was then joined, the scenario goes, in the late 1960s by the public flotation of Geers Gross, Boase Massimi Pollet (BMP), KMP and Collett Dickenson Pearce (CDP). The 1970s marked a general period of rationalization, largely driven by a marked recession in 1974–5. It also was the moment of the Second Wave's emergence. The Second Wave in fact was formed in two phases. The launch of Saatchi and Saatchi in 1970 marked, in this account, the preliminary formation of the Second Wave while the second phase begins in the late 1970s. This second phase is in fact the more significant event in terms of the formation of a distinctive wave. These years – from 1977 to 1982 – saw the coming into being of Abbot Mead Vickers, SMS, Wight Collins Rutherford Scott (WCRS), Gold Greenless Trott (GGT), Lowe Howard-Spink, Leagas Delaney, Valin Pollen and Bartle Bogle Hegarty (BBH). These formed the high profile agencies of the 1980s, and were most associated with the creative developments within British advertising through the decade. The Third Wave began in 1987 with the formation of Devito Butterfield Day Hockney (BDDH), and their self-conscious plundering of the term from Alvin Toffler, together with, notably, Howell Henry Chaldecott Lury (HCCL) and Woolams Moira Gaskin O'Malley. The Third Wave's "third way" was set out by BDDH in the following terms: as a shift away from a situation in which "clients are offered an imperfect choice between agencies that are strong on service and agencies that are strong on creativity and planning. [We aim to be a bridge] between one – boring multinationals and wallpaper advertising – and two – sharp, witty advertising – but bugger the client or the deadline" (*Marketing Week*, 12/2/88: 48).

4. This evidence of account gains is drawn from, "BBH: smooth going against the grain", *Marketing Week*, 3/3/89: 42–6.

5. The agency won £30 million worth of new accounts in 1986 (ibid.).

6. "Below-the-line" services essentially include all the areas of marketing and promotion excluding television, press and poster advertising. Direct marketing is the key "below-the-line service". See Chapter 3.

7. "Beach" and "The Getaway People" were featured in the television programme *Washes whiter*, BBC TV, 1990.

## Chapter 7

1. There was further good reason for the IPA to attempt to clarify the nature of the new consumer segmentations. These ways of representing consumers had, by the the mid to late 1980s, become more than the intellectual property of market researchers and agency folk. In both the quality and popular press, the new consumer segmentations were appropriated in the construction of popular languages of identity. Thus, for example, the *Daily Telegraph* (7/10/87: 29) asked, "Are you a social resister or a belonger?", while the *Sunday Times* dissected the "New couple": "they're young, they're glamorous, they're rich, they're monogamous and (thank goodness) they love to go shopping" (*Sunday Times*, 12/4/87: 88). The most celebrated cross-overs from the research documents of market researchers to popular commentary, however, were the "yuppies" – groups of consumers defined as "urban, trendy and, above all, affluent. They're hard working and hard spending" (*Marketing*, 2/6/86: 20). What was at stake in this, and the other, popular appropriations of market research segmentations was the resonance of the segmentations in giving shape to the felt movements of culture.
2. These percentages are drawn from USA figures. SRI restricted access to its UK based figures to its clients.

## Chapter 8

1. These were, respectively: John Bartle, Leslie Butterfield, Damon O'Malley and Adam Lury.
2. See *Campaign*'s report on the APG seminars, *Campaign*, 11/11/83: 14.
3. In starting with the planner–client relationship, Scorah was contesting a prevalent view which suggested that planners were overly concerned with the imput of consumers at the expense of clients' opinions.
4. A fuller account of this process is offered by Damon O'Malley in Cowley (1987).
5. This account of the K-Shoes planning process is formed from a interview I conducted with Liz Watts in 1989.
6. Other hostile attacks on planning can be found in, "Time to topple these myths", *Campaign*, 12/8/88: 42–3 and "What pushed Murray chick out the GGT nest?", *Campaign*, 18/3/88: 20. In the latter article, David Trott, Creative Director at GGT, is alleged to have likened planners to parrots: "They sit on your shoulder while you're working and crap down your back. And when you've finished, they crap on your

work." Trott's invocation of the parrot metaphor is a corruption of Don Cowley's (of the APG) use of the metaphor. For Cowley, of course, the metaphor of the parrot was to be read positively. It attempted to indicate the way planning could assist creatives.
7. The acquisition of direct marketing companies by agencies was linked to the model of expansion exemplified by Saatchi and Saatchi. See Chapter 6.
8. I discuss some of these examples in Chapter 10.

## Part IV

### Chapter 9

1. *Esquire*, published by The National Magazine Company, was launched in 1933. *GQ* was started by The National Magazine Company as a trade magazine, *Apparel Arts*, in 1957. It was bought by Condé Nast in 1979 and significantly restyled.
2. D. Hebdige comments on these adverts in Hebdige 1988, Ch. 6.
3. In September 1985, IPC launched a new "general interest magazine" for 15–19 year old men, called *The Hit*. *The Hit* was very much a product of the debates within advertising and magazine publishing that I chart in this chapter. IPC were confident that *The Hit* – with its strong editorial emphasis on music and lifestyle – would be successful. However, six weeks after its launch, and with confirmed sales lower than anticipated, IPC moved to close down *The Hit*. The magazine's short publication run haunted the trade debates through 1985–9 on "general interest men's magazines". For trade commentaries on *The Hit*, see *Media Week*, 17/5/85: 12; *Media Week*, 6/9/85: 21; *Campaign*, 15/11/85: 15.

### Chapter 10

1. Logan explicitly alludes to the influence of *Paris Match* and *Life* in an interview in *Direction*, September 1988: 32.
2. For extended discussion on these aspects of "Two tone", see Hebdige 1987: 106–17.
3. Jon Savage's regular contributions confidently moved between established pop journalism and the language of critical theory in unpacking the dynamics of pop. Frith & Horne (1987) advance an important argument about the role of art education in furnishing British pop practitioners with this particular, critical vocabulary. The involvement of individuals associated with *The Face* – Robert Elms, Neil Spencer and Neville Brody – with "Red Wedge", the alliance of musicians and other

media practitioners in support of the Labour Party, was indicative of a left of centre politics which also surfaced in the magazine and accented its critical vocabulary.

4. McRobbie (1980) reflects briefly on the coverage *Subculture* received from the *New Musical Express* at the time of its publication.

5. McDermott (1987), points to the influence of Brody's graphic design on a wide range of other art directors and designers. The development of "style" sections in the broadsheet newspapers – such as the *Guardian* – owed much to the success of *The Face*'s journalistic and editorial approach. A similar influence were also clear on television magazine programmes such as *Network 7*, broadcast on Channel 4 between 1987 and 1989, and *Def II*, produced by Janet Street-Porter for BBC 2 and involving many of the team originally involved in *Network 7*.

6. In issue number 6, *Arena* produced a feature called "Ideal standards". This piece set out the key elements of the *Arena* man's wardrobe. Or, as the feature put it, "every homme should have one". These were: a Prince of Wales check suit; an important watch; a pair of chinos and polo shirt; brogues; Levi's 501s, a pair of good white socks and loafers; and a good raincoat.

7. See *Arena*, Autumn/Winter 1989: 164–71.

8. See Wozencroft 1988: 8–9.

9. A similar mixture of a post-permissive masculine heterosexual script and the masculine codes of romance informed: "Bathing beauties", *GQ* August/September 1990; "Play mistress for me", *GQ*, April/May 1989; "Fast girls, fast cars", *GQ*, February/March 1989, as well as the regular section, "All about Adam".

## Chapter 11

1. I have learnt much from Richard Dyer's suggestive analysis of masculine visual representations in Dyer (1989). Andy Medhurst, drawing on Dyer, also makes some useful points about masculinity and visual representation in Medhurst (1985).

2. Post-Renaissance Western Art has provided a particular legacy in relation to the formation of a distinctive regime of masculine–feminine forms of spectatorship.

3. The organization of spectatorship in relation to television suggests a further marking of the look: namely, the marking of the spectatorial look as "familial". On the centrality of the family audience to popular television, see Morley (1986); Ellis (1982).

4. Neale (1983) advances a rigid bifurcation between identification and a desiring look.

5. The concept of *bricolage* is developed by D. Hebdige (1979). I. Chambers also deploys it in Chambers (1986).

6. These observations on "Hard times" culture draw on Robert Elms, "Hard times", *The Face*, September 1982; Janice Winship, "Back to the future", *New Socialist*, September 1986 and Mort (1988).
7. The notion of "Italianicity" as the "condensed essense" of Italianness is appropriated from Roland Barthes (1977).

## Conclusion

1. This formulation of economic processes setting limits and exerting certain pressures on cultural production is taken from Raymond Williams (1980).
2. The advertising agency Grey Advertising Ltd produced a report in 1990 on advertising to men. *About men, reflections on the male experience in the 1990s*, offered a critical commentary on the "new man" imagery, arguing that it did not address the aspirations of a large proportion of men. Its author, Neil Saunders, argued that there "has been the temptation to try to shift men too quickly from one extreme to the other" (*Campaign*, 14/6/90: 9). On advertising and the "new lad", see "Ads by lads", *Independent on Sunday*, 3/9/95: 10.
3. See GQ, December/January 1990/1 "The perfect blonde". "The siren call of the perfect blonde lures men into stormy waters, washing them up on the shores of dangerous sex"; GQ, June 1992 14-page feature "How to pull chicks".
4. An even more elaborated rendering of the "new lad" was found in *Loaded*, launched in March 1994 and marking IPC's return to the young male general interest market.
5. The cultural politics forged in relation to AIDS activism provides one model of this operationalizing of a politics of representation. This has involved both a critical and engaged reading of popular representation and a process of counter cultural production based around a clearly imagined community and form of cultural authority. At the heart of this cultural politics has been the concern to produce representational forms through which people with AIDS can represent their experience in their own terms; in particular, as Crimp argues, to contest the desexualization of AIDS. This process of cultural production also aims to frame the way in which AIDS is imagined in wider public debate. Such interventions in cultural production have required an engagement with the apparatuses of representation and a negotiation of the culture of the practitioners in these apparatuses (notably, gallery curatorship). See Boffin & Gupta (1990); Crimp (1992); Hall (1992).

# Bibliography

Aglietta, M. 1982. World capitalism in the eighties, *New Left Review* (August/September), 5–42.

Allen, J. & D. Massey 1988. *The economy in question*. London: Sage.

Amin, A. & K. Robins 1990. The re-emergence of regional economies? The mythical geography of flexible accumulation. *Environment and Planning D: Society and Space* 8, 7–34, London: Pion.

Ang, I. 1985. *Watching Dallas*. London: Methuen.

B & MR Reports 1989. *The UK market for men's suits*. London: Business & Marketing Research.

Barthes, R. 1972. *Mythologies*. London: Fontana.

Barthes, R. 1977. The rhetoric of the image. In *Image, music, text*, S. Heath (ed.), 32–51. London: Fontana.

Benjamin, W. 1973. *Charles Baudelaire: a lyric poet in the era of high capitalism*. London: New Left Books.

Bennett, T. 1986. Introduction: popular culture and the "turn" to Gramsci. In *Popular culture and social relations*, T. Bennett, C. Meuer, J. Woollacott (eds), xi–xix. Milton Keynes: Open University Press.

Bennett, T. 1992. Putting policy into cultural studies. See Grossberg et al. (1992), 23–37. London: Routledge.

Blackwell, L. & J. Burney 1990. *Retail future*. London: Thames & Hudson.

Boffin, T. & S. Gupta (eds) 1990. *Escatic antibodies, resisting the aids mythology*. London: Rivers Oram Press.

Bourdieu, P. 1984. *Distinction, a social critique of the judgement of taste*. London: Routledge.

Bowlby, R. 1985. *Just looking, consumer culture in Dreiser, Gissing and Zola*. London: Macmillan.

Bristow, J. 1991. *Empire boys, adventures in a man's world*. London: Harper Collins.

Broadbent, S. (ed.) 1990. *Advertising Works 5*.

Brown, M. 1984. Divide or describe? A critical appraisal of the major segmentation procedures. In *Marketing appraisal*. The Institute of Practitioners in Advertising, Bulletin No. 198, London.

Burchell, G., C. Gordon, P. Miller 1991. *The Foucault effect*. Hemel Hempstead: Harvester Wheatsheaf.

The Burton Group 1980, 1985, 1987, 1989. *Annual report*.

Butler, J. 1990. *Gender trouble, feminism and the subversion of identity*. London: Routledge.

Butler, J. 1993. *Bodies that matter, on the discursive limits of "sex"*. London: Routledge.

Chambers, I. 1986. *Popular culture, the metropolitan experience*. London: Methuen.

Chapman, R. 1988. The great pretender: variations on the new man theme. See Chapman & Rutherford (1988), 225–48.

Chapman, R. & J. Rutherford (eds) 1988. *Male order. Unwrapping masculinity*. London: Lawrence & Wishart.

Cohn, N. 1971. *Today there are no gentlemen*. London: Weidenfeld & Nicolson.

Copjec, J. 1989. The orthopsychic subject: film theory and the reception of Lacan. *October* (Summer): 53–71.

Coward, R. (with M. Black) 1981. Linguistic, social and sexual relations: a review of Dale Spender's man-made language. *Screen Education* (Spring), 69–85.

Coward, R. 1984. *Female desire, women's sexuality today*. London: Paladin.

Cowie, E. 1990. Fantasia. In *The woman in question*, P. Adams & E. Cowie (eds), 149–97. London: Verso.

Cowley, D. 1987. *How to plan advertising*. London: Cassell.

Crewe, L. & Z. Forster 1993. Markets, design and local agglomeration: the role of the small independent retailer in the workings of the fashion system. *Environment and Planning D: Society and Space* 11(2), 213–30.

Crimp, D. 1992. Portraits of people with AIDS. See Grossberg et al. (1992), 117–33.

Cote, K. 1987. Branders chase lifestyles. In *Marketing appraisal*. The Institute of Practitioners in Advertising, Bulletin No. 281, London.

Cutler, T., C. Haslam, J. Williams, K. Williams 1987. The end of mass production? *Economy and Society* 16(3), 112–84.

Davies, G. 1989. *What next?* London: Arrow Books.

Dawson, G. 1991. The blond bedouin: Lawrence of Arabia, imperial adventure and the imagining of English–British masculinity. In *Manful assertions, masculinities in Britain since 1800*, J. Tosh & M. Roper (eds), 113–44. London: Routledge.

Dawson, G. 1994. Soldier heroes: British adventure, Empire and the imagining of masculinities. London: Routledge.

De Vroey, M. 1984. A regulation approach interpretation of contemporary crisis. *Capital and Class* (Summer), 45–65.
Docker, J. & A. Roberts 1987. Lifestyle or brandstyle: which is better to segment by? In *Marketing appraisal*. The Institute of Practitioners in Advertising, Bulletin No. 288, London.
Donald, J. 1989. The *mise en scene* of desire. In *Fantasy and cinema*, J. Donald (ed.), 1–15. London: British Film Institute.
Du Gay, P. 1991 Enterprise culture and the ideology of excellence. *New Formations* (Summer), 45–61.
Dyer, R. 1985. Male sexuality in the media. In *The sexuality of men*, A. Metcalf & M. Humphries (eds), 28–43. London: Pluto Press.
Dyer, R. 1989. Don't look now. In *Zoot suits and second-hand dresses, an anthology of fashion and music*, A. McRobbie (ed.), 198–207. London: Macmillan.
Dyer, R. 1993. Coming out as going in: the image of the homosexual as a sad young man. In *The matter of images, essays on representation*, 73–92. London: Routledge.
Ellis, J. 1982. *Visible fictions, cinema, television, video*. London: Routledge.
Evans, C. & M. Thornton 1989. *Women and fashion, a new look*. London: Quartet Books.
Fitch, R. & J. Woudhuysen 1988. The strategic significance of design. In *The changing face of British retailing*, E. McFayden (ed.), 14–21. London: Newman.
Foucault, M. 1972. *The archaeology of knowledge*, London: Tavistock.
Foucault, M. 1977a. *Discipline and punish, the birth of the prison*. London: Penguin.
Foucault, M. 1977b. History of systems of thought. In *language, counter-memory, practice – selected essays and interviews*, D. F. Bouchard (ed.), 199–204. Oxford: Oxford University Press.
Foucault, M. 1978. *The history of sexuality, an introduction*. London: Penguin.
Foucault, M. 1980. "Two lectures" and "The history of sexuality". In *Power/knowledge: selected interviews and other writings 1972-1977*, C. Gordon, (ed.), 78–108 and 183–93 Brighton: Harvester Wheatsheaf.
Foucault, M. 1981. The order of discourse. In *Untying the text, a post-structuralist reader*, R. Young (ed), 48–78. London: Routledge & Kegan Paul.
Foucault, M. 1982. The subject and power. In *Michel Foucault: beyond structuralism and hermeneutics*, H. Dreyfus & P. Rabinow (eds), 208–28. Brighton: Harvester.
Foucault, M. 1985. *The uses of pleasure*. London: Penguin.
Foucault, M. 1988. The political technology of individuals. In *Technologies of the self, a seminar with Michel Foucault*. L. Martin, H. Gutman, P. Hutton (eds), 143–65. London: Tavistock.
Foucault, M. 1991. Politics and the study of discourse. In *The Foucault*

*effect*, G. Burchell, C. Gordon, P. Miller (eds), 53–72. Hemel Hempstead: Harvester Wheatsheaf.

Freud, S. 1977 [1905]. Three essays on the theory of sexuality. In *Pelican Freud library*, vol VIII, 33–170. London: Penguin. [Hereafter PFL.]

Freud, S. 1984 [1914]. On narcissism: an introduction. In PFL, vol. XI, 59–98.

Freud, S. 1984 [1915]. Instincts and their vicissitudes. In PFL, vol. XI, 105–38.

Freud, S. 1977 [1921]. Group psychology and the analysis of the ego. In PFL, vol. XII, 91–178.

Freud, S. 1977 [1924]. The dissolution of the Oedipus complex. In PFL, vol. VIII, 313–22.

Freud, S. 1977 [1927]. Fetishism. In PFL, vol. VIII, 345–58.

Freud, S. 1977 [1931]. Female sexuality. In PFL, vol. VIII, 367–92.

Frisby, D. 1985. *Fragments of modernity*. London: Polity.

Frith, S. & S. Horne 1987. *Art into pop*. London: Routledge.

Gammon, L. & M. Marshment 1988. *The female gaze*. London: Women's Press.

Gardner, C. 1987. The new retail theatre. *Design* (April), 5.

Gardner, C. & J. Sheppard 1989a. Chronic consumption. *The Listener* (12 October), 4–5.

Gardner, C. & J. Sheppard 1989b. *Consuming passion, the rise of retail culture*. London: Unwin Hyman.

Gershuny, J. & I. Miles 1983. *The new service economy: the transformation of employment in industrial societies*. New York: Praeger.

Green, N. 1990. *The spectacle of nature, landscape and bourgeois culture in nineteenth century France*. Manchester: Manchester University Press.

Grossberg, L., C. Nelson, P. Treichler (eds) 1992. *Cultural studies*. London: Routledge.

Hall, C. & L. Davidoff 1987. *Family fortunes, men and women of the English middle class 1780–1850*. London: Hutchinson.

Hall, C. 1992. Missionary stories: gender and ethnicity in England in the 1830s and 1840s. See Grossberg et al. (1992), 240–76.

Hall, S. 1988. *The hard road to renewal*. London: Verso.

Hall, S. 1992. Cultural studies and its theoretical legacies. See Grossberg et al. (1992), 277–94.

Hall, S. 1980. Encoding/decoding. In *Culture, media, language*, S. Hall, D. Hobson, A. Lowe, P. Willis (eds), 128–38. London: Hutchinson.

Hall, S. & M. Jacques (eds) 1989. *New times*. London: Lawrence & Wishart.

Hebdige, D. 1979. *Subculture, the meaning of style*. London: Methuen.

Hebdige, D. 1987. *Cut'n'mix, culture, identity and Caribbean music*. London: Comedia.

Hebdige, D. 1988. The bottom line on planet one, squaring up to the face. In *Hiding in the light, on images and things*, 155–80. London: Comedia.

Hirst, P. & J. Zeitlin 1989. Flexible specialisation and the competitive failure of UK manufacturing. *Political Quarterly* 60(2), 164–78.

Hirst, P. & J. Zeitlin 1991. Flexible specialisation versus post-Fordism: theory, evidence and policy implications. *Economy and Society* 20(1), 1–56.

Hunter, I. 1993. Subjectivity and Government. *Economy and Society* 22(1), 123–39.

*I-D* Magazine 1989. *A decade of I-Deas, the encylopedia of the 80s*. London: Penguin.

Jessop, B. 1988. Regulation theory, post-Fordism and the state: more than a reply to Werner Bonefield. *Capital and Class* (Spring), 147–69.

Jessop, B. 1990. Regulation theories, retrospect and prospect. *Economy and Society* 19(2), 153–215.

Jessop, B., K. Bonnett, S. Bromley 1990. Farewell to Thatcherism? Neoliberalism and "new times". *New Left Review* (January/February), 81–102.

Jessop, B., K. Bonnett, T. Ling, S. Bromley 1987. Popular capitalism, flexible accumulation and left strategy. *New Left Review* (March/April), 104–23.

Jessop, B., K. Bonnett, T. Ling, S. Bromley 1988. *Thatcherism*, Oxford: Polity.

Jordans 1989. *Britain's advertising industry*. Bristol: Jordans & Sons Ltd.

Key Note Report 1987. *Men's clothing retailers*. London: Key Notes Publications.

Key Note Report 1989. *Men's clothing retailers*. London: Key Notes Publications.

Lacan, J. 1968. The mirror phase as formative of the function of the I. *New Left Review* (March/April), 71–77.

Lacan, J. 1977. *The four fundamental concepts of psychoanalysis*. London: Penguin.

Laclau, E. 1990. *New thoughts on the revolution in our time*. London: Verso.

Lash, S. & J. Urry 1987. *The end of organised capitalism*. Cambridge: Polity.

Leborgne, D. & A. Lipietz 1988. New technologies, new modes of regulation: some spatial implications. *Environment and Planning D: Society and Space* 6(3), 263–80.

Leys, C. 1985. Thatcherism and British manufacturing: a question of hegemony. *New Left Review* (May/June), 5–25.

Lipietz, A. 1982. Towards global Fordism. *New Left Review* (March/April), 33–47.

Lipietz, A. 1984. Imperialism or the beast of the apocalypse. *Capital and Class* (Spring) 81–109.

Lipietz, A. 1987. *Mirages and miracles*, London: Verso.

Marks and Spencer 1989. *Information pack*. London: St Michael's.

McDermott, C. 1987. *Street style: British design in the 80s*. London: Design Council.

McRobbie, A. 1980. Settling accounts with subcultures: a feminist critique. *Screen Education* (Spring), 37–49.

McRobbie, A. (ed.) 1989. *Zoot suits and second-hand dresses*. London: Macmillan.

Massey, D. 1984 *Spatial divisions of labour, social structures and the geography of production*. London: Macmillan.

Massey, D. 1994. *Space, place and gender*. Cambridge: Polity.

Medhurst, A. 1985. Can chaps be pin-ups? *Ten 8* (July), 3–9.

Meegan, R. 1988. A crisis of mass production. In *The economy in question*, J. Allen & D. Massey (eds), 136–83. London: Sage.

Mercer, C. 1991. Neverending stories, the problem of reading in cultural studies. *New Formations* (Summer), 63–74.

Mercer, K. 1988. Recoding narratives of "race" and nation. *Black film/ British cinema*. London: Institute of Contemporary Arts.

Mercer, K. 1992. Skin head sex thing. *New Formations* (Autumn), 1–23.

Merck, M. 1987. Difference and its discontents. *Screen* 28(1), 2–9.

Metcalf, A. & M. Humphries (eds) 1985. *The sexuality of men*. London: Pluto Press.

Mitchell, J. 1984. Psychoanalysis: a humanist humanity or a linguistic science? In *Women: the longest revolution*, 236–45. London: Penguin.

Moore, S. 1988. Here's looking at you, kid! In *The female gaze*, M. Marshment & L. Gamman (eds), 45–59. London: Women's Press.

Morley, D. 1986. *Family television, cultural power and domestic leisure*. London: Routledge.

Morley, D. 1992. *Television, audiences and cultural studies*. London: Comedia.

Mort, F. 1987. *Dangerous sexualities, medico-moral politics in England since 1830*. London: Routledge & Kegan Paul.

Mort, F. 1988 Boy's own? Masculinity, style and popular culture. In *Male order. Unwrapping masculinity*, R. Chapman & J. Rutherford (eds), 193–224. London: Lawrence & Wishart.

Mort, F. 1992. Consumer cultures, political discourses and the problem of cultural politics. Paper presented at the Theory, Culture and Society Conference, University of Pittsburgh, USA.

Mouffe, C. 1991. *The return of the political*. London: Verso.

Mulvey, L. 1989. *The visual and other pleasures*. London: Macmillan.

Murray, F. 1987. Flexible specialisation in the "Third Italy". *Capital and Class* (Winter), 84–95.

Murray, R. 1987. Ownership, control and the market. *New Left Review*

(July/August), 87–112.

Murray, R. 1989. Fordism and post-Fordism. In *New times, the changing face of politics in the 1990s*, S. Hall & M. Jacques (eds), 38–53. London: Lawrence & Wishart.

Neale, S. 1983. Masculinity as spectacle. *Screen* 24(6), 2–16.

*Next directory* 1989. Leicester: Next plc.

*Next in-store catalogue* 1987. Leicester: Next plc.

O'Donahugue, D. 1989. *Lifestyles and psychographics.* The Institute of Practitioners in Advertising, London

Packard, V. 1981 [1957]. *The hidden persuaders.* London: Penguin.

Pilditch, J. 1974. The changing face of design. *Retail and Distribution Management* (January/February), 26–9.

Pollert, A. 1988. Dismantling flexibility. *Capital and Class* (Spring), 42–75.

Pryke, M. 1991. An international city going "global": spatial change in the City of London. *Enviroment and Planning D: Society and Space* 9, 197–222.

Rabinow, P. 1984. *The Foucault reader.* London: Penguin.

Radway, J. 1984. *Reading the romance: women, patriarchy and popular literature.* London: Verso.

Reeves, R. 1961. *Reality in advertising.* London: MacGibbon & Kee..

Roper, M. 1991. Yesterday's model: product fetishism and the British company man, 1945–1985. In *Manful assertions, masculinities in Britain since 1800*, J. Tosh & M. Roper (eds), 190–211. London: Routledge.

Rose, J. 1986. *Sexuality in the field of vision.* London: Verso.

Rutherford, J. 1988. Who's that man? See Chapman & Rutherford (1988), 21–67.

Saatchi and Saatchi 1985. *Annual report.*

Sayer, A. 1986. New developments in manufacturing: just-in-time system. *Capital and Class* (Winter), 43–61.

Schwarz, B. 1984. The language of constitutionalism. In *Formations of nation and people*, 1–18, London: Routledge & Kegan Paul.

Schwarz, B. 1986. Conservatism, nationalism and imperialism. In *Politics and ideology*, J. Donald & S. Hall (eds). Milton Keynes: Open University Press.

Scott, A. J. 1988. Flexible production systems and regional development. *International Journal of Urban and Regional Studies* 12(2), 171–85.

Sudjic, D. 1990. *Rei Kawabuko and Comme des Garcons*, London: Thames & Hudson.

Tagg, J. 1988. The democracy of the image. In *The burden of representation. Essays on photographies and histories*, J. Tagg (ed.), 34–59. London: Macmillan.

Tosh, J. & M. Roper (eds) 1991. *Manful assertions, masculinities in Britain since 1800.* London: Routledge.

Walkerdine, V. 1985. Video replays. In *Formations of fantasy*, V. Burgin & J. Donald (eds). London: Routledge & Kegan Paul.

Weeks, J. 1985 *Sexuality and its discontents*. London: Routledge.

Weeks, J. 1991. *Against nature*. London: Rivers Oram Press.

Weeks, J. 1982. Foucault for historians. *History Workshop Journal* 14, Autumn: 106–20.

Williams, R. 1980. *Problems in materialism and culture*. London: New Left Books.

Willis. P. 1979. Shop floor culture, masculinity and the wage form. In *Working class culture: studies in history and theory*, J. Clarke, C. Chritcher, R. Johnson (eds), 185–210. London: Hutchinson.

Wilson, E. 1992. The invisible flaneur. *New Left Review* (January/February), 90–110.

Woudhuysen, J. 1988. How design got high street cred. *Campaign* (16 September), 38–40.

Wozencroft, J. 1988. *The graphic language of Neville Brody*. London: Thames & Hudson.

Zeitlin, J. 1988. The clothing industry in transition. *Textile History* 19(2), 211–38.

Zeitlin, J. 1989. Local industrial strategies: introduction. *Economy and Society* 18(4), 1–7.

Zizek, S. 1989. The undergrowth of enjoyment: how popular culture can serve as an introduction to Lacan. *New Formations* (Spring), 7–29.

## Newspapers, journals and periodicals

*Admap*
*Arena*
*Barclays Review*
*Benn's Media Directory*
*Campaign*
*City Limits*
*Daily Telegraph*
*Design*
*Direction*
*DR (Drapers Record)*
*Employment Gazette*
*The Economist*
*The Face*
*Fashion Weekly*
*Financial Times*
*GQ*

*Guardian*
*I-D*
*Independent*
*Independent on Sunday*
*Marketing*
*Marketing Review*
*Marketing Week*
*Media Week*
*New Socialist*
*New Statesman & Society*
*The Observer*
*Retail and Distribution Management*
*The Spectator*
*The Times*
*Vogue*

# Index

Lightning Source UK Ltd.
Milton Keynes UK
UKOW01f0615170217
294639UK00002B/3/P

9 780312 163333